RANDOM HOUSE
WEBSTER'S
grammar, usage, and punctuation

RANDOM HOUSE REFERENCE

NEW YORK   TORONTO   LONDON   SYDNEY   AUCKLAND

TABLE OF CONTENTS

INTRODUCTION xi

SECTION 1 — *Grammar*

PARTS OF SPEECH 3

Nouns 4

Pronouns 6

   Case 9

   Ambiguous References 16

   Common Pronoun Mistakes 17

Verbs 21

   Transitive Verbs 22

   Intransitive Verbs 22

   Ergative Verbs 22

   Copula Verbs 23

   Auxiliary Verbs 26

   Phrasal Verbs 26

   Verbal Forms 27

   Regular and Irregular Verbs 30

   Conjugation of Tricky Verbs 37

   Tense 53

   Mood 62

Voice 64

Verbals 66

Determiners 66

Adjectives 67

Nouns and Pronouns as Adjectives 67

Special Adjectives 68

Adverbs 69

Sentence Adverbs 70

Adjective or Adverb? 70

Using Adjectives after Linking Verbs 71

Using Adjectives or Adverbs
after Direct Objects 72

Words That Can Be Either
Adjectives or Adverbs 73

Using Adjectives and Adverbs
to Make Comparisons 73

Prepositions 78

Common Prepositions 78

Phrasal Prepositions (Two or More Words) 79

Prepositional Phrases 79

Placement of Prepositions 80

Prepositional Phrases as
Adverbs and Adjectives 80

Preposition or Adverb? 81

Conjunctions 81

Coordinating Conjunctions 81

Correlative Conjunctions 82

Subordinating Conjunctions......................84
Subordinating Conjunction or Preposition?.....85
Conjunctive Adverb or Transitional Phrase?....85
Transitional Phrase 86
Transitional Phrase or
Coordinating Conjunction?......................87

Interjections...87

Pluralization 89

PHRASES 93

Noun Phrases 93

Verb Phrases 93

Prepositional Phrases.............................94

Verbal Phrases 94

CLAUSES 96

Independent Clauses...............................96

Dependent Clauses................................96

Adjective Clauses..................................97

Adverb Clauses 97

Noun Clauses 98

Elliptical Clauses..................................98

SENTENCES 100

Subjects and Predicates 100

Hard-to-Locate Subjects 101

Sentence Complements 102

Forming Sentences 104

Review of Sentence Forms 107

Sentence Functions 107

Sentence Errors 109

Agreement of Sentence Parts 117

SHIFTS 126

Shifts in Tense 126

Shifts in Voice 127

Shifts in Mood 128

Shifts in Person 129

Shifts in Perspective 131

Shifts in Number 132

Shifts in Tone and Style 133

Shifts in Direct and Indirect Quotations 135

PARALLELISM 137

Parallel Structure 137

Parallel Items in Series 139

Parallel Outlines and Lists 140

SECTION QUIZ 141

SECTION II — *Usage*

COMMON ERRORS 153

COMMONLY CONFUSED WORDS 186

**AVOIDING INSENSITIVE
AND OFFENSIVE LANGUAGE** 215

Sexism 216

Race, Ethnicity, and National Origin 219

Age 220

Sexual Orientation 221

*Avoiding Depersonalization of Persons
with Disabilities or Illnesses* 221

*Avoiding Patronizing or Demeaning
Expressions* 222

*Avoiding Language that Excludes or
Unnecessarily Emphasizes Differences* 223

SECTION QUIZ 224

SECTION III — *Spelling*

Spelling Rules 233

Words Commonly Misspelled 235

Using a Spell-Checker 243

Rules of Word Division 243

SECTION QUIZ 245

SECTION IV — *Punctuation*

[.] *Period* 253

[?] *Question Mark* 254

[!] *Exclamation Point* 255

[,] *Comma* 255

[;] *Semicolon* 260

[:] *Colon* 262

[—] *Dash* 264

[...] *Ellipsis* 266

[( )] *Parentheses* 267

[[ ]] *Brackets* 268

[""] *Quotation Marks* 270

Italics/Underlining 274

[/] *Forward Slash*

(Also Called "Solidus" or "Virgule") 276

['] *Apostrophe* 277

[-] *Hyphen* 279

Capitalization 282

Pronunciation 284

Abbreviations...................................... 287

Rules for Using Numbers 291

SECTION QUIZ **294**

Section v — *Writing*

GETTING STARTED **301**

WRITING A TERM PAPER **303**
The Subject....................................... 303
Library Research................................. 304
Internet Research 305
Outline 306
Writing 306
Footnotes... 308
Bibliographies 318
Sample Entries 318
Citing Internet Sources 319

Section vi — *Prefixes, Suffixes, and Roots*

COMMON PREFIXES AND THEIR MEANINGS **323**

COMMON SUFFIXES AND THEIR MEANINGS **329**

COMMON ROOTS AND THEIR MEANINGS 337

GLOSSARY OF TERMS 351

INDEX 359

INTRODUCTION

WHETHER it's spoken or written, language exists so that we may communicate with one another. Sometimes we communicate informally about everyday matters: The stove is broken. Someone missed a bus. The rent is due. Sometimes, the communication is more formal: an acceptance speech at an awards ceremony or a presentation to coworkers.

No doubt, language is complicated. It has structure. It has rules. Some of these rules are written in stone, some are not. Why, you ask, is it necessary for you to know the definition of a transitive verb, a determiner, a phrasal preposition, or a misplaced modifier? Why is it necessary to know the difference between a colon and a semicolon? Because when you understand how sentences are created, that knowledge will help you communicate more directly and effectively. To use an analogy, if you are in charge of bringing a large ship to a specific destination not only safely and soundly, but also expeditiously, the more you know about how the ship is constructed and how it works, the easier your task will be.

Having said that, there is one fundamental difference between this analogy and our language. Once a ship is built, it's rare that the structure will change. Not so with language, which is constantly evolving. *Random House Webster's Grammar, Usage, and Punctuation* in its new and expanded form will give you the most up-to-date information on:

- Understanding the parts of speech
  and elements of a sentence

- Avoiding common grammatical, stylistic, and spelling errors

- Improving your writing skills

Plus you can test your knowledge with quizzes at the end of each section. In the Usage part of the book, you'll find a section on Commonly Confused Words. The fact is, English *can* be confusing, and no one, no matter how well educated or how verbally accomplished, is ever totally free from error. Do you know for certain the difference between *adverse* and *averse*? Do you know when it should be *me* or *I*? *He* or *him*?

Random House Webster's Grammar, Usage, and Punctuation is your one-stop reference for answers to these questions. It's simple and easy to use, with a detailed table of contents and index so you can easily locate a particular subject, as well as a glossary of terms. If your goal is effective communication, this clear and precise guide to the English language is the tool that will help get you there.

SECTION 1

Grammar

PARTS OF SPEECH

THE English language has nine basic classes of words, or parts of speech: **nouns, pronouns, verbs, adjectives, determiners, adverbs, prepositions, conjunctions**, and **interjections**.

Words often serve more than one grammatical function, depending on their position, meaning, and use in a sentence. Therefore, the same word can be a different part of speech in different sentences. For example, the word *help* can be either a verb or a noun.

Help as a noun:

The offer of **help** was greatly appreciated.

(Here *help* is the name of something.)

Help as a verb:

They **help** the community by volunteering their time to tutor illiterate adults.

(Here *help* expresses an action.)

Since words can work in different ways, you must determine how the word is functioning within a sentence before you can label it as a specific part of speech. You cannot assume that any word will always be the same part of speech and fulfill the same grammatical function.

Words and phrases from different parts of speech often modify other words and phrases. For instance, an adjective modifies a noun by describing the noun (a **blue** hat). An adverb modifies an adjective, a verb, or another adverb by giving more specific information about it (a **light-blue** hat; He spoke **quickly**; He spoke **very quickly**).

NOUNS

A *noun* is a word used to name a person, place, thing, idea, state, or quality.

Person	Place	Thing
Mary	library	flowers
Edward	Ontario	mutiny
American	coastline	computer
cousin	Paris	house
Mr. Jones	city	rabbit

Idea	State	Quality
democracy	hunger	integrity
equality	poverty	courage
Hinduism	happiness	sincerity
justice	rage	decency
evil	joy	bravery

Some of the nouns listed above can be further classified into specific types.

Common nouns name any of a class of people, places, or things:

girl
city
river
road

Proper nouns name specific people, places, and things:

Lisa
Vienna
Ohio River
Main Street

Collective nouns name groups of people or things:

team
clan
flock
tribe
pack
committee

Mass nouns name qualities or things that cannot be counted and do not have plural forms:

laughter
sand
valor
exhaustion
anger
wheat

Compound nouns are made up of two or more words. The words may be separate, hyphenated, or combined:

boarding pass
mother-in-law
housework
runaway
airport
schoolroom

PRONOUNS

A *pronoun* is a word that takes the place of a noun.

> Ellen has been working on the project for a long time. **She** spends eight hours a day on it. **Her** time is well spent, however, as **she herself** recognizes.

ANTECEDENTS

An *antecedent* is the noun, phrase, clause, or sentence to which a pronoun refers. Use a singular pronoun to refer to a singular antecedent and a plural pronoun to refer to a plural antecedent. In the above example, the antecedent of the pronoun *she* is *Ellen*; the antecedent of the pronoun *it* is *project*.

TYPES OF PRONOUNS

Personal pronouns refer to the one speaking, the one spoken to, or the one spoken about. Personal pronouns that refer to the speaker are known as *first-person pronouns*; those that refer to the person spoken to are known as *second-person pronouns*; those that refer to the person, place, or thing spoken about are known as *third-person pronouns*.

Singular

First person	I	me	my, mine
Second person	you	you	your, yours
Third person	he	him	his
	she	her	her, hers
	it	it	its

Plural

First person	we	us	our, ours
Second person	you	you	your, yours
Third person	they	them	their, theirs

Intensive pronouns and reflexive pronouns end in *-self* or *-selves*.

myself	ourselves
yourself	yourselves
himself	themselves
herself	themselves
itself	

Intensive pronouns add emphasis to a noun or pronoun:

I **myself** have never given much thought to the matter.

Mary hung the striped wallpaper **herself**.

Reflexive pronouns show that the subject of the sentence also receives the action of the verb:

I treated **myself** to a new pair of shoes.

Michael kept telling **himself** that it was not his fault.

Interrogative pronouns are used to ask questions. These pronouns do not have to have a specific antecedent.

which   what   who   whom   whose

What did you call me for in the first place?

Whom have you called about this matter?

Whose is that?

Relative pronouns are used to tie together or relate groups of words. Relative pronouns begin subordinate clauses.

which   **what**   **who**   **whom**   **whose**

Debbie enrolled in the class that her employer recommended.

Charles has a friend **who** lives in Toronto.

Demonstrative pronouns are used to point out nouns, phrases, or clauses. They can be placed before or after their antecedents.

this   **that**   **these**   **those**

This is the book I told you about last week.

That is a perfect place to sit down and have lunch.

Is **that** the house with the Japanese garden in the backyard?

Indefinite pronouns take the place of a noun but do not have to have a specific antecedent. Following is a list of some common indefinite pronouns.

all	everyone	none
another	everything	nothing
any	few	one
anybody	little	other
anyone	many	others
anything	more	several
both	most	some
each	much	somebody
either	neither	someone
every	nobody	something
everybody	no one	

Indefinite pronouns can have a specific antecedent or no specific antecedent.

Specific Antecedent

The **casserole** was so delicious that **none** was left by the end of the meal.

A **few** of the **relatives** usually lend a hand when my husband undertakes one of his home-repair projects.

No Specific Antecedent

Someone arrived at the party early, much to the embarrassment of the unprepared host and hostess.

Everyone stayed late, too.

CASE

The majority of English words rely on their position within a sentence (not their form) to show their function. The placement of a word determines whether it is a subject or object. Certain nouns and pronouns, however, also change their form to indicate their use.

Case is the form of a noun or pronoun that shows how it is used and how it relates to other words in a sentence.

English has three cases: **nominative, objective,** and **possessive.** In general, pronouns take the nominative case when they function as the subject of a sentence or clause and the objective case when they function as the object of a verb or a preposition. Pronouns and nouns take the possessive case to indicate ownership.

Nouns change form only in the possessive case: for example, a **dog's** bone, **Maria's** hair. Some pronouns, in contrast, change form in the nominative, objective, and possessive cases. The following table shows how personal pronouns change form in the three different cases.

Nominative	Objective	Possessive
I	me	my, mine
you	you	your, yours
he	him	his
she	her	her, hers
it	it	its
we	us	our, ours
you	you	your, yours
they	them	their, theirs

NOMINATIVE CASE

The *nominative case* is sometimes called the *subjective case* because it is used when pronouns function as subjects. The following examples illustrate how personal pronouns are used in the nominative case.

Subject of a Verb

We understand that they will be late.

Neither **she** nor **I** will be attending.

Appositive Identifying a Subject

An *appositive* is a word or a phrase appearing next to a noun or pronoun that explains or identifies it and is equivalent to it:

Both physicists, **Marie Curie and he**, worked on isolating radium.

Mr. Brown, **our English teacher**, went on the class trip with us.

Predicate Nominative

The *predicate nominative* is the noun or pronoun after a linking verb that renames the subject. The linking verb *to be* functions as an equal sign (=): the words on either side must be in the same case.

It is **I**.

The primary supervisor is **she**.

The fastest runners are **Lenore** and **he**.

Since the predicate nominative can sound overly formal in speech, many people use the colloquial: It's **me**. It's **her**. In formal speech and edited writing, however, the nominative forms should be used: It must be **he**. The person at the door was **she**, not her husband. This is **she**. In some instances, revising the sentence can produce a less artificial sound.

Predicate nominative

The delegates who represented the community at last evening's town board meeting were **he** and **I**.

Revision

He and **I** were the delegates who represented the community at last evening's town board meeting.

OBJECTIVE CASE

The *objective case* is used when a personal pronoun is a direct object, indirect object, or object of a preposition.

Direct Object

Bob's jokes embarrassed **me**.

When you reach the station, call either **him** or **me**.

Indirect Object

The glaring sun gave **my friends** and **me** a headache.

My aunt brought **us** pottery from Mexico.

Please give **him** some money.

Object of a Preposition

The cat leaped onto the bed and curled up beside **me**.

They fully understood why she had come with **us** rather than with **him**.

Let's keep the understanding between **you** and **me**.

Case after *Than* or *As*

If the word following *than* or *as* begins a clause, the pronoun takes the nominative case. If the word following *than* or *as* does not begin a clause, the pronoun takes the objective case. In some instances, the case depends on the meaning of the sentence. To help decide whether the sentence requires a pronoun in the nominative or objective case, complete the clause.

She has been working at Smithson longer than **he** (has).

Kevin is more proficient at marketing than **I** (am).

They are going to be informed as quickly as **we** (are).

I have stayed with Julia as long as **she** (has stayed with her).

I have stayed with Julia as long as (I have stayed with) **her**.

USES OF WHO AND WHOM

The form of the pronoun *who* depends on its function within a clause.

Subordinate Clauses and *Who/Whom*

In subordinate clauses, use *who* and *whoever* for all subjects, *whom* and *whomever* for all objects, regardless of whether the clause itself acts as a subject or object:

Distribute the food to **whoever** needs it.
> (Since *whoever* is the subject of *needs*, it is in the nominative case. The entire clause *whoever needs it* is the object of the preposition to.)

We did not realize **whom** the specialist had called.
> (Since *whom* is the object of *called*, it is in the objective case. The entire clause *whom the specialist had called* is the object of the verb *realize*.)

Frederick is the lawyer **whom** most people hire for this type of work.
> (Since *whom* is the object of *hire*, it is in the objective case. The clause *whom most people hire for this type of work* modifies the noun *lawyer*.)

She is the candidate **who** everyone thinks will win.
> (Since *who* is the subject of *will win*, it is in the nominative case. The clause *who everyone thinks will win* modifies the noun *candidate*.)

There is only one doctor **who** I know makes house calls.
> (Since *who* is the subject of *makes*, it is in the nominative case. The clause *who makes house calls* modifies the noun *doctor*.)

He will speak to **whoever** will listen.
> (Since *whoever* is the subject of *will listen*, it is in the nominative case. The clause *whoever will listen* is the object of the preposition *to*.)

Questions and *Who/Whom*

Use *who* at the beginning of a question about a subject; use *whom* at the beginning of a question about an object.

In informal speech, the distinction is not always made, and *who* is used for the first word of a question, regardless of whether the question is about a subject or an object.

To determine whether to use *who* or *whom*, you can use a personal pronoun to construct an answer to the question. The case of the personal pronoun determines whether *who* (nominative) or *whom* (objective) is required:

Who left the car doors open?
(Possible answer to the question: "He left the car doors open." Since *he* is in the nominative case, the question is about a subject and thus requires *who*.)

Whom should I see about this invoice?
(Possible answer to the question: "You should see him." Since *him* is in the objective case, the question is about an object and thus requires *whom*.)

POSSESSIVE CASE

Use the *possessive case* of a pronoun to show ownership.

The possessives *my, mine; your, yours; her, hers; our, ours;* and *their, theirs* have two different forms. Which one you use depends on whether the possessive comes before a noun or takes the place of a noun. *His* and *its* are used in either position.

Use the possessive pronouns *my, her, your, our, their* before a noun:

My cat sleeps all day.

Where is **your** umbrella?

Joan left **her** coat in the theater.

Our son is graduating from high school this year.

Use the possessive pronouns *mine, hers, yours, ours, theirs* alone to indicate possession:

This idea was **mine**, not **yours**.

Is this article really **hers**?

Do you believe that it's **theirs**?

The red one is **ours**.

In most instances you should use the possessive case before gerunds. A *gerund* is the -*ing* form of the verb (*swimming, snoring*) used as a noun. Possessive pronouns and nouns often precede gerunds, as in:

The landlord objected to **my** (not *me*) having guests late at night.

My shoveling the snow saved the mail carrier a nasty fall.

Do you mind **my** eating the rest of the cake?

She wholeheartedly supported **his** exercising.

My colleagues were annoyed by **my** coughing.

A possessive is not used before a gerund if its use would create a clumsy sentence. In these instances, you should rewrite the sentence entirely to eliminate the awkward construction.

Awkward

The neighbors spread the news about **somebody's** wanting to organize a block party.

Revision

We heard from the neighbors that somebody wants to organize a block party.

Note: Never use an apostrophe with a possessive pronoun. The following personal pronouns are already possessive and have no need for an apostrophe: *my, mine, your, yours, her, hers, its, our, ours, their,* and *theirs.* Do not confuse the contraction *it's* (for *it is*) with the possessive pronoun *its.*

AMBIGUOUS REFERENCES

Make sure that the reference is clear when two pronouns could logically refer to either of two antecedents. The following examples demonstrate how ambiguities can occur.

Unclear

The manager told Mrs. Greenberger that **she** will have to train her new people by June.

As the sentence is written, it is unclear whether the manager or Mrs. Greenberger will have to train the new people and whose new people have to be trained.

Clearer

Since Mrs. Greenberger will have to train her new people by June, she decided to take her vacation in the fall.

If the reference to an antecedent is not specific, confusion can arise. An unclear pronoun reference can usually be clarified by rearranging the sentence or by using the noun rather than the pronoun, as the following examples show.

Unclear

When you have finished with the stamp and bound the report, please return **it** to the storeroom.

Clearer

When you have finished with the stamp and bound the report, please return the stamp to the storeroom.

Sometimes, using *it*, *they*, and *you* incorrectly will result in a sentence that is vague or wordy. Removing the pronoun, eliminating excess words, or revising the sentence helps produce a clearer and more vigorous style.

Wordy

In the cookbook **it** says that wooden chopping blocks should be disinfected with bleach.

Better

The cookbook says that wooden chopping blocks should be disinfected with bleach.

Wordy

They say you should use a cold steam vaporizer instead of the traditional hot steam one.

Better

The doctor recommends using a cold steam vaporizer instead of the traditional hot steam one.

COMMON PRONOUN MISTAKES

Some of the most common grammatical errors involve the use of pronouns. Is it *me* or *I*? *He* or *him*? If a sentence *sounds* grammatically correct, does that mean it always is? Here is a list of pronoun mistakes to watch out for:

1. **Using the wrong form when pronouns serve as the subjects for the verb.**

   Him and me loved to sing. This should be: *He and I loved to sing.* Many pronoun mistakes occur when two or more pronouns are included in a sentence. To figure out what pronoun to use, simply eliminate the other pronoun. Would you say "Him loved to sing"? Or "Me loved to sing"? When broken down this way, the answers "he" and "I" are obvious.

2. **Using the wrong pronoun when the pronoun is the object of a preposition.**

   The present is from Danny and I. It should be: *The present is from Danny and me.* The pronoun in this case is the object of a preposition—from—so it must be the objective case of the pronoun. Using the same logic as in example #1, would you say, "The present is from I"?

3. **Problems with the noun or pronoun following a linking verb.**

   The chief of the police department is him. It should be: *The chief of the police department is he.* Yes, it sounds awkward. But this is a predicate nominative following the linking verb "to be," so you have to be able to substitute the pronoun at the beginning of the sentence as you do at the end of the sentence—i.e., *He is the chief of the police department.*

4. **Using the wrong pronoun with the objective case.**

   The noise on the street gave my companions and I a huge headache. It should be: *The noise on the street gave my companions* *and me a huge headache.* Again, use the trick from example #1 and #2, and take out "my companions." You are left with, *The noise gave me a headache.*

5. Confusing "who" and "whom."

Who should I write to regarding this matter? It should be: *Whom should I write to regarding this matter?* To figure out who or whom, answer your own question: If the answer is "him" (i.e., you should write *him*) then use *whom.* If the answer is "he" (as in the following example: *Who do we think will win the race? We think* he *will win the race*) then use *who.*

6. Using the possessive case with a gerund.

The teacher objected to me doing homework in class. It should be: *The teacher objected to my doing homework in class.* The gerund form of the verb—doing—requires the possessive pronoun.

7. Difficulties with comparisons.

The Smiths have a larger backyard than us. It should be: *The Smiths have a larger backyard than we.* To determine the correct form, simply add the "understood" verb: *The Smiths have a larger backyard than we (do). She can jump higher than I (can).*

8. Confusing pronouns involved in neither . . . nor.

Neither she nor him will be going to the picnic. It should be: *Neither she nor he will be going to the picnic.* In this case, the pronoun serves as a subject, so you use the nominative (he) case. In cases such as these, the pronouns should always match: she/he, we/them, etc.

9. **Confusing agreement with a noun and pronouns.**

The two runners, John and him, get into shape by using the tread-mill. It should be: *The two runners, John and he, get into shape by using the treadmill.* Eliminate "The two runners," and you'll see "John and he get into shape . . ." makes sense.

10. **Odd Encounters with the Objective Case.**

Let's you and I go to the store. It should be: *Let's you and me go to the store.* This is an odd-sounding one. But the fact is that "Let's" is a contraction for "Let us," and since "us" is the objective case, the pronouns must be, too. An easy way to simplify this one is to simply say, "Let's go to the store."

Here are some more tricky pronoun examples:

1. The Wilsons have a smaller car than **we/us.**

   The first sentence should be "The Wilsons have a smaller can than **we.**" You can tell if you simply add the verb "have" that is missing but implied. "The Wilsons have a smaller cat than we [have]."

2. The teacher has no difficulties about **us/our** using a calculator during the math test.

   You always use a possessive pronoun if it falls before a gerund—i.e., the *-ing* form of the verb. So, this should be, "The teacher has no difficulties about **our** using a calculator during the math test."

3. Distribute the candy to **whomever/whoever** wants it.

   The use of a pronoun *who* depends on its function within a clause. Since, in the sentence above, *whoever* is the subject of *needs,* it is in the nominative case. So, it should be, "Distribute the candy to whoever wants it."

4. Bruce is the carpenter **who/whom** most people hire for their trim work.

   Since *whom* is the object of *hire,* it is the objective case, so it should be, "Bruce is the carpenter whom most people hire for their trim work."

5. Everyone has **his or her/their** idea of who will win the election.

   "Everyone" is a singular pronoun, despite how it may sound, and so all pronouns in the phrase should be singular as well, "Everyone has his or her idea of who will win the election."

VERBS

A *verb* is a word that expresses an action, an occurrence, or a state of being.

Action	Occurrence	State of Being
jump	become	be
swim	happen	seem
throw		
speak		

Action verbs can describe mental actions as well as physical actions. The verb *think,* for example, describes a mental action, one that cannot be seen. Additional examples of action verbs that describe unseen mental actions include *understand, welcome, enjoy, relish, ponder, consider*, and *deliberate*. Action verbs are divided into two groups, **transitive** and **intransitive**, depending on how they function within a sentence.

TRANSITIVE VERBS

A *transitive verb* is a verb that requires a direct object to complete its meaning. The direct object receives the action of the verb:

My son **ate** the last piece of chocolate cake.

My sister **baked** another cake.

Please **call** your mother.

Sally **read** twenty-five books during the summer.

INTRANSITIVE VERBS

An *intransitive verb* is a verb that does not need a direct object to complete its meaning:

When they heard about it, my friends **laughed**.

Even the baby **giggled**.

Please **sit** down.

I **worked** hard all winter.

ERGATIVE VERBS

Some verbs can treat the same noun as both a subject and an object. An *ergative* is a verb that allows the subject of the intransitive form to be the object of the transitive form:

The boat **capsized**.

They **capsized** the boat.

The dress **buttons** down the front.

She **buttoned** her dress.

Marie **sat**.

He **sat** the baby in her highchair.

The boat **sank** to the bottom of the lake.

They deliberately **sank** the boat.

The doorbell **rang**.

They **rang** the doorbell.

COPULA VERBS

A *copula*, or *linking verb*, describes an occurrence or a state of being. It connects parts of a sentence.

A sentence contains a linking verb if you can substitute an equal sign (=) for the verb and the equation works. So, if you take the linking verb "appear," and put it in a sentence, "The man appears ill," we can take out the verb and substitute "The man = ill." You *cannot* do this with, say, the sentence, "John ate a pizza." "John = pizza" makes no sense. *Ate* is not a linking verb.

The most common linking verb is the verb *to be*. For example,

The building is white.

The parents are exhausted.

The table is large.

My mother was president of the PTA.

You could be hungry if you don't eat.

The dog is lost.

Note that there are some cases where "to be" does *not* serve as a linking verb:

John is home.

The bicycle is in the basement.

Following are some other linking verbs.

appear	grow	seem
become	lie	smell
continue	look	sound
fall	prove	stay
feel	run	taste
get	remain	turn

The supports **looked** fragile.

The actor **seemed** nervous when the play began.

It **sounds** like a fire alarm.

I **became** increasingly certain that he was lying.

The butter **turned** rancid.

The test **proved** extremely difficult.

The little girl **fell** asleep.

You'll also notice that quite a few linking verbs relate to the senses, and that's one way to single them out.

The roast **smelled** delicious.

The drink **tasted** bitter.

The room **smelled** musty.

The verbs on the list do not always function as linking verbs. To determine whether the word is functioning as a linking verb or as an action verb, examine its role in the sentence.

Linking verb

The child **grew** tired by the end of the evening.

The milk **smells** sour.

The lemonade **tastes** too sweet.

Action verb

My mother **grows** the best tomatoes I have ever eaten.

Can you **smell** those roses?

Have you **tasted** the lemonade?

A *subject complement* (noun, pronoun, or adjective) follows a linking verb and describes or identifies the subject.

My sister is **a pediatrician**.

The lemonade tastes **sour**.

Is that **you**?

I feel **sick**.

A subject complement is frequently a subject nominative. Since the linking verb serves as an equal sign, the words on both sides of it must be in the same case, i.e., the nominative case.

We all assumed that it was **he**.

I am waiting for my mother to call. Is that **she**?

AUXILIARY VERBS

An *auxiliary verb*, or *helping verb*, is used with a main verb to form a verb phrase. The three helping verbs are *be*, *do*, and *have*.

Are you **enjoying** the play?

Did you **complete** the project on time?

Have you ever **eaten** at the Chinese restaurant on 12th Street?

MODAL VERBS

There is another class of auxiliary verbs called *modals*. These verbs express ability, possibility, obligation, permission, intention, and probability. The modal auxiliaries are *can*, *could*, *may*, *might*, *shall*, *should*, *will*, *would*, and *must*. *Dare*, *had better*, *have to*, *need*, *ought to*, and *used to* are also used as modals.

I **might work** late tonight.

Can you **help** me?

Could you please **help** me?

You really **should** not **do** that.

May I please **have** a cup of coffee?

I **must go** to the office early tomorrow morning.

You **had better do** your homework before you go out.

You **ought to try** it.

PHRASAL VERBS

A *phrasal verb* is a combination of a verb and one or more adverbs or prepositions. The meaning of the phrase is often idiomatic and is not predictable from the individual parts. Examples of phrasal verbs are: *call off, catch on, get along with, put up with, send for, show up, stand up to, take off, throw away.*

It won't take you long to **catch on** to the new routine.

She has trouble **getting along with** her coworkers.

What time did they finally **show up**?

You ought to **stand up** to him.

Did your flight **take off** on time?

She has **thrown away** several opportunities.

VERBAL FORMS

All English verbs have four basic *forms*, or principal parts: the **infinitive**, the **past**, the **past participle**, and the **present participle**.

INFINITIVE FORM

The *infinitive* is the basic form of a verb:

to grin
to talk
to snore
to walk
to drop

The *bare infinitive* is the form found in dictionaries, without *to*:

grin
talk
snore
walk
drop

The infinitive (*to* + the bare form of a verb) can begin a clause that acts as an object. Main verbs that invite infinitives as objects include *ask*, *beg*, *expect*, *help*, *intend*, *like*, *mean*, *prefer*, *want*, *wish*, *would hate*, and *would like*:

> We would like **to go** to Paris in June.
>
> They had not expected **to go** to Italy last winter.
>
> I would have liked **to hear** at least one of Mozart's operas during my trip to Vienna last year.
>
> She wanted **to win** that award.

PERFECT INFINITIVE FORM

The *perfect infinitive* (*to have* + the past participle) is used with a main verb in the present tense to express action that will be completed by a future date:

> They expect **to have seen** three plays by the time they return.
>
> We hope **to have moved** into our new house by Christmas.

The perfect infinitive is also used with *would like/love* to express a wish that was not realized:

> She would like **to have won** that award.
>
> He would love **to have bought** a new car.

PAST FORM

The *past* form is used to form the past tense. It indicates that the verb's action took place in the past. The past form of regular verbs is formed by adding -*d* or -*ed* to the infinitive, sometimes requiring the doubling of a final consonant. (See pp. 30–37 for irregular verbs.)

grinned
talked
snored
walked
dropped

PAST PARTICIPLE

The *past participle* is used with at least one helping verb and/or modal verb to form the *perfect tenses.* The past participle of regular verbs is the same as the past form. (See pp. 31–37 for irregular verbs.)

grinned
talked
snored
walked
dropped

The past participle can also be used as an adjective:

Where is the **finished** product?

My nephew refuses to eat **cooked** vegetables.

PRESENT PARTICIPLE

The *present participle* is used with the verb *to be* to create *progressive forms,* which show continuing action. The present participle is formed by adding *-ing* to the infinitive. The final consonant is often doubled with this addition.

grinning
talking
snoring

walking

dropping

Like the past participle, the present participle can be used as an adjective:

Stand clear of the **closing** doors.

She picked up the **crying** child.

REGULAR AND IRREGULAR VERBS

The majority of English verbs are regular and change their form by adding -*ing*, -*ed*, or -*d* to the infinitive. However, many verbs do not follow this pattern. These irregular verbs form their past tense and past participle in a number of ways: Some change an internal vowel and add -*n* to the past participle; some retain the same spelling in all three forms or in the past tense and past participle; some follow no discernible pattern.

The following list includes the most common irregular verbs. For information about verbs not included below, consult a dictionary. If a verb is regular, the dictionary will usually give only the infinitive. If the verb is irregular, the dictionary will include the past tense and past participle along with the infinitive; if only two forms are given, the past tense and the past participle are identical.

COMMON IRREGULAR VERBS

Present Tense	Past Tense	Past Participle
arise	arose	arisen
awake	awoke	awoken
be	was/were	been

Present Tense	Past Tense	Past Participle
bear	bore	borne, born
beat	beat	beaten
become	became	become
befall	befell	befallen
begin	began	begun
behold	beheld	beheld
bend	bent	bent
bet	bet, betted	bet
bid	bid, bade	bid, bidden
bide	bode/bided	bided
bind	bound	bound
bleed	bled	bled
bite	bit	bitten
blow	blew	blown
break	broke	broken
breed	bred	bred
bring	brought	brought
build	built	built
burn	burned, burnt	burned, burnt
burst	burst	burst
buy	bought	bought
catch	caught	caught

Present Tense	Past Tense	Past Participle
chide	chided/chid	chided/chid/chidden
choose	chose	chosen
cling	clung	clung
come	came	come
creep	crept	crept
cut	cut	cut
deal	dealt	dealt
dig	dug	dug
dive	dived, dove	dived
do	did	done
draw	drew	drawn
dream	dreamed, dreamt	dreamed, dreamt
drink	drank	drunk
drive	drove	driven
dwell	dwelled/dwelt	dwelled/dwelt
eat	ate	eaten
fall	fell	fallen
feed	fed	fed
feel	felt	felt
fight	fought	fought
find	found	found
flee	fled	fled

Present Tense	Past Tense	Past Participle
fling	flung	flung
fly	flew	flown
forbid	forbade,	forbidden,
	forbad	forbid
forget	forgot	forgotten,
		forgot
forgive	forgave	forgiven
forsake	forsook	forsaken
freeze	froze	frozen
frostbite	frostbit	frostbitten
get	got	got, gotten
give	gave	given
go	went	gone
grind	ground	ground
grow	grew	grown
hang (suspend)	hung	hung
hang (execute)	hanged	hanged
hear	heard	heard
hide	hid	hidden
hold	held	held
inlay	inlaid	inlaid
keep	kept	kept
kneel	knelt/kneeled	knelt/kneeled

Present Tense	Past Tense	Past Participle
know	knew	known
lay (put down)	laid	laid
lead	led	led
leap	leaped/lept	leaped/lept
learn	learned/learnt	learned/learnt
lend	lent	lent
lie (rest; recline)	lay	lain
light	lighted/lit	lit
lose	lost	lost
make	made	made
mean	meant	meant
meet	met	met
mislead	mislead	mislead
mistake	mistook	mistaken
mow	mowed	mowed/mown
overcome	overcame	overcome
overdo	overdid	overdone
overtake	overtook	overtaken
overthrow	overthrew	overthrown
pay	paid	paid
picnic	picnicked	picnicked
plead	pled	pled
prove	proved	proved/proven

Present Tense	Past Tense	Past Participle
ride	rode	ridden
ring	rang	rung
rise	rose	risen
run	ran	run
say	said	said
see	saw	seen
seek	sought	sought
sell	sold	sold
set	set	set
sew	sewed	sewed, sewn
shake	shook	shaken
shear	shore	shorn
shine	shone	shone
shoe	shoed	shoed/shod
shoot	shot	shot
shrink	shrank	shrunk
sing	sang, sung	sung
sink	sank	sunk
sit	sat	sat
slay	slew	slain
sleep	slept	slept
slide	slid	slid
sling	slung	slung

Present Tense	Past Tense	Past Participle
smite	smote	smitten
sow	sowed	sowed/sown
speak	spoke	spoken
speed	sped	sped
spend	spent	spent
spill	spilled/spilt	spilled/spilt
spin	spun	spun
spring	sprang	sprung
stand	stood	stood
steal	stole	stolen
stick	stuck	stuck
stink	stank	stunk
stride	strode	stridden
strike	struck	struck
strive	strove	striven
swear	swore	sworn
sweep	swept	swept
swim	swam	swum
swing	swung	swung
take	took	taken
teach	taught	taught
tear	tore	torn
think	thought	thought
thrive	thrived/throve	thrived/thriven

Present Tense	Past Tense	Past Participle
throw	threw	thrown
tread	trod	trodden
understand	understood	understood
uphold	upheld	upheld
wake	woke,	woken,
	waked	waked
wear	wore	worn
weave	weaved/wove	weaved/woven
weep	wept	wept
win	won	won
wind	wound	wound
withdraw	withdrew	withdrawn
withstand	withstood	withstood
wring	wrung	wrung
write	wrote	written

CONJUGATION OF TRICKY VERBS

All of us who have learned a foreign language have struggled with the eccentricities of verb conjugations, especially with irregular verbs. The same difficulties exist in English. Here are some examples.

TO BEAR						
	Present	Past	Future	Conditional	Present Participle	Past Participle
First person singular	I bear	bore	will bear	would bear	bearing	born
First person plural	We bear	bore	will bear	would bear		
Second person singular	You bear	bore	will bear	would bear		
Second person plural	You bear	bore	will bear	would bear		
Third person singular	He/she/ it bears	bore	will bear	would bear		
Third person plural	They bear	bore	will bear	would bear		

TO BITE						
	Present	Past	Future	Conditional	Present Participle	Past Participle
First person singular	I bite	bit	will bite	would bite	biting	bitten
First person plural	We bite	bit	will bite	would bite		
Second person singular	You bite	bit	will bite	would bite		

	Present	Past	Future	Conditional	Present Participle	Past Participle
Second person plural	You bite	bit	will bite	would bite		
Third person singular	He/she/it bites	bit	will bite	would bite		
Third person plural	They bite	bit	will bite	would bite		

TO CHOOSE						
	Present	Past	Future	Conditional	Present Participle	Past Participle
First person singular	I choose	chose	will choose	would choose	choosing	chosen
First person plural	We choose	chose	will choose	would choose		
Second person singular	You choose	chose	will choose	would choose		
Second person plural	You choose	chose	will choose	would choose		
Third person singular	He/she/it chooses	chose	will choose	would choose		
Third person plural	They choose	chose	will choose	would choose		

TO CLING						
	Present	**Past**	**Future**	**Conditional**	**Present Participle**	**Past Participle**
First person singular	I cling	clung	will cling	would cling	clinging	clung
First person plural	We cling	clung	will cling	would cling		
Second person singular	You cling	clung	will cling	would cling		
Second person plural	You cling	clung	will cling	would cling		
Third person singular	He/she/it clings	clung	will cling	would cling		
Third person plural	They cling	clung	will cling	would cling		

TO DRAW						
	Present	**Past**	**Future**	**Conditional**	**Present Participle**	**Past Participle**
First person singular	I draw	drew	will draw	would draw	drawing	drawn
First person plural	We draw	drew	will draw	would draw		
Second person singular	You draw	drew	will draw	would draw		

	Present	Past	Future	Conditional	Present Participle	Past Participle
Second person plural	You draw	drew	will draw	would draw		
Third person singular	He/she/ it draws	drew	will draw	would draw		
Third person plural	They draw	drew	will draw	would draw		

TO DRINK						
	Present	Past	Future	Conditional	Present Participle	Past Participle
First person singular	I drink	drank	will drink	would drink	drinking	drunk
First person plural	We drink	drank	will drink	would drink		
Second person singular	You drink	drank	will drink	would drink		
Second person plural	You drink	drank	will drink	would drink		
Third person singular	He/she/ it drinks	drank	will drink	would drink		
Third person plural	They drink	drank	will drink	would drink		

TO FLY						
	Present	Past	Future	Conditional	Present Participle	Past Participle
First person singular	I fly	flew	will fly	would fly	flying	flown
First person plural	We fly	flew	will fly	would fly		
Second person singular	You fly	flew	will fly	would fly		
Second person plural	You fly	flew	will fly	would fly		
Third person singular	He/she/it flies	flew	will fly	would fly		
Third person plural	They fly	flew	will fly	would fly		

TO FORBID						
	Present	Past	Future	Present Conditional	Past Participle	Participle
First person singular	I forbid	forbade/ forbad	will forbid	would forbid	forbiding	forbidden
First person plural	We forbid	forbade/ forbad	will forbid	would forbid		
Second person singular	You forbid	forbade/ forbad	will forbid	would forbid		

	Present	Past	Future	Conditional	Present Participle	Past Participle
Second person plural	You forbid	forbade/ forbad	will forbid	would forbid		
Third person singular	He/she/ it forbids	forbade/ forbad	will forbid	would forbid		
Third person plural	They forbid	forbade/ forbad	will forbid	would forbid		

TO FORSAKE

	Present	Past	Future	Conditional	Present Participle	Past Participle
First person singular	I forsake	forsook	will forsake	would forsake	forsaking	forsaken
First person plural	We forsake	forsook	will forsake	would forsake		
Second person singular	You forsake	forsook	will forsake	would forsake		
Second person plural	You forsake	forsook	will forsake	would forsake		
Third person singular	He/she/ it forsakes	forsook	will forsake	would forsake		
Third person plural	They forsake	forsook	will forsake	would forsake		

TO HIDE						
	Present	Past	Future	Conditional	Present Participle	Past Participle
First person singular	I hide	hid	will hide	would hide	hiding	hidden
First person plural	We hide	hid	will hide	would hide		
Second person singular	You hide	hid	will hide	would hide		
Second person plural	You hide	hid	will hide	would hide		
Third person singular	He/she/ it hides	hid	will hide	would hide		
Third person plural	They hide	hid	will hide	would hide		

TO KNEEL						
	Present	Past	Future	Present Conditional	Past Participle	Participle
First person singular	I kneel	knelt/ kneeled	will kneel	would kneel	kneeling	knelt/ kneeled
First person plural	We kneel	knelt/ kneeled	will kneel	would kneel		
Second person singular	You kneel	knelt/ kneeled	will kneel	would kneel		

	Present	Past	Future	Conditional	Present Participle	Past Participle
Second person plural	You kneel	knelt/ kneeled	will kneel	would kneel		
Third person singular	He/she/ it kneels	knelt/ kneeled	will kneel	would kneel		
Third person plural	They kneel	knelt/ kneeled	will kneel	would kneel		

TO LIE (REST, RECLINE)

	Present	Past	Future	Conditional	Present Participle	Past Participle
First person singular	I lie	lay	will lie	would lie	lying	lain
First person plural	We lie	lay	will lie	would lie		
Second person singular	You lie	lay	will lie	would lie		
Second person plural	You lie	lay	will lie	would lie		
Third person singular	He/she/ it lies	lay	will lie	would lie		
Third person plural	They lie	lay	will lie	would lie		

TO LIGHT						
	Present	Past	Future	Conditional	Present Participle	Past Participle
First person singular	I light	lighted/ lit	will light	would light	lighting	lit
First person plural	We light	lighted/ lit	will light	would light		
Second person singular	You light	lighted/ lit	will light	would light		
Second person plural	You light	lighted/ lit	will light	would light		
Third person singular	He/she/ it lights	lighted/ lit	will light	would light		
Third person plural	They light	lighted/ lit	will light	would light		

TO PLEAD						
	Present	Past	Future	Conditional	Present Participle	Past Participle
First person singular	I plead	pled	will plead	would plead	pleading	pled
First person plural	We plead	pled	will plead	would plead		
Second person singular	You plead	pled	will plead	would plead		

	Present	Past	Future	Conditional	Present Participle	Past Participle
Second person plural	You plead	pled	will plead	would plead		
Third person singular	He/she/ it pleads	pled	will plead	would plead		
Third person plural	They plead	pled	will plead	would plead		

TO RING						
	Present	**Past**	**Future**	**Conditional**	**Present Participle**	**Past Participle**
First person singular	I ring	rang	will ring	would ring	ringing	rung
First person plural	We ring	rang	will rung	would ring		
Second person singular	You ring	rang	will ring	would ring		
Second person plural	You ring	rang	will ring	would rung		
Third person singular	He/she/ it rings	rang	will ring	would ring		
Third person plural	They ring	rang	will ring	would ring		

TO RISE						
	Present	Past	Future	Conditional	Present Participle	Past Participle
First person singular	I rise	rose	will rise	would rise	rising	risen
First person plural	We rise	rose	will rise	would rise		
Second person singular	You rise	rose	will rise	would rise		
Second person plural	You rise	rose	will rise	would rise		
Third person singular	He/she/it rises	rose	will rise	would rise		
Third person plural	They rise	rose	will rise	would rise		

TO SHRINK						
	Present	Past	Future	Conditional	Present Participle	Past Participle
First person singular	I shrink	shrank	will shrink	would shrink	shrinking	shrunk
First person plural	We shrink	shrank	will shrink	would shrink		
Second person singular	You shrink	shrank	will shrink	would shrink		

	Present	Past	Future	Conditional	Present Participle	Past Participle
Second person plural	You shrink	shrank	will shrink	would shrink		
Third person singular	He/she/it shrinks	shrank	will shrink	would shrink		
Third person plural	They shrink	shrank	will shrink	would shrink		

TO SLAY

	Present	Past	Future	Conditional	Present Participle	Past Participle
First person singular	I slay	slew	will slay	would slay	slaying	slain
First person plural	We slay	slew	will slay	would slay		
Second person singular	You slay	slew	will slay	would slay		
Second person plural	You slay	slew	will slay	would slay		
Third person singular	He/she/it slays	slew	will slay	would slay		
Third person plural	They slay	slew	will slay	would slay		

TO SMITE						
	Present	Past	Future	Conditional	Present Participle	Past Participle
First person singular	I smite	smote	will smite	would smite	smiting	smitten
First person plural	We smite	smote	will smite	would smite		
Second person singular	You smite	smote	will smite	would smite		
Second person plural	You smite	smote	will smite	would smite		
Third person singular	He/she/it smites	smote	will smite	would smite		
Third person plural	They smite	smote	will smite	would smite		

TO SPRING						
	Present	Past	Future	Conditional	Present Participle	Past Participle
First person singular	I spring	sprang	will spring	would spring	springing	sprung
First person plural	We spring	sprang	will spring	would spring		
Second person singular	You spring	sprang	will spring	would spring		

	Present	Past	Future	Conditional	Present Participle	Past Participle
Second person plural	You spring	sprang	will spring	would spring		
Third person singular	He/she/ it springs	sprang	will spring	would spring		
Third person plural	They spring	sprang	will spring	would spring		

TO SWIM						
	Present	**Past**	**Future**	**Conditional**	**Present Participle**	**Past Participle**
First person singular	I swim	swam	will swim	would swim	swimming	swum
First person plural	We swim	swam	will swim	would swim		
Second person singular	You swim	swam	will swim	would swim		
Second person plural	You swim	swam	will swim	would swim		
Third person singular	He/she/ it swims	swam	will swim	would swim		
Third person plural	They swim	swam	will swim	would swim		

TO TREAD						
	Present	**Past**	**Future**	**Conditional**	**Present Participle**	**Past Participle**
First person singular	I tread	trod	will tread	would tread	treading	trodden/ trod
First person plural	We tread	trod	will tread	would tread		
Second person singular	You tread	trod	will tread	would tread		
Second person plural	You tread	trod	will tread	would tread		
Third person singular	He/she/ it treads	trod	will tread	would tread		
Third person plural	They tread	trod	will tread	would tread		

TO WRING						
	Present	**Past**	**Future**	**Conditional**	**Present Participle**	**Past Participle**
First person singular	I wring	wrung	will wring	would wring	wringing	wrung
First person plural	We wring	wrung	will wring	would wring		
Second person singular	You wring	wrung	will wring	would wring		

	Present	Past	Future	Conditional	Present Participle	Past Participle
Second person plural	You wring	wrung	will wring	would wring		
Third person singular	He/she/it wrings	wrung	will wring	would wring		
Third person plural	They wring	wrung	will wring	would wring		

TENSE

Tense refers to the form of a verb that indicates the time of the action, occurrence, or state of being expressed by the verb. Tense is different from time. The present tense, for instance, shows present time, but it can also indicate future time or a generally accepted belief.

English has two groups of tenses: the **simple tenses** (present, past, and future) and the **perfect tenses** (present perfect, past perfect, and future perfect).

SIMPLE TENSES

The *simple tenses* generally show that an action or state of being is taking place now, in the future, or in the past relative to the speaker or writer. The simple tenses indicate a finished, momentary, or habitual action or condition.

Present:	smile (smiles)	go (goes)
Past:	smiled	went
Future:	will (shall) smile	will (shall) go

Note: Shall is rarely used except in formal speaking and writing, to express determination, and in laws or directives.

I **shall** call the governor myself.

We **shall** overcome.

You **shall** not go!

All new students **shall** report to the dean upon arrival.

Present Tense

Except when the subjects are singular nouns or third-person singular pronouns, the present tense is the same as the infinitive form of the verb (I walk—to walk, you skip—to skip, we jump—to jump, they catch—to catch). With singular nouns or third-person singular pronouns, *-s* or *-es* is added to the infinitive (Robert **walks,** she **skips,** he **jumps,** it catches).

The *present tense* is used:

To state present action

Nick **prepares** the walls for painting.

To show present condition

The secretary **is** efficient.

To show that an action occurs regularly

Louise **prepares** a report for her supervisor every week.

To show a condition that occurs regularly

The traffic **is** usually backed up at the bridge in the evening.

To indicate future time, as an alternative to the future tense when a specific time is indicated

The income tax refund **arrives** tomorrow.

To state a generally held belief

Haste **makes** waste.

To state a scientific truth

A body in motion **tends** to stay in motion.

To discuss literary works, films, etc.

In *Hamlet*, Claudius **poisons** his brother, **marries** his former sister-in-law, and **seizes** the throne.

To narrate historical events as if they were happening in the present time (the "historical present")

In 1781 Cornwallis **surrenders** to Washington at Yorktown.

Past Tense

The *past tense* of regular verbs is formed by adding -*d* or -*ed* to the infinitive. The past tense of irregular verbs is formed in a variety of ways. Consult the table on pages 30–37 for forms of irregular verbs.

The *past tense* is used:

To show actions and conditions that began and ended in the past, or were true at a particular time in the past

Johnny **walked** the dog last night.

Joan **was** very happy.

To show recurring past actions that do not extend to the present

During World War II, Eric **saw** the fighting through the lens of a camera.

Future Tense

The *future tense* is formed by using the modal verbs *will* or *shall* plus the bare infinitive form of the verb.

The *future tense* is used:

To show a future action
Tomorrow the sun **will set** at 6:45 p.m.

To show a future condition
They **will be** excited when they see the presents.

To indicate intention
The Board of Education has announced that it **will begin** repairs on the pool as soon as possible.

To show probability
The decrease in land values in the Northeast **will** most likely **continue** into next year.

PERFECT TENSES

The *perfect tenses* indicate that one action was or will be finished before an indicated time.

Present:	have (has) smiled	have (has) gone
Past:	had smiled	had gone
Future:	will (shall) have smiled	will (shall) have gone

Present Perfect

The *present perfect* tense is formed by using the present tense of the auxiliary verb *have* plus the past participle of the main verb.

The *present perfect* tense is used:

To show completed action
Martin **has finished** talking to his clients.

To show past action or condition continuing into the present
We **have been waiting** for a week.

To show action that occurred at an unspecified past time
I **have reviewed** all the new procedures.

Past Perfect

The *past perfect* tense is formed by using the past tense of the auxiliary verb *have* plus the past participle of the main verb.

The *past perfect* tense is used:

To show one action or condition completed before another
By the time her employer returned, Linda **had completed** all her assigned tasks.

To show an action that occurred before a specific past time
By 1930 insulin **had been** isolated, refined, and distributed.

To show that something that was assumed or expected did not in fact happen
We **had hoped** to have the new cabin ready by the first of June.

Future Perfect

The *future perfect* tense is formed by using the auxiliary verbs *will* and *have* plus the past participle of the main verb.

The *future perfect* tense is used:

To show a future action or condition completed before another
By the time you read this letter, Bill **will have left** California for Mexico.

To show that an action will be completed by a specific future time

By tomorrow the bonds **will have lost** more than fifty percent of their face value.

PROGRESSIVE FORMS

Progressive forms are verb phrases that show continuing action. They are created by using the present participle of the main verb with forms of the verbs *to be* and *to have.*

Present Progressive

The *present progressive* is used to show continuing action or condition. It is formed with the present form of the verb *to be* plus the present participle:

I **am finishing** the painting while the children are at camp.

Medicine **is becoming** increasingly specialized.

Past Progressive

The *past progressive* is used to show an action or condition continuing in the past and to show two past actions occurring simultaneously. It is formed with the past form of the verb *to be* plus the present participle:

She **was becoming** disenchanted with the protein diet.

Garth fell off his bike while he **was watching** a cat climb a tree.

Future Progressive

The *future progressive* is used to show continuing future action and to show continuing action at a specific future time. It is formed with *will* plus *be* plus the present participle:

She **will be studying** all night.

Will you **be traveling** to Japan again in the spring?

Present Perfect Progressive

The *present perfect progressive* is used to show that an action or condition is continuing from the past into the present and/or the future. It is formed with the present form of the verb *to have* plus *been* plus the present participle:

The amount of pollution **has been increasing** sharply.

I **have been waiting** for a train for fifteen minutes.

Past Perfect Progressive

The *past perfect progressive* is used to show that a continuing past action has been interrupted by another. It is formed with *had* plus *been* plus the present participle:

Alice **had been taking** a detour through town until the new bridge was finished.

The workers **had been planning** a strike when the management made a new offer.

Future Perfect Progressive

The *future perfect progressive* is used to show that an action or condition will continue until a specific time in the future. It is formed with *will* plus *have* plus *been* plus the present participle:

By Monday I **will have been working** on that project for a month.

In September they **will have been traveling** for nearly a year.

USING TENSES

The sequence of tenses refers to the relationship among the verbs within a sentence or in sentences that follow each other. Illogical shifts in verb tenses confuse readers and muddle meaning. For clarity and sense, all the verbs must accurately reflect changes in time in the real world. Using tenses correctly allows you to express the desired sequence of events correctly.

Simultaneous Actions

If the actions described occur at approximately the same time, the tenses of all the verbs must be the same.

> The audience **applauded** when the conductor **mounted** the podium.

> Although we **have analyzed** the data, we **have** not **been able** to come to a firm conclusion.

> William Carlos Williams **was** a pediatrician in Paterson, New Jersey, who **wrote** some of the most distinctive verse of the twentieth century.

Actions Occurring at Different Times

If the verbs within a sentence describe actions that have occurred, are occurring, or will occur at different times, the tenses of the verbs must be different to express the different time sequence.

> The conference **had been over** for an hour by the time I **arrived**.

> I **asked** if he **had consulted** his attorney last week.

> Joe **was** worried that his dog **had bitten** the mail carrier.

Conditional Sentences

When the realization of the situation described in the main clause depends on something else, a conditional clause is used. Conditional clauses usually begin with *if* or *unless*.

> We'll stay home **if** it rains.

> We'll go **unless** it rains.

If the situation described is likely to occur, use the present tense in the conditional clause and *will* (or *won't*) in the main clause:

> If you **take** the train, you **will be** in the center of the city by 3:00.

> If you **wear** boots, your feet **won't get** cold.

If the situation described is imaginary or unlikely to occur, use the past tense form in the conditional clause and *would, might,* or *could* in the main clause.

> If I **had** her address, I **could send** her flowers.

> If wishes **were** horses, beggars **would ride**.

> If he **called** me, I **might go**.

If you want to describe a conditional situation that occurred in the past, use the past perfect form in the conditional clause and *would have* in the main clause.

> If they **had arrived** on time, we **would have been** able to go to a movie.

> The curtains **would** not **have gotten** wet if I **had remembered** to close the windows.

Using Participles Logically

The present participle expresses action occurring at the same time as that of the main verb.

> **Chewing** his pencil absently, Jeremy stared out the window at the mountains in the distance.

The present perfect participle expresses action occurring before that of the main verb.

Having operated the terminal for a month, the assistant knew how to repair the malfunction.

MOOD

The *mood* of a verb shows how the writer or speaker regards what he or she is saying. The form of the verb changes to indicate the mood. In English, there are three moods: the **indicative**, the **imperative**, and the **subjunctive**.

INDICATIVE MOOD

The *indicative* mood is used to state a fact or to ask a question:

Henry James **wrote** The Turn of the Screw.

We **hold** soccer games only on Saturdays.

Did T. S. Eliot **have** a great impact on twentieth-century literature?

Do you **hold** soccer games only on Saturdays?

IMPERATIVE MOOD

The *imperative* mood is used to give directions or express commands. Frequently, the subject (usually *you*) is understood rather than stated:

Get up!

We'll go to Mario's for dinner.

Turn left at the convenience store.

SUBJUNCTIVE MOOD

The *subjunctive* mood has traditionally been used to state wishes or desires, requirements, suggestions, or conditions that are contrary to fact. Its form looks different only in the present and past tenses of the verb *to be* and in the third-person singular present tense of all other verbs.

Although it has largely disappeared from English, the subjunctive survives in sentences with conditional clauses that are contrary to fact and in subordinate clauses after verbs like *wish*. In these cases, the subjunctive requires the form *were*:

He acted as if he **were** the owner.

If I **were** you, I would write them a letter.

I wish I **were** more organized.

The subjunctive is required in clauses expressing resolution, demand, or recommendation. In these cases, the subjunctive requires the bare infinitive form of the verb:

I move that the minutes **be** accepted.

He recommended that she **hire** an attorney.

They demanded that he **come** immediately.

The subjunctive is also used in certain idioms and set phrases:

Far **be** it from me . . .

If need **be** . . .

Be that as it may.

The people **be** damned.

Come rain or **come** shine.

As it **were** . . .

Suffice it to say . . .

Come what may . . .

VOICE

Voice shows whether the subject of a verb acts or is acted upon. There are two voices, **active** and **passive**. Only transitive verbs (those that take objects) can show voice.

ACTIVE VOICE

When the subject of the verb does the action, the verb is in the *active voice:*

> I **hit** the ball across the field.

> The subject, *I*, does the action, *hit*.

PASSIVE VOICE

When the subject of the verb receives the action, the verb is in the *passive voice:*

> The ball **was hit** by me.

> The subject, *the ball*, receives the action, *was hit*.

To convert an active verb to a passive verb, a form of *to be* is used with the past participle.

Active

The storms **damaged** many homes.

Mary's dog **bit** Christopher.

Keats **wrote** "The Eve of St. Agnes."

Eileen **will make** dinner.

Passive

Many homes **were damaged** by the storms.

Christopher **was bitten** by Mary's dog.

"The Eve of St. Agnes" **was written** by Keats.

Dinner **will be made** by Eileen.

WHEN TO USE THE ACTIVE VOICE

In general, use the active voice to emphasize the performer of the action. Except for a small number of specific situations, which are described below, the active voice is usually clearer and more powerful than the passive voice.

WHEN TO USE THE PASSIVE VOICE

The passive voice is preferable to the active voice:

When you do not wish to mention the performer of the action

A mistake **has been made**.

A check **has been returned** marked "insufficient funds."

When it is necessary to avoid vagueness

Furniture **is manufactured** in Hickory, North Carolina.
   (Recasting this sentence in the active voice—"They manufacture furniture in Hickory, North Carolina"—results in the vague *they*.)

When the performer of the action is not known

Plans for fifty units of low-income housing **were unveiled** at today's county meeting.

The computer **was stolen**.

When the result of the action is more important than the person performing the action

The driver **was arrested** for speeding.

The chief suspect **was freed** on bail pending trial.

VERBALS

A *verbal* is a verb form—a *participle*, a *gerund*, or an *infinitive*—used as another part of speech. Verbals can function as nouns, adjectives, or adverbs.

Verbals can be modified by adverbs and adverbial phrases. They can also take objects and complements, but they cannot function as the only verb form in a sentence. The verbal phrase includes the verbal and the words related to it.

Signs **hung on this wall** will be removed.
(*Hung on this wall* is a participial phrase functioning as an adjective and modifying *signs*.)

Eating a low-fat diet reduces the risk of many diseases.
(*Eating a low-fat diet* is a gerund phrase functioning as a noun. It is the subject of the verb *reduces*.)

She likes **to read science fiction novels**.
(*To read science fiction novels* is an infinitive phrase functioning as a noun. It is the object of the verb *likes*.)

DETERMINERS

A *determiner*, sometimes also called a *noun marker*, is a word that determines the use of a noun without actually modifying it. Determiners are placed before nouns or noun phrases.

Examples of determiners are the articles *a*, *an*, and *the*; the demonstrative pronouns *this*, *that*, *these*, and *those*; the possessive pronouns *my*, *your*, *her*, *his*, *our*, *their*; and indefinite pronouns such as *some* and *each*.

ADJECTIVES

An *adjective* is a word that modifies (describes) a noun or a pronoun.

The illness has affected **twelve** people in the apartment complex.

We could give you **additional** reasons why that would not be a **wise** decision, but we believe these will suffice.

You have had **enough** cookies for one day.

The **gold** earrings go with that outfit much better than the **silver** ones do.

The **eerie** noise seems to come from the basement.

This is the **third** time I've asked you to clean your room!

The **red**, **white**, and **blue** eye shadow proclaimed her patriotism but did little for her appearance.

NOUNS AND PRONOUNS AS ADJECTIVES

Nouns and pronouns can also function as adjectives.

The **produce** stand is open all night.

He has always enjoyed **piano** concertos.

We look forward to our **coffee** break.

Some common phrases in which nouns are used as adjectives:

amusement park	**dance** class
apple pie	**flood** control
art history	**flower** bed
beach towel	**horse** trailer
child care	**truth** serum

The demonstrative pronouns *this*, *that*, *these*, *those*; the interrogative pronouns *which* and *what*; and the indefinite pronouns *some*, *another*, *both*, *few*, *many*, *most*, *more*, etc., can all function as adjectives as well.

Are **those** socks yours or his?

This bus is rarely on time in the winter.

Which chores do you dislike the least?

What hobbies and sports do you enjoy the most?

Some people have managed to get tickets for the concert.

Any fan who wanted tickets had to be at the stadium at 4 a.m.

SPECIAL ADJECTIVES

There are also two special kinds of adjectives: *proper adjectives* and *compound adjectives*.

An adjective derived from a proper noun is called a *proper adjective*. Many of these adjectives are forms of people's names, as in *Emersonian*, from the nineteenth-century writer Ralph Waldo Emerson.

Kafkaesque situation
Shavian wit (Shaw)
Italian food
Chinese silk
March madness

An adjective made up of two or more words is called a *compound adjective*. The words in a compound adjective may be combined or hyphenated.

nearsighted	**open-and-shut**	**close-by**
soft-shelled	**hardworking**	

Note: A compound that is not hyphenated when it is another part of speech becomes hyphenated when it acts as an adjective placed before a noun.

Compare:

Is there a grocery store **close by**?

a **close-by** grocery store

ADVERBS

An *adverb* is a word that modifies (describes) a verb, an adjective, or another adverb.

Adverbs add description and detail to writing by more closely focusing the meaning of a verb, an adjective, or another adverb. They can sometimes provide a wider range of description than adjectives alone. They describe by telling *where, when, how,* or *to what extent.*

The pot boiled **over**.

The rain came **down**.

Yesterday it snowed; **today** it all melted.

The children **often** talk about going to Disneyland.

I **quickly** changed the topic.

The days are **slowly** getting longer.

Wash your hands **thoroughly**, please.

The child has **fully** recovered from her illness.

SENTENCE ADVERBS

Sentence adverbs are adverbs that modify or comment on the sentence as a whole or on the conditions under which the sentence is spoken.

Frankly, I don't believe him.

Really, you are too clever for me.

Compare:

"Things will be all right," she said **hopefully**.
(The adverb *hopefully* modifies *said*.)

"**Hopefully**, things will be all right," she said.
(The sentence adverb *hopefully* modifies the full statement.)

ADJECTIVE OR ADVERB?

How can you tell if a word is an adjective or an adverb? Many adverbs end in -*ly*, but this is not a reliable way to distinguish adverbs from adjectives. Not all adverbs end in -*ly* (*far, fast, little, well*). There are some adjectives that end in -*ly* (*curly, surly, lovely*) and some adverbs that have two different forms. The best test for determining whether a word is an adjective or an adverb is to determine its purpose in the sentence. Adjectives modify nouns. Adverbs modify adjectives, verbs, and other adverbs. Ultimately, the part of speech is determined by a word's function in the sentence, not by its ending.

Examples of adverbs that have two forms:

He aims **high** in his political ambitions.

I don't care for **highly** seasoned food.

Look **sharp**!

The car swerved **sharply** to the left.

Don't arrive too **late**.

He has been sick a lot **lately**.

Don't talk so **loud**.

"I want to go home," my daughter said **loudly**.

Winter is drawing **near**.

He **nearly** fell into the ditch.

You did it **wrong** again.

You were blamed **wrongly**.

In some instances, the choice of form depends on the idiomatic use of the word. *Nearly,* for example, is used to mean *almost,* while *near* is used to mean *close in time. Slow* is used in spoken commands with short verbs that express motion, such as *drive* and *run* (Drive slow), and combined with present participles to form adjectives (a slow-moving vehicle). *Slowly* is commonly found in writing and is used in both speech and writing before a verb (He slowly swam across the cove) as well as after a verb (He swam slowly through the waves).

In general, the short forms are used more often in informal speech and writing; the long forms are found more often in formal discourse.

USING ADJECTIVES AFTER LINKING VERBS

A *linking verb* connects a subject with its complement (a **noun, pronoun,** or **adjective** that completes the meaning of the verb). Do not use an adverb after a linking verb.

The words that follow linking verbs are called *subject complements.* The most common linking verbs include forms of *to be;*

verbs such as *appear, seem, believe, become, grow, turn, prove,* and *remain*; and sensory verbs such as *sound, look, hear, smell, feel,* and *taste.*

> The dog **smelled** bad.
>
> The girl **appeared** content.
>
> The cold milk **tasted** good.
>
> That **sounds** wonderful.
>
> She **grew** thoughtful.

USING ADJECTIVES OR ADVERBS
AFTER DIRECT OBJECTS

If the verb's direct object is followed by a word that describes the verb, that word must be an adverb.

> He muttered the words **angrily**.
>> (The adverb *angrily* modifies the verb *muttered*.)

On the other hand, if the direct object is followed by a word that describes the object, the word must be an adjective.

> The red pepper made the soup **spicy**.
>> (The adjective *spicy* modifies the noun *soup*.)

Compare the following pairs of sentences:

> His mother called him **quiet**.
>> (The adjective *quiet* modifies the pronoun *him*.)

> His mother called him **quietly**.
>> (The adverb *quietly* modifies the verb *called*.)

> The evaluation committee considered the firm's work **complete**.
>> (The adjective *complete* modifies the noun *work*.)

The evaluation committee considered the firm's work **completely**.
(The adverb *completely* modifies the verb *considered*.)

WORDS THAT CAN BE EITHER
ADJECTIVES OR ADVERBS

Depending on how they are used, some words can function as either adjectives or adverbs.

Adverb

I think you ought to go to bed **early** tonight.

Janine is fortunate that she lives **close** to public transportation.

Adjective

I had an **early** appointment this morning.

That certainly was a **close** call!

USING ADJECTIVES AND ADVERBS
TO MAKE COMPARISONS

Many adjectives and adverbs take different forms when they are used to make comparisons. The three forms are the **positive degree**, the **comparative degree**, and the **superlative degree**.

POSITIVE DEGREE

The *positive* degree is the basic form of the adjective or the adverb, the form listed in the dictionary. Since the positive degree does not indicate any comparison, the adjective or adverb does not change form.

COMPARATIVE DEGREE

The *comparative* form indicates a greater degree by comparing two things. In the comparative form, adjectives and adverbs add *-er* or *more*.

SUPERLATIVE DEGREE

The *superlative* form indicates the greatest degree of difference or similarity by comparing three or more things. In this form, adjectives and adverbs add *-est* or *most*.

CHOOSING BETWEEN *LESS/LEAST/MORE/MOST* AND *-ER/-EST*

A number of one- or two-syllable adjectives and adverbs use *-er* to form the comparative degree and *-est* to form the superlative degree. In some instances, these words use *more* and *most* when necessary to avoid awkwardness:

Positive	Comparative	Superlative
clear	clearer	clearest
poor	poorer	poorest
rich	richer	richest
pretty	prettier	prettiest
heavy	heavier	heaviest
steady	steadier	steadiest
childlike	more childlike	most childlike
youthful	more youthful	most youthful
golden	more golden	most golden

Most adjectives and adverbs of three or more syllables and nearly all adverbs ending in *-ly* use *more/less* and *most/least* to form the comparative and superlative degrees:

Positive	Comparative	Superlative
customary	more/ less customary	most/ least customary
regular	more/ less regular	most/ least regular
admiring	more/ less admiring	most/ least admiring
slowly	more/ less slowly	most/ least slowly
harshly	more/ less harshly	most/ least harshly
rudely	more/ less rudely	most/ least rudely

IRREGULAR ADJECTIVES AND ADVERBS

Some adverbs and adjectives are irregular in the comparative and superlative degrees, as shown in the table below:

Adjectives

Positive	Comparative	Superlative
good	better	best
bad	worse	worst
little	littler, less	littlest, least
many	more	most

Adverbs

Positive	Comparative	Superlative
well	better	best
badly	worse	worst

COMPARATIVE OR SUPERLATIVE?

In general, you will use the comparative form to compare two things; use the superlative form to compare three or more things.

Twiskers was the **smarter** of the two hamsters.

Marc was the **taller** of the two second-graders.

Louisa is the **quicker** of the two runners.

Of the six hamsters, Twiddles is the **smartest**.

Among the six of you, Robert is the **tallest**.

Of all the runners, Louisa is the **quickest**.

DOUBLE COMPARISONS

Do not use double comparatives or double superlatives.

Amanda gets a bigger allowance because she is **older** (not *more older*) than I am.

She is the **nicest** (not *most nicest*) girl in the class.

COMPLETING COMPARISONS

Be careful not to omit words needed to complete comparisons.

Incomplete:

Steve's salary is **less than** his wife.

Complete:

Steve's salary is **less than** that of his wife.

or

Steve's salary is **less than** his wife's.

Incomplete:

Cooking with herbs is **more healthful than** fat.

Complete:

Cooking with herbs is **more healthful than** cooking with fat.

Incomplete:

Rainy days in Tucson are **as rare as** Santa Fe.

Complete:

Rainy days in Tucson are **as rare as** they are in Santa Fe.

Incomplete:

Denver is **farther from** Pueblo than Boulder.

Complete:

Denver is **farther from** Pueblo than it is from Boulder.

Incomplete:

New York City **has more** movie theaters.

Complete:

New York City **has more** movie theaters than any other city in the state.

Note: There are a number of words whose positive degree describes their only form. Words such as *central, dead, empty, excellent, impossible, infinite, perfect, straight,* and *unique* cannot have a greater or lesser degree. Therefore, something cannot be *more unique* or *most infinite.*

In general, you should avoid using comparative or superlative forms for adjectives and adverbs that cannot be compared.

PREPOSITIONS

A *preposition* is a word used to connect and relate a noun or pronoun to some other word in the sentence.

COMMON PREPOSITIONS

about	beside	inside	since
above	besides	into	through
across	between	like	throughout
after	beyond	near	till
against	but	of	to
along	by	off	toward
amid	concerning	on	under
among	despite	onto	underneath
around	down	opposite	until
as	during	out	up
at	except	outside	upon
before	excepting	over	with
behind	for	past	within
below	from	regarding	without
beneath	in	round	

PHRASAL PREPOSITIONS (TWO OR MORE WORDS)

according to

along with

apart from

as for

as of

as regards

aside from

because of

by means of

by reason of

by way of

except for

in addition to

in case of

in front of

in lieu of

in place of

in regard to

in spite of

instead of

on account of

out of

up to

with reference to

with regard to

with respect to

with the exception of

PREPOSITIONAL PHRASES

A preposition always has an object, which is a noun or pronoun. The preposition with its object and any modifiers is called a *prepositional phrase*. A prepositional phrase can be made up of any number of words:

toward the mountain

away from the ocean

by the side of the cliff

in front of the bushes

on account of his gross negligence

with the exception of three players

PLACEMENT OF PREPOSITIONS

A preposition usually precedes its object, but it may also follow its object. A preposition may also come at the end of the sentence:

What did Allison do that **for**?

Josh and Kate had many things to talk **about**.

For a week, she couldn't get the horrible scene **out of** her mind.

In addition to having a superb academic record, he was an out-standing athlete and humanitarian.

We know which chair you are hiding **behind**.

PREPOSITIONAL PHRASES AS
ADVERBS AND ADJECTIVES

Prepositional phrases can function as adverbs or adjectives.

Prepositional Phrases as Adverbs

He hammered rapidly **underneath the overhang**.

The children flew their new dragon kite **on the beach**.

Charles drove **through the night**.

Prepositional Phrases as Adjectives

Melinda is the girl **with the missing front tooth**.

The reporter **in the red dress** asked the first question.

New York is a city that has something **for everyone**.

She was carrying a bag **of groceries**.

PREPOSITION OR ADVERB?

To distinguish between prepositions and adverbs, remember that prepositions, unlike adverbs, can never function alone within a sentence. A preposition must always have an object.

Prepositions

The children went **into** the house.

Crowds of people were skiing **down** the icy slopes.

Adverbs

They went **in**.

After the fifth book fell **down**, we decided it was time to rearrange the bookshelves.

CONJUNCTIONS

A *conjunction* is a word used to connect words, phrases, or clauses.

The three kinds of conjunctions are **coordinating, correlative,** and **subordinating.** Adverbs can also be used to link related ideas. When adverbs are used in this way, they are called *conjunctive adverbs.*

COORDINATING CONJUNCTIONS

A *coordinating conjunction* connects sentence parts (individual words, phrases, or clauses) of equal rank. Following are the most common coordinating conjunctions:

and	for	nor	yet
but	or	so	

And shows connections:

> The children cleaned up quickly **and** quietly.
>
> We went to a concert, **and** the children went to a movie.

But, nor, and *yet* show contrast:

> The living room was extremely elegant **but** surprisingly comfortable.
>
> My supervisor will never give us half days on Friday, **nor** will she agree to our other demands.
>
> She took good care of the houseplant, **yet** it wilted and lost its leaves anyway.

Or shows choice:

> You can have the spaghetti and meatballs **or** the veal and peppers.
>
> We can have a picnic in the park, **or** we can drive out to the lake.

So shows result:

> All the stores were closed, **so** we ended up eating peanut butter and jelly sandwiches.

For shows causality:

> Laura stayed in the office late all week, **for** she had to finish the project by Friday.

CORRELATIVE CONJUNCTIONS

Correlative conjunctions also link sentence parts of equal grammatical rank. These conjunctions always work in pairs to connect words, phrases, or clauses.

both . . . and
either . . . or
neither . . . nor
not only . . . but also
not . . . but
whether . . . or

Both the bank **and** the post office are closed on national holidays.

Either you agree to ratify our contract now, **or** we will have to return to the bargaining table.

The envelopes are **neither** in the drawer **nor** in the cabinet.

Not only the children **but also** the adults were captivated by the dancing bears at the circus.

Not the renters **but** the homeowners were most deeply affected by the recent change in the tax laws.

Whether you agree to implement my plan **or** not, you have to concede that it has merit.

Note: The two elements connected by correlative conjunctions must be in parallel form.

Incorrect:

Neither the dripping cat **nor** the dog that was muddy was welcome in my foyer.

The hosts paid attention **not only** to the refreshments, **but** they **also** were paying attention to the music.

Correct:

Neither the dripping cat **nor** the muddy dog was welcome in my foyer.

The hosts paid attention **not only** to the refreshments **but also** to the music.

SUBORDINATING CONJUNCTIONS

A *subordinating conjunction* is a word that connects two thoughts by making one subordinate to, or dependent on, the other. To "subordinate" suggests making one statement less important than the other:

> **Although** some people tried to repair the tennis courts, they were unable to gain sufficient public backing.

The main idea, "they were unable to gain sufficient public backing," is an independent clause (complete sentence); the subordinate idea, "Although some people tried to repair the tennis courts," is a dependent clause that functions here as an adverb. Either clause may come first in the sentence.

Common Subordinating Conjunctions

after	if	till
although	if only	unless
as	in order that	until
as long as	now that	when
as of	once	whenever
as soon as	rather than	where
as though	since	whereas
because	so that	wherever
before	than	while
even if	that	
even though	though	

> **Although** traffic was light every morning, he was unable to arrive at work on time.
>
> The little girl overheard her parents arguing in the next room **even though** they were whispering.

We ordered pizza **so that** we wouldn't have to go out in the rain.

Don't forget **that** your taxes are due on the fifteenth of the month.

Until you make up your mind, we won't be able to leave.

Please do the dishes **before** you go to the movies.

Do you know **where** he lives?

That is more **than** I can afford.

SUBORDINATING CONJUNCTION OR PREPOSITION?

A word such as *until*, *before*, *since*, *till*, or *after* can function as either a preposition or a subordinating conjunction. To distinguish between the two parts of speech, remember that subordinating conjunctions, unlike prepositions, connect two complete ideas.

Subordinating conjunctions

Please drop this tape off at the video store **since** you are driving in that direction anyway.

After you finish reading that book, may I borrow it?

Prepositions

I have had a headache **since** this morning.

After lunch I am going shopping **for** a new pair of shoes.

CONJUNCTIVE ADVERB OR TRANSITIONAL PHRASE?

A *conjunctive adverb* is an adverb that connects two clauses or sentences by describing their relationship to each other.

Common Conjunctive Adverbs

also	incidentally	nonetheless
anyway	indeed	otherwise
besides	instead	still
consequently	likewise	then
finally	meanwhile	therefore
furthermore	moreover	thus
hence	nevertheless	undoubtedly
however	next	

The electric company promised that power would be restored by tomorrow; **meanwhile**, we are using a generator.

The memo required an immediate response; **consequently**, we sent a fax.

You should not be angry at them for arriving early; **undoubtedly**, they were nervous and overestimated the time that the drive would take.

TRANSITIONAL PHRASE

Expressions that are used to link complete ideas are called *transitional phrases*.

Common Transitional Phrases

after all	for example
as a result	in addition
at any rate	in fact
at the same time	in other words
by the way	on the contrary
even so	on the other hand

The school building is in great disrepair; **for example**, the roof is leaking, the paint is peeling, and the heating system works erratically.

The voters rejected an increase in the school tax; **as a result**, the repairs will not be done this year.

There is a great public clamor for better schools; **at the same time**, no one wants to spend the necessary money.

Note: A semicolon is used before a conjunctive adverb or a transitional phrase that is placed between main clauses. The adverb or phrase itself is set off by a comma.

TRANSITIONAL PHRASE OR COORDINATING CONJUNCTION?

To distinguish between transitional phrases and coordinating conjunctions, ask yourself if the item can be moved. Conjunctive adverbs and transitional phrases can be moved within a sentence; coordinating conjunctions cannot:

The taxi was late; **however**, we arrived in time to catch the entire first act.

The taxi was late; we arrived, **however**, in time to catch the entire first act.

The taxi was late; we arrived in time to catch the entire first act, **however**.

INTERJECTIONS

An *interjection* is a word used to express strong emotion. It functions independently within a sentence.

In Latin, the word *interjection* means "something thrown in." In a sense, interjections are "thrown in" to add strong feeling.

Interjections have a long and storied history in literature. Shakespeare was fond of them. He uses the interjection *Zounds!* twenty times in his plays. It's a euphemism for "God's wounds," a popular epithet back then, but considered too blunt to be spoken directly. *Alas!* was another favorite. And what about Scrooge's famous "Bah! Humbug!" or "Leapin' lizards," a favorite of Little Orphan Annie?

Sometimes an interjection can become a trademark. The late baseball player and commentator Phil Rizzuto, used to exclaim, "Holy Cow!" when he witnessed a particularly spectacular play. Before him, Mel Allen used to cry out, "How about that!"

Almost any verb can be employed as an interjection. We use the example below of *help*. But you could just as well use the verb *run,* for example: "Run! The building's on fire." Or "Duck! The plaster's falling." Or "Hide! The police are here."

For maximum effect, you should use interjections sparingly in your writing. Since they are independent from the rest of the sentence, they can be set off by commas or followed by an exclamation point.

Common Interjections

ah	hey	tsk
alas	hmm	uhh
bah	nonsense	well
bravo	oh	whoa
darn	ouch	wow
fine	shh	yes
help	so	

Darn! The cat got out again.

Oh, I didn't expect you so early.

Hey! Do you know what you're doing?

Yes! He made that shot!

Fine—we'll go to your mother's for dinner.

Help! My cat's up a tree.

So! It was you!

PLURALIZATION

Making a word a plural—or, as it's defined, "indicating that a word has more than one referent, as in *men* (the plural of *man*)"— is not always easy.

Generally speaking, to make a plural of a noun you add *-s, -es,* or *-ies*. Most nouns are made plural by adding an *s*. As in:

building	buildings
goat	goats
hut	huts
pencil	pencils

However, this is not always the case. Nouns ending in *ch*, *s*, *sh*, ss, *x*, and *z* make their plural by adding *-es*.

batch	batches
dish	dishes
bass	basses
box	boxes
bus	buses

If the noun ends with a *y*, preceded by a consonant, then you change the *y* to an *i* and add *-es*.

tabby	tabbies
sky	skies
try	tries

If, however, the noun ends with a *y* and is preceded by a vowel, then simply add *-s*.

day	days
toy	toys
donkey	donkeys
jay	jays

The following is a list of irregular plurals for which there is no single rule that can apply to all:

aircraft	aircraft
alumnus	alumni
analysis	analyses
antenna	antennae/antennas
appendix	appendices
axis	axes
bacterium	bacteria
beau	beaux
blues	blues
bureau	bureaus/bureaux
cactus	cacti
child	children
corpus	corpora
crisis	crises
criterion	criteria

curriculum	curricula
datum	data
deer	deer
ellipsis	ellipses
fish	fish
focus	foci/focuses
foot	feet
formula	formulae/formulas
fungus	fungi/funguses
genus	genera
goose	geese
hypothesis	hypotheses
index	indeces/indexes
knife	knives
loaf	loaves
louse	lice
means	means
medium	media
memorandum	memoranda
moose	moose
mouse	mice
nebula	nebulae/nebulas
nucleus	nuclei
oasis	oases
offspring	offspring
ox	oxen
paralysis	paralyses
parenthesis	parentheses
person	people
phenomenon	phenomena
radius	radii
series	series

sheep	sheep
species	species
stimulus	stimuli
stratum	strata
swine	swine
thesis	theses
tooth	teeth
vertebra	vertebrae/vertebras
vita	vitae
volcano	volcanoes
wife	wives
woman	women

PHRASES

A *PHRASE* is a group of related words that does not contain both a subject and a verb. Phrases are classified as **noun phrases, verb phrases, prepositional phrases,** and **verbal phrases** (participial phrases, gerund phrases, and infinitive phrases).

NOUN PHRASES

A *noun phrase* contains a noun and one or more modifiers.

> The **brilliant sunshine** only made the **old house** look more dilapidated.
>
> I have heard that she is **a very interesting speaker**.
>
> **A tall blue heron** stood motionless on the shore.

VERB PHRASES

A *verb phrase* contains a main verb and an auxiliary verb.

> The cat **has eaten** the carnations.
>
> **Let's go** to the movies.
>
> **Can** you **read** his handwriting?

PREPOSITIONAL PHRASES

A *prepositional phrase* is a group of words that opens with a preposition and ends with a noun or pronoun.

Prepositional phrases can function as adjectives, as adverbs, or, occasionally, as nouns.

Prepositional phrases used as adjectives

The price **of the dinner** was exorbitant.

My house is the one **between the twisted oak tree and the graceful weeping willow**.

Prepositional phrases used as adverbs

The joggers ran **with determination**.

My flight is scheduled to leave **at 6 p.m.**

Prepositional phrases used as nouns

After lunch is too late.

Beyond the oak tree is out-of-bounds.

VERBAL PHRASES

A *verbal* is a verb form used as another part of speech. Participles, infinitives, and gerunds are verbals. The verbal and all the words related to it are called a *verbal phrase*.

Participial phrases function as adjectives. They can be placed before or after the word they describe.

Shaking with fear, the defendant stood before the jury. [present participle]

She got a hot dog **drenched in mustard**. [past participle]

Gerund phrases function as nouns. Gerunds always end in *-ing*:

Swimming laps three times a week helps her stay in shape.

Hiking in the Rockies is my idea of a great vacation.

Infinitive phrases can function as nouns, adjectives, or adverbs. An infinitive phrase always begins with the word *to*:

To shop in that store is a nightmare. [noun]

We plan **to fly to Houston** on Monday. [noun]

He gave us a lot of homework **to do**. [adjective]

She struggled **to overcome** her disability. [adverb]

CLAUSES

A *CLAUSE* is a group of related words that contains both a subject and a verb. There are two types of clauses: **independent** (main) and **dependent** (subordinate).

INDEPENDENT CLAUSES

An *independent* (main) clause can stand alone as a complete sentence.

> Swimming is suitable for people of all ages.
>
> He missed his train.
>
> Marcia plans to open a catering business.

DEPENDENT CLAUSES

A *dependent* (subordinate) clause functions as a part of speech that relates to an element in the main clause.

> Swimming, **which is very good exercise**, is suitable for people of all ages.
>
> **Because he overslept**, he missed his train.
>
> Marcia, **who won the blue ribbon in the cooking contest**, plans to open a catering business.

FUNCTIONS OF DEPENDENT CLAUSES

A dependent clause functions as a part of speech—as an adjective, an adverb, or a noun.

ADJECTIVE CLAUSES

An *adjective clause* is a subordinate clause that modifies a noun or pronoun. It usually begins with a relative pronoun: *which, what, whatever, who, whose, whom, whoever, whomever,* or *that*. It may also begin with words such as *when, where, before, since,* or *why*. An adjective clause almost always follows the word it modifies:

> We hired the candidates **who came with the strongest recommendations**.
>
> The child **whom you saw in the magazine** is my niece.
>
> Did Fred tell you the reason **why he was late for work this morning**?
>
> Good restaurants **where one can eat cheaply** are very rare in this town.

ADVERB CLAUSES

An *adverb clause* is a subordinate clause that modifies a verb, an adjective, an adverb, or a verbal. Adverb clauses usually begin with subordinating conjunctions. (See page 84 for a list of subordinating conjunctions.) Unlike adjective clauses, adverb clauses can be separated from the word they modify and can be placed anywhere in the sentence. If the clause is placed at the beginning or in the middle of a sentence, it is often set off by commas.

Since the guests were so convivial, I soon forgot my troubles.

Did you visit the Metropolitan Museum **when you were in New York?**

I decided, **after I lost an important document**, to make backup copies of all my files.

NOUN CLAUSES

A *noun clause* is a subordinate clause that acts as a noun. Noun clauses can function as subjects, objects, and predicate nouns within sentences. They begin either with a relative pronoun or with a word such as *how*, *why*, *where*, *when*, *if*, or *whether*.

Noun clauses can be difficult to identify. Since so many different words can be used to begin a noun clause, you cannot decide on the basis of the opening word alone. You must discover the function of the clause within the sentence to identify it as a noun clause.

Whoever washes the dishes will be allowed to choose which program to watch. [subject]

Do you know **where they went on vacation?** [direct object]

They talked about **whether they could take the time off from work**. [object of a preposition]

That is **what I meant**. [predicate nominative]

ELLIPTICAL CLAUSES

An *elliptical clause* is a subordinate clause that is grammatically incomplete but nonetheless clear because the missing element can be understood from the rest of the sentence. The word *elliptical* comes from *ellipsis*, which means "omission." The verb from the second part of the comparison may be missing, or the relative pronouns *that*, *which*, and *whom* may be omitted from adjectival clauses. Often, elliptical clauses begin with *as* or *than*, although any subordinating conjunction that makes logical sense can be used. In the following examples, the omitted words are supplied in parentheses:

Chad's younger cousin is as tall as he (**is**).

Aruba is among the islands (**that**) they visited on their recent cruise.

When (**he was**) only a child, Barry was taken on a tour around the world.

Although (**they were**) common fifty years ago, passenger pigeons are extinct today.

SENTENCES

SUBJECTS AND PREDICATES

There are two basic parts to every sentence: the **subject** and the **predicate**.

The simple subject is the noun or pronoun that identifies the person, place, or thing the sentence is about. The complete subject is the simple subject and all the words that modify it.

The predicate contains the verb that explains what the subject is doing. The simple predicate contains only the verb; the complete predicate contains the verb and any complements and modifiers.

Subject

The motorcycle

Calico cats

One of Hawthorne's direct blood relatives

Farmingdale, in the town of Oyster Bay,

Predicate

veered away from the boulder.

are always female.

was the famous "hanging judge" of the Salem witchcraft trials.

has recently begun a massive recycling project.

HARD-TO-LOCATE SUBJECTS

COMMANDS OR DIRECTIONS

In some instances, the subject can be difficult to locate. In commands or directions, for instance, the subject is often not stated because it is understood to be *you*.

Subject	Predicate
(you)	Please unload the dishwasher and tidy the kitchen.
(you)	Just tell me what happened that evening.

QUESTIONS

In questions, too, subjects can be difficult to locate because they often follow the verb rather than come before it. Rewriting the question as a statement will make it easier to find the subject.

Question:
Are **you** planning to go to Oregon this weekend or next?

Rewritten as a statement:
You are planning to go to Oregon this weekend or next.

SENTENCES BEGINNING WITH THERE OR HERE

If you are having trouble locating the subject of a sentence beginning with *there* or *here*, try rephrasing the sentence:

There is **your wallet** on the table.

Here are **the peaches** from the farmer's market.

Rewritten:
Your wallet is there on the table.

The peaches from the farmer's market are here.

INVERTED SENTENCES

Inverted sentences place the subject after the verb for emphasis.

High on the cliff above the ocean stood **the diver**.

On a rack behind the door hung **a dripping raincoat**.

Even more significant was **the lack of a firm objective**.

SENTENCE COMPLEMENTS

Along with a verb, complete predicates may contain a complement. A *complement* is a word or word group that completes the meaning of the verb.

There are four primary kinds of sentence complements: **direct objects, indirect objects, object complements**, and **subject complements** (nouns, pronouns, and adjectives).

DIRECT OBJECTS

A *direct object* is the noun, pronoun, or word acting as a noun that completes the meaning of a transitive verb by receiving the action. (Intransitive verbs do not have direct objects.) To help decide if a word is a direct object, ask *What?* or *Whom?* after an action verb:

Martha won **the stuffed dog**.
(What did she win? *The stuffed dog.*)

The hurricane destroyed **the beach and the boardwalk**.
(What did the hurricane destroy? *The beach and the boardwalk.*)

The waiter served **Jack**.
(Whom did the waiter serve? *Jack*.)

INDIRECT OBJECTS

An *indirect object* is a noun or pronoun that names the person or thing that something is done to or given to. Indirect objects are located after the verb and before the direct object. They are found only in sentences that have direct objects. Indirect objects answer the questions *To whom? For whom? To what?* or *For what?*

My aunt lent **me** her motorcycle.
(To whom did my aunt lend her motorcycle? *To me*.)

I gave **my daughter** a computer for her birthday.
(To whom did I give a computer? *To my daughter*.)

Maria sent **Serge** an invitation.
(To whom did Maria send an invitation? *To Serge*.)

OBJECT COMPLEMENTS

An *object complement* is a noun or adjective immediately following a direct object. It either renames or describes the direct object.

She called him **a fool**.

We made the platypus **our mascot**.

They named the kitten **Ivan the Terrible**.

SUBJECT COMPLEMENTS

Subject complements, like object complements, are found in the predicate of a sentence.

A *subject complement* is a noun, pronoun, or adjective that follows a linking verb and gives further information about the subject of a sentence.

A predicate noun or pronoun follows a linking verb to identify the subject of a sentence:

> The new head of the division will be **Elizabeth Fabian**.
>
> Which of those two phones is **the newer one**?

A predicate adjective follows a linking verb to describe the subject of a sentence:

> The vegetable soup smells **delicious**.
>
> My daughter's stamp collection grows **larger** and **more valuable** every day.

FORMING SENTENCES

Independent and dependent clauses can be combined in various ways to create four basic types of sentences: **simple**, **compound**, **complex**, and **compound-complex**.

SIMPLE SENTENCES

A *simple sentence* is one independent clause, a group of words containing one subject and one predicate. This does not mean, however, that a simple sentence must be short. Both the subject and the verb may be compounded. In addition, a simple sentence may contain describing phrases. By definition, though, a simple sentence cannot have a subordinate clause or another independent clause.

Heather shopped.

The carpenter and the electrician arrived simultaneously.

The shingle flapped, folded, and broke off.

Either my mother or my grandmother bought and wrapped this lovely crystal decanter.

Freezing unexpectedly, the water in the copper lines burst the gaskets.

COMPOUND SENTENCES

A *compound sentence* is two or more independent clauses joined together. Since the clauses in a compound sentence are independent, each can be written as an individual sentence. A compound sentence does not have dependent clauses. The independent clauses can be connected by a comma and a coordinating conjunction (*and, but, or, for, so, yet*) or by a semicolon. If the clauses are very short, the comma before the coordinating conjunction may be omitted.

Mary went to the concert, but Bill stayed home with the baby.

You may mail the enclosed form back to our central office, or you may call our customer service representative at the number listed above.

Eddie typed the report in three hours; Donna spent five hours editing it.

I ate lunch and then I took a nap.

COMPLEX SENTENCES

A *complex sentence* contains one independent clause and one or more subordinate clauses. To distinguish it from the other clauses, the independent clause in a complex sentence is called the main clause. In a complex sentence, each clause has its own subject and verb. The subject in the main clause is called the subject of the sentence; the verb in the main clause is called the main verb. An independent clause can stand alone as a complete sentence; a dependent clause cannot.

In the following examples, the main clauses are in boldface type.

> As we were looking over your sign-in sheets for May and June, **we noticed a number of minor problems**.
>
> While Mary went to the concert, **Bill stayed home with the baby**.
>
> **No one responded** when she rang the front doorbell.
>
> **The owners of the small mountain inns rejoiced** when the snow fell.

COMPOUND-COMPLEX SENTENCES

A *compound-complex sentence* has at least two independent clauses and at least one dependent clause. The compound-complex sentence is so named because it shares the characteristics of both compound and complex sentences. Like the compound sentence, the compound-complex has at least two main clauses. Like the complex sentence, it has at least one subordinate clause. The subordinate clause can be part of an independent clause.

In the following examples, the main clauses are in boldface type.

> Since my memo seems to outline our requirements fully, **we are circulating it to all the departments; please notify us** if we can be of any further assistance.
>
> When the heat comes, **the lakes dry up**, and **farmers know that their crops will fail**.

REVIEW OF SENTENCE FORMS

The following five sentence forms are the basic templates on which all sentences are built.

1. Subject + intransitive verb

    Bond prices fell.

2. Subject + transitive verb + direct object

    Bobbie hummed the song.

3. Subject + transitive verb + direct object + object complement

    The committee appointed Eric secretary.

4. Subject + linking verb + subject complement

    The procedure was tedious.

    The gift was a silk scarf.

5. Subject + transitive verb + indirect object + direct object

    The clerk gave us the receipt.

SENTENCE FUNCTIONS

In addition to the form they take, sentences can also be classified according to function. There are four main types of sentences: **declarative**, **interrogative**, **imperative**, and **exclamatory**.

DECLARATIVE SENTENCES

A *declarative sentence* makes a statement and always ends with a period:

On Thursday we are going to see a movie.

We have been waiting for two weeks for the movie to open here.

The reviews were excellent.

INTERROGATIVE SENTENCES

An *interrogative sentence* asks a question and always ends with a question mark:

Are we going to see the movie on Tuesday?

How long have you been waiting for the movie to open?

What did the reviewers say about it?

IMPERATIVE SENTENCES

An *imperative sentence* makes a command. In many instances, the subject of an imperative sentence is understood to be *you* and is thus not stated. In other instances, the sentence may be phrased as a question but does not end with a question mark.

Take this money in case you change your mind.

Clean up that mess!

Will you please reply at your earliest convenience.

Would someone please move those books to the top shelf.

EXCLAMATORY SENTENCES

An *exclamatory sentence* conveys strong feeling and always ends with an exclamation point. Many exclamatory sentences are very strongly stated declarative sentences. Since the exclamatory sentence conveys strong emotions, it is not found much in formal writing.

They still haven't called!

The dress is ruined!

SENTENCE ERRORS

Sentence errors fall into three main divisions: parts of sentences set off as though they were complete (**fragments**), two or more sentences incorrectly joined (**run-ons**), and sentence parts misplaced or poorly connected to the rest of the sentence (**misplaced, dangling,** or **squinting modifiers**).

FRAGMENTS

A *fragment* is part of a sentence presented as though it were a complete sentence. The fragment may lack a subject or verb or both, or it may be a subordinate clause not connected to a complete sentence. Since fragments are not complete sentences, they do not express complete thoughts.

No subject:

Ran to catch the bus.

Ate all the chocolate hidden in the drawer.

No main verb:

The box sitting in the trunk.

The man in the room.

No subject or main verb:

Feeling happy.

Acting poorly.

Subordinate clause:

When I woke him up early this morning.

If it is as pleasant as you expect today.

CORRECTING FRAGMENTS

Fragments are often created when phrases and subordinate clauses are punctuated as though they were complete sentences. Remember that phrases can never stand alone because they are groups of words that do not have subjects or verbs. To correct phrase fragments, add the information they need to be complete.

Subordinate clauses, on the other hand, do contain subjects and verbs. Like phrases, however, they do not convey complete thoughts. You can complete them by connecting them to main clauses. They can also be completed by dropping the subordinating conjunction. Correct each fragment in the way that makes the most logical sense within the context of the passage.

Phrase fragment:

a big house

Corrected:

A big house at the end of the block burned down last night.
  (Fragment becomes subject; predicate is added.)

My sister recently bought a big house.
  (Fragment becomes direct object; subject and verb are added.)

She earned enough money for a big house.
  (Fragment becomes object of the preposition; subject, verb, and direct object are added.)

Did you hear about his newest acquisition, the big house on Maple Street?

(Fragment becomes appositive; subject, verb, and prepositional phrase are added.)

Subordinating clause fragment:
If it is as pleasant as you expected today.

Corrected:
It is as pleasant as you expected today.
   (Subordinating conjunction dropped.)

If it is as pleasant as you expected today, we will be able to go to the beach.
   (Fragment connected to a main clause.)

RUN-ONS

A *run-on* is two complete ideas incorrectly joined. Run-ons are generally classified as either comma splices or fused sentences. A *comma splice* incorrectly joins two independent clauses with a comma.

Mary walked into the room, she found a mouse on her desk.

The vest was beautiful, it had intricate embroidery.

My daughter loves *Buffy the Vampire Slayer*, she watches it every week.

A *fused sentence* runs two independent clauses together without an appropriate conjunction or punctuation mark:

Many people are afraid of computers they do not realize how easy it is to learn basic tasks.

All the word processing programs come with built-in lessons you can learn to do basic word processing in an afternoon or less.

The online spell-checker and thesaurus are especially handy they do not take the place of a good dictionary.

CORRECTING RUN-ON SENTENCES

There are four ways to correct both comma splices and fused sentences.

1. Separate the clauses into two sentences.

   Mary walked into the room. She found a mouse on her desk.

   Many people are afraid of computers. They do not realize how easy it is to learn basic tasks.

2. Insert a comma and coordinating conjunction between clauses to create a compound sentence.

   Mary walked into the room, and she found a mouse on her desk.

   Many people are afraid of computers, for they do not realize how easy it is to learn basic tasks.

3. Insert a semicolon between the clauses.

   Mary walked into the room; she found a mouse on her desk.

   Many people are afraid of computers; they do not realize how easy it is to learn basic tasks.

4. Subordinate one clause to the other to create a complex sentence.

When Mary walked into the room, she found a mouse on her desk.

Many people are afraid of computers because they do not realize how easy it is to learn basic tasks.

MISPLACED MODIFIERS

A *misplaced modifier* occurs when the modifier looks as if it is describing the wrong word in the sentence.

As a general rule, a modifier should be placed as close as possible to the word it modifies. When a word, phrase, or clause is placed too far from the word it modifies, the sentence may fail to convey the intended meaning and therefore produce ambiguity or amusement. When this occurs, the modifier is called *misplaced*.

Words misplaced:

To get to the ski slope we **nearly** drove five hours.

I **almost** drank a whole quart of water.

Revised:

To get to the ski slope we drove **nearly** five hours.

I drank **almost** a whole quart of water.

Phrases misplaced:

We all stared at the woman who was talking to the governor **with green spiked hair**.

Roasted whole, those who shied away from garlic will delight in this new vegetable.

The professor explained how her grading system worked **on Monday**.

Revised:

We all stared at the woman **with green spiked hair** who was talking to the governor.

Those who shied away from garlic will delight in this new vegetable when it is **roasted whole**.

On Monday the professor explained how her grading system worked.

Clauses misplaced:

I bought Brie in the new shop on North Road **that cost $8.00 a pound**.

We saved the balloons for the children **that had been left on the table**.

Revised:

I bought Brie **that cost $8.00 a pound** in the new shop on North Road.

We saved the balloons **that had been left on the table** for the children.

DANGLING MODIFIERS

A *dangling modifier,* also called an unattached modifier, occurs when a modifier does not logically or grammatically describe anything in the sentence because the noun or pronoun to which a phrase or clause refers is either in the wrong place or missing. Like misplaced modifiers, dangling modifiers cause confusion.

Examples of dangling modifiers:

While reading the paper, the birds on the railing caught my eye.

Biking up the hill, a Jaguar went roaring past.

Drinking a cup of coffee, the cat leaped on the table.

The evening passed contentedly, reading and listening to music.

Sitting on the riverbank, the sun glinted on the rippling waves.

After closing the door, the room got very warm.

In planning a European trip, consideration of the amount of luggage is needed.

To graduate with honors, exceptional ability and hard work are needed.

When traveling, my passport is in my inside pocket.

Revised:

While I was reading the paper, the birds on the railing caught my eye.

As I was biking up the hill, a Jaguar went roaring past.

While I was drinking a cup of coffee, the cat leaped on the table.

We passed the evening contentedly, reading and listening to music.

Sitting on the riverbank, I watched the sun glinting on the rippling waves.

After I had closed the door, the room got very warm.

In planning a European trip, one needs to consider the amount of luggage one can carry.

To graduate with honors, one needs exceptional ability and hard work.

When traveling, I carry my passport in my inside pocket.

Or

When I am traveling, my passport is in my inside pocket.

SQUINTING MODIFIERS

A *squinting modifier* is one that may refer to either a preceding or following word and therefore causes ambiguity and confusion.

Examples of squinting modifiers:

We said **when we were coming back from the Cape** that we would like to buy some local produce.

Exercising **often** gives me energy.

The case that the prosecution had prepared **quickly** forced it to declare the defendant's sister a hostile witness.

Revised:

We said we would like to buy some local produce **when we were coming back from the Cape**.

Or

When we were coming back from the Cape, we said we would like to buy some local produce.

Often, exercising gives me energy.

Or

It gives me energy to exercise **often**.

The case that the prosecution had **quickly** prepared forced it to declare the defendant's sister a hostile witness.

Or

The case that the prosecution had prepared forced it to **quickly** declare the defendant's sister a hostile witness.

AGREEMENT OF SENTENCE PARTS

Agreement is what it sounds like—matching. Specifically, agreement refers to the matching of number, person, and gender within a sentence. Subjects and verbs must agree in number (singular or plural) and person (first, second, or third). Pronouns and their antecedents (the words to which they refer) must also match in gender (masculine, feminine, or neuter).

Sentences that do not maintain agreement among all their elements sound clumsy and can be ambiguous.

SUBJECT-VERB AGREEMENT

A subject must agree with its verb in number. A singular subject takes a singular verb. A plural subject takes a plural verb.

First, find the subject; then determine whether it is singular or plural. The subject is the noun or pronoun that is doing the action. Often, it will be located at the beginning of the sentence, as in the following example:

I recommend that company highly.

Here, the subject *I* is doing the action *recommend*.

Sometimes the subject will follow the verb, as in questions and in sentences beginning with *here* and *there*. In the following example, the verb *are* comes before the subject *roads*:

There **are two roads** you can take.

The same is true of the placement of the subject and verb in the following question, as the verb "is" comes before the subject *briefcase*:

Where **is your briefcase**?

After you have located the subject, decide whether it is singular or plural. In English, confusion can arise because most present-tense verbs add -s or -es when their subject is third-person singular (He *runs* fast. She *studies* a lot.), whereas nouns ending in -s or -es are plural (*potatoes*, *computers*). The following table shows how regular English verbs are conjugated in the present tense:

Singular	Plural
I dream	we dream
you dream	you dream
he, she, it dreams	they dream

There are a number of plural nouns that are regarded as singular in meaning, as well as other nouns that can be both singular and plural, depending on the context of the sentence. *Acoustics, athletics, economics, gymnastics, mathematics, physics, politics,* and *statistics,* for example, are often treated as singular nouns.

Acoustics is the branch of physics that deals with sound.

The acoustics in the new hall **are** excellent.

Gymnastics is an Olympic sport.

Verbal gymnastics are his forte.

Statistics is the science that deals with the collection and analysis of numerical data.

The statistics show that the town's population has increased by twenty-two percent in the past decade.

Often, a phrase or clause will intervene between a subject and a verb. These intervening words should not affect subject-verb agreement, as illustrated in the following examples.

The supervisor of the department, together with her sales force, **is taking** the 8:30 shuttle to Washington.

The deputies to the mayor **are** exploring alternate methods of disposing of newspapers.

A display of luscious foods sometimes **encourages** impulse buying.

The profits earned this quarter **are** much higher than we had expected.

Singular subjects connected by *or, nor, either . . . or,* or *neither . . . nor* take a singular verb if both subjects are singular, a plural verb if both subjects are plural.

Either your supervisor or your colleague has to take responsibility for the error.

Either supervisors or colleagues have to take responsibility for the error.

Neither the sled nor the snow shovel has been put away.

Either the clown or the magician is scheduled to appear at the library on Sunday afternoon.

Neither boots nor shoes are included in the one-day sale.

If a subject consists of both singular and plural nouns or pronouns connected by *or* or *nor,* the verb usually agrees with the closer noun or pronoun.

In the following sentence, the plural verb *want* agrees with the plural noun *students:*

Neither the teacher nor the students want to be here.

Notice that the verb becomes singular when *teacher* and *students* are reversed:

Neither the students nor the teacher wants to be here.

This is one rule of thumb. For many people, the presence of one plural subject, no matter what its position, signals the use of a plural verb. Either method is correct; however, your writing must be consistent. Choose one of these rules and stick with it. Some writers place the plural subject closer to the verb to avoid awkwardness:

Neither we nor she has distributed the memo yet.

Neither she nor we have distributed the memo yet.

Either Martha, Ruth, or the Champney girls are planning to organize the graduation party.

Two or more subjects, phrases, or clauses connected by *and* take a plural verb. Whether the individual subjects are singular or plural, together they form a compound subject, which is plural:

The president and her advisers were behind schedule.

The faculty and staff have planned a joint professional retreat.

Derek and his dog jog before work every morning.

Sleeping late Sunday morning and reading the paper help me relax after a long week at work.

Traditionally, when the subjects joined by *and* refer to the same object or person or stand for a single idea, the entire subject is treated as a unit. Most often, the personal pronoun or article before the parts of the compound subject indicates whether the subject is indeed seen as a unit. As with other matters of agreement, this varies widely in actual use:

Unit as singular:
Ham and Swiss is my favorite sandwich.
  (*Ham and Swiss* is treated as a type of sandwich.)

My mentor and friend guides me through difficult career decisions.
  (*Mentor* and *friend* are the same person.)

Unit as plural:
Ham and Swiss make a great sandwich.
  (Each ingredient is treated as separate.)

My mentor and my friend guide me through difficult career decisions.
  (*Mentor* and *friend* are two different people.)

Mixed units:
Ham and eggs was once considered a nutritious and healthful breakfast; now, **cereal and fresh fruit are** considered preferable.

Nouns that refer to weight, extent, time, fractions, portions, or amount considered as one unit usually take a singular verb; those that indicate separate units usually take a plural verb.

In the first two examples below, the subjects are considered as single units and therefore take a singular verb. In the last two, the subjects are considered as individual items and therefore take a plural verb.

Seventy-five cents is more than enough to buy what you want at the penny carnival.

Three-fourths of the harvest was saved through their heroic efforts.

Half of the nails were rusted.

Fifty pounds of homegrown tomatoes are being divided among the eager shoppers.

COLLECTIVE NOUNS

Collective nouns (nouns that are singular in form but denote a group of persons or objects) may be either singular or plural, depending on the meaning of the sentence.

Common Collective Nouns

assembly	couple	minority
association	crowd	number
audience	family	pair
board	flock	part
class	group	percent
commission	half	press
committee	herd	public
company	jury	series
corporation	legion	staff
council	majority	

You should determine agreement for each collective noun on a sentence-by-sentence basis. If the sentence implies that the group named by the collective noun acts as a single unit, use a singular verb. If the sentence implies that the group named by the collective noun acts individually, use a plural verb.

The budget committee is voting on a new accountant this week.

The budget committee are in complete disagreement about the choice of a new accountant.

The team are trying on their new game jerseys.

The jury, not the judge, **makes** the final decision.

Gotthelf & Company is hosting its annual holiday party this Friday evening.

The phrases *the number* and *the total* are usually singular, but the phrases *a number* and *a total* are usually plural:

The number of new members is astonishing.

A number of new members were at the meeting.

When the collective nouns *couple* and *pair* refer to people, they are usually treated as plurals:

The pair are hosting a New Year's open house.

The couple have bought a large apartment with a view of the river.

Note: In British English, a collective noun naming an organization regarded as a unit is usually treated as plural:

Gotthelf & Company are hosting their annual holiday party this Friday evening.

The team have eight games scheduled for September.

PRONOUN-ANTECEDENT AGREEMENT

A pronoun must agree with its antecedent—the word to which the pronoun refers—in number and gender.

Traditionally, certain indefinite pronouns were always considered singular, some were always considered plural, and some could be both singular and plural. As language changes, however, many of these rules are changing. *None*, for example, was traditionally treated as a singular pronoun even though it has been used with both singular and plural verbs since the ninth century. Today when the sense is "not any persons or things," the plural is more commonly used:

The rescue party searched for survivors, but **none were** found.

When *none* is clearly intended to mean "not one" or "not any," it is followed by a singular verb:

> Of all my court cases, **none has been** more stressful than yours.
>
> **None of us is** going to the concert.

The following lists, therefore, are presented as general guidelines, not hard-and-fast rules. In general, use singular verbs with indefinite pronouns.

Indefinite pronouns that are most often considered singular

anybody	everybody	nothing
anyone	everyone	one
anything	everything	somebody
each	many a	someone
either	neither	
every	nobody	

Indefinite pronouns that are always considered plural

both	many	several
few	others	

Indefinite pronouns that can be considered singular or plural

all	more	none
any	most	some

Each of the people observes all the safety regulations.

Few are comfortable during a job interview.

Some of the water is seeping into the wall, but **most of the files remain** dry.

All the food has been donated to charity.

All the children have had cake and ice cream.

The effort to avoid the sexist implications of *he* has led to the general acceptance, in informal speech and writing, of *they*, *their*, and *them* to refer to indefinite pronouns:

Everyone began putting on **their** coats.

If **anybody** calls, tell **them** I'll call back after 10:00.

In formal speech and writing, *he* or *she* is still preferred to refer to indefinite pronouns.

Everyone handed in **his** test.

Anyone who wants **her** children to succeed will stress the importance of education to them.

SHIFTS

A *SHIFT* is an unnecessary or illogical change of tense, voice, mood, person, number, tone or style, viewpoint, or direct and indirect quotations within a sentence, paragraph, or essay. Shifts confuse your reader and distort the meaning of your writing.

SHIFTS IN TENSE

A shift in *tense* occurs when the tenses of verbs within a sentence or paragraph do not logically match.

Confusing:
Throughout the eighties the junk-bond market **rose** steadily; as a result, small investors **invest** heavily from 1985 to 1989.

Revised:
Throughout the eighties the junk-bond market **rose** steadily; as a result, small investors **invested** heavily from 1985 to 1989.

Confusing:
Last night I **was watching** my favorite television show. Suddenly the show is interrupted for a special news bulletin. I **lean forward** and **will** eagerly **watch** the screen for information.

Revised:
Last night I **was watching** my favorite television show. Suddenly the show was **interrupted** for a special news bulletin. I **leaned forward** and eagerly **watched** the screen for information.

Note: If you are using the present tense to narrate events in a literary work, be careful not to slip into the past tense.

SHIFTS IN VOICE

Voice shows whether the subject of the verb acts or is acted upon. (See page 64–65.) When the subject of the verb does the action, the sentence is said to be in the *active voice:*

Dave hit a home run.

When the subject of the verb receives the action, the sentence is said to be in the *passive voice:*

The home run was hit by Dave.

You should avoid changing from active voice to passive voice within a sentence.

Confusing:
As **we finished** our coffee, **the servers were seen** clearing the adjacent tables.

Revised:
As **we finished** our coffee, **we saw** the servers clearing the adjacent tables.

Confusing:
The **cook mixed** the bread dough until it was blended, and then **it was set** in the warm oven to rise.

Revised:

The **cook mixed** the bread dough until it was blended and then **set** it in the warm oven to rise.

Or

The bread dough was mixed until it was blended, and then **it was set** in the warm oven to rise.

SHIFTS IN MOOD

The *mood* of a verb indicates the manner in which it is used. English has three moods: **indicative, subjunctive,** and **imperative.** (See page 62–63.)

Confusing:

Stroke the paint on evenly, but **you should not dab** it on corners and edges. [Shift from imperative to indicative]

Revised:

Stroke the paint on evenly, but **don't dab** it on corners and edges.

Or

You should stroke the paint on evenly, but **you shouldn't dab** it on corners and edges.

Confusing:

The cleaning service **asked** that they get better hours and **they want** to work fewer weekends as well. [Shift from subjunctive to indicative]

Revised:

The cleaning service **asked** that they get better hours and that they work fewer weekends as well.

Or

The cleaning service **asked** to work better hours and fewer weekends.

Or

The cleaning service **wants** to work better hours and fewer weekends.

Confusing:
If the rain **stopped** and the sun **comes out**, we **could have** a picnic. [Shift from subjunctive to indicative]

Revised:
If the rain **stopped** and the sun **came out**, we **could have** a picnic.

Or

If the rain **stops** and the sun **comes out**, we **can have** a picnic.

SHIFTS IN PERSON

Person is the form a pronoun or verb takes to show the person or persons speaking: the first person (*I, we*), the second person (*you*), or the third person (*he, she, it, they*). As the pronouns indicate, the first person is the person speaking, the second person is the person spoken to, and the third person is the person, concept, or thing spoken about.

Shifts between second- and third-person pronouns cause the most confusion. The following examples illustrate common shifts in person and different ways to revise such shifts.

Confusing:

When **one** shops for an automobile, **you** should research various models in consumer magazines and read all the advertisements as well as speak to salespeople. [Shift from the third to the second person]

Revised:

When **you** shop for an automobile, **you** should research various models in consumer magazines and read all the advertisements as well as speak to salespeople.

Or

When **one** shops for an automobile, **one** should research various models in consumer magazines and read all the advertisements as well as speak to salespeople.

Or

When **people** shop for an automobile, **they** should research various models in consumer magazines and read all the advertisements as well as speak to salespeople.

Confusing:

When **a person** applies themselves diligently, **you** can accomplish a surprising amount.

Revised:

When **people** apply themselves diligently, **they** can accomplish a surprising amount.

Or

When **you** apply yourself diligently, **you** can accomplish a surprising amount.

Or

When **a person** applies himself or herself diligently, **he or she** can accomplish a surprising amount.

SHIFTS IN PERSPECTIVE

Shifts in *perspective* are related to shifts in person that change the vantage point from which a story is told. As with other shifts, there will be occasions when it is desirable to shift perspective; however, unnecessary shifts confuse readers.

Effectively shifting perspective is often a matter of slowing down. Sometimes when we write, we get caught up in the story, and we skip a few steps when writing down our thoughts. We have to remember that although we fully understand the event we are describing, the reader does not. So, take your time with your description.

In the following example, the perspective shifts from above the water to below without adequate transition.

Confusing:
The frothy surface of the ocean danced with bursts of light, and the fish swam lazily through the clear water and waving plants.

Revised:
The frothy surface of the ocean danced with bursts of light; below, the fish swam lazily through the clear water and waving plants.

Confusing:
Bill, Jim, and Steve thought they were lost, and the wind trembled in the trees making them afraid.

Revised:

Bill, Jim, and Steve thought they were lost. When the wind trembled in the trees, it made them afraid.

Confusing:

The university went to great lengths to oppose the action and the public prepared to rebel.

Revised:

The university went to great lengths to oppose the action. Meanwhile, the public prepared to rebel.

SHIFTS IN NUMBER

Number indicates one (singular) or more than one (plural). Shifts in number occur with nouns and personal pronouns because both change form to show differences in number. Confusion with number occurs especially often between a pronoun and its antecedent and between words whose meanings relate to each other. Remember to use singular pronouns to refer to singular antecedents and plural pronouns to refer to plural antecedents.

Confusing:

If **a person** does not keep up with household chores, **they** will find that things pile up with alarming speed.

Revised:

If **a person** does not keep up with household chores, **he or she** will find that things pile up with alarming speed.

Or

If **people** do not keep up with household chores, **they** will find that things pile up with alarming speed.

Confusing:
All the repair stations have **a good reputation**.

Revised:
All the repair stations have **good reputations**.

PERSON AND NUMBER WITH COLLECTIVE NOUNS

Maintaining consistency of person and number is especially tricky with collective nouns since many can be either singular or plural, depending on the context. Once you establish a collective noun as singular or plural within a sentence, maintain consistency throughout.

Confusing:
Because **my company** bases **their** bonus on amount of income generated yearly, we must all do our share to enable **it** to give a generous bonus.

Revised:
Because **my company** bases **its** bonus on amount of income generated yearly, we must all do our share to enable **it** to give a generous bonus.

Or

Because **my company** bases **their** bonus on amount of income generated yearly, we must all do our share to enable **them** to give a generous bonus.

Confusing:

The jury is divided on whether or not **they** should demand additional evidence.

Revised:

The jury are divided on whether or not **they** should demand additional evidence. [Jury functioning as separate individuals]

SHIFTS IN TONE AND STYLE

Tone is the writer's attitude toward his or her readers and subject. As pitch and volume convey tone in speaking, so word choice and sentence structure help convey tone in writing. Tone can be formal or informal, humorous or earnest, distant or friendly, pompous or personal. Obviously, different tones are appropriate for different audiences.

Style is a writer's way of writing. Style comprises every way a writer uses language. Elements of style include tone, word choice, figurative language, grammatical structure, rhythm, and sentence length and organization.

A piece of writing is more powerful and effective if consistent tone and style are maintained throughout.

Shift:

Reporters who assert that freedom of the press can be maintained without judicial intervention are out of their minds. [Shift from elevated diction to colloquial]

Revised:

Reporters who assert that freedom of the press can be maintained without judicial intervention are greatly mistaken.

Shift:

Their leave-taking was marked by the same affability that had characterized their entire visit with us. Later, we discussed what cool dudes they were. [Shift from standard English to colloquial]

Revised:

Their leave-taking was marked by the same affability that had characterized their entire visit with us. Later, we discussed their good humor, consideration, and generosity.

SHIFTS IN DIRECT AND INDIRECT QUOTATIONS

Direct quotations use quotation marks to report a speaker's exact words: "I'll be the referee for today's game," Ms. Marin said. Usually, direct quotations are also marked by a phrase such as *she said* or *he remarked*, which indicates the speaker.

Indirect quotations report what was said, but not necessarily in the speaker's own words: Ms. Marin said that she would be the referee for today's game. Since the remarks do not have to be reproduced exactly, indirect quotations do not use quotation marks. Often, a reported statement will be introduced by *that, who, how, if, what, when,* or *whether*.

Illogical shifts between direct and indirect quotations can become wordy and confuse readers. As the following examples show, these errors can usually be eliminated by recording a speaker's remarks with logic and consistency regardless of whether you choose to use direct quotations, indirect quotations, or a combination of the two.

Wordy:

Poet and critic T. S. Eliot said that he feels that the progress of an artist was like a long process of sacrifice of self, "a continual extinction of personality."

Revised:

Poet and critic T. S. Eliot said that the progress of an artist was like a long process of self-sacrifice, "a continual extinction of personality."

Or

Poet and critic T. S. Eliot said that to progress, artists must sacrifice and extinguish the self.

Confusing:

Jill asked whether we had cut down the storm-damaged tree and was there any further damage.

Revised:

Jill asked whether we had cut down the storm-damaged tree and if there was any further damage.

Or

Jill asked, "Did you cut down the tree damaged by the storm? Was there any further damage?"

Confusing:

My son said he was very busy and would I please take the cat to the vet.

Revised:

My son said he was very busy and asked if I would take the cat to the vet.

PARALLELISM

PARALLEL STRUCTURE

Parallelism, or parallel structure, means that grammatical elements that share the same function will share the same form. Parallel structure ensures that ideas of equal rank are expressed in similar ways and that separate word groups appear in the same grammatical forms.

Individual words, phrases, clauses, or sentences can be paralleled. For example, adjectives are paired with adjectives, and verbs correspond with matching verbs in tense, mood, voice, and number. Parallel structure helps coordinate ideas and strengthen logic and symmetry.

Study the following pairs of examples. Note how much more smoothly the sentences flow when the constructions are parallel.

Not parallel:
Lindsey was hot, cranky, and needed food.

Parallel:
Lindsey was hot, cranky, and hungry.

Not parallel:
Sam is organized, efficient, and works hard.

Parallel:
Sam is organized, efficient, and industrious.

Not parallel:
Knowing how to win is important, but it is even more important to know how to lose.

Parallel:
Knowing how to win is important, but knowing how to lose is even more important.

Not parallel:
We can go out to eat, or ordering a pizza would do as well.

Parallel:
We can go out to eat, or we can order a pizza.

Not parallel:
He has plundered our seas, ravaged our coasts, and was burning our towns.

Parallel:
He has plundered our seas, ravaged our coasts, and burned our towns.

Not parallel:
The only good is knowledge, and evil is the only ignorant thing.

Parallel:
The only good is knowledge, and the only evil is ignorance.

Not parallel:
Cursed be the social wants that sin against the strength of youth!
Cursed be the social ties that warp us from the living truth!

Cursed be the sickly forms that err from honest nature's rule!

The gold that gilds the straighten'd forehead of the fool is also cursed.

Parallel:

Cursed be the social wants that sin against the strength of youth!

Cursed be the social ties that warp us from the living truth!

Cursed be the sickly forms that err from honest nature's rule!

Cursed be the gold that gilds the straighten'd forehead of the fool.

PARALLEL ITEMS IN SERIES

Items in a series have greater impact when arranged in parallel form. The items can be words, phrases, or clauses:

Passions, prejudices, fears, and neuroses spring from ignorance, and take the form of myth and illusions.
   —*Sir Isaiah Berlin*

When any of the four pillars of the government, religion, justice, counsel, and treasure, are mainly shaken or weakened, men have need to pray for fair weather.
   —*Francis Bacon*

In the opening of *A Tale of Two Cities*, Charles Dickens arranged paired items in a series for a powerful effect:

It was the best of times, it was the worst of times,

it was the age of wisdom, it was the age of foolishness,

it was the epoch of belief, it was the epoch of incredulity,

it was the season of Light, it was the season of Darkness,

it was the spring of hope, it was the winter of despair . . .

PARALLEL OUTLINES AND LISTS

Arranging outlined ideas and lists in parallel structure helps solidify logic. Maintaining one format (for example, complete sentences, clauses, or phrases) throughout serves to order ideas, as the following sentence outline shows:

I. **Cigarette smoke harms the health of the general public.**

    A. Cigarette smoke may lead to serious diseases in nonsmokers.

        1. It leads to lung disease.

            a. It causes emphysema.

            b. It causes cancer.

        2. It leads to circulatory disease.

            a. It causes strokes.

            b. It causes heart disease.

    B. Cigarette smoke worsens less serious health conditions in nonsmokers.

        1. It aggravates allergies.

        2. It intensifies pulmonary infections.

SECTION QUIZ

NOW that you've read the section on Grammar, see how much you've learned by taking the quiz below.

I. **Classify the following nouns as either proper, collective, common, or compound.**

   1. stream
   2. tribe
   3. schoolroom
   4. Paris
   5. girl
   6. Broadway
   7. housework
   8. boy
   9. Stanley

II. **Which of these is the nominative case and which the objective case?**

   1. him
   2. they
   3. them
   4. I
   5. her

6.   it

7.   we

8.   us

III.   **Are the verbs in the following sentences transitive or intransitive?**

1.   Please *telephone* your brother.

2.   Even the old lady *laughed.*

3.   I *worked* hard all winter.

4.   Steve *wrote* fifteen books in ten years.

5.   Please *sit* down.

6.   My brother *drank* the last bottle of soda.

IV.   **Each of the bolded terms is in one of the perfect tenses. Name which tense.**

1.   We **have been working** for a week.

2.   By tomorrow, the stocks **will have lost** more than ninety percent of their face value.

3.   We **had hoped** to have the boat painted by the end of March.

V.   **Each of the bolded terms is in one of the progressive forms. Name which form.**

1.   The office workers **had been planning** a party when it rained.

2.   By Tuesday, **I will have been working** on this assignment for a year!

3. He **will be studying** all evening.

4. Sports **is becoming** progressively dangerous.

5. Jenny fell asleep while she **was watching** a woman on television.

VI. **Determine if the sentence is in the active or passive voice.**

1. Tommy was scratched by Bill's cat.

2. Many boats were damaged by the storm.

3. Stacey will make the dessert.

4. The pie will be made by Frank.

VII. **Determine if the bolded term is used as an adjective or adverb.**

1. I believe she ought to go to bed **early** tonight.

2. I had an **early** date this weekend.

3. That was some **close** call!

4. Bill is lucky he lives **close** to the subway.

VIII. **Determine whether the bolded term is a preposition or an adverb.**

1. They all went **in**.

2. The men went **into** the cave.

3. After the third stone fell **down**, we knew it was time to leave.

4. Lots of students were skiing **down** the slope.

IX.   **Determine whether the language below is a transitional phrase or a conjunctive adverb.**

1.   in fact

2.   still

3.   thus

4.   by the way

5.   indeed

6.   at any rate

X.   **Determine if the bolded language is an adjective clause or adverb clause.**

1.   Do you know **where they went on their honeymoon**?

2.   Did Tim tell you the reason **why he didn't get the work done**?

3.   Did you see the Eiffel Tower **when you were in Paris**?

XI.   **Are these sentences grammatically correct? If not, why not?**

1.   If I was you, I would mail them a letter.

2.   Rainy days in Tucson are as rare as Santa Fe.

3.   The leaders paid attention not only to the people but they were also paying attention to the pets.

XII.   **Which part of the sentence is the subject and which is the predicate?**

1.   The bicycle veered away from the crowd.

2.   Calico cats are always female.

3. One of Mr. Miller's distant relatives was the notorious "Shoeless" Joe Jackson of the Chicago "Black Sox."

4. Virginia Beach, a resort near the North Carolina border, has recently expanded its commercial base from tourism to fishing.

XIII. True or false? The following are complete sentences.

1. Drank all the soda in the refrigerator.

2. I leaped for joy.

3. Feeling sad.

4. When I woke him up early this morning.

5. This is the right time.

ANSWERS

To learn more about the subjects covered in this quiz, refer back to the page numbers listed below.

I. Classify the following nouns as either proper, collective, common, or compound. (See pages 4–5 for more information.)

1. stream   *common*

2. tribe   *collective*

3. schoolroom   *compound*

4. Paris   *proper*

5. girl   *common*

6. Broadway   *proper*

7. housework   *compound*

8. toy   *common*

9. Stanley   *proper*

II. **Which of these is the nominative case and which the objective case? (See pages 9–12 for more information.)**

1. him   *objective*

2. they   *nominative*

3. them   *objective*

4. I   *nominative*

5. her   *objective*

6. it   *nominative*

7. we   *nominative*

8. us   *objective*

III. **Are the verbs in the following sentences transitive or intransitive? (See page 22 for more information.)**

1. Please *telephone* your brother.   *transitive*

2. Even the old lady *laughed*.   *intransitive*

3. I *worked* hard all winter.   *intransitive*

4. Steve *wrote* fifteen books in ten years.   *transitive*

5. Please *sit* down.   *intransitive*

6. My brother *drank* the last bottle of soda.   *transitive*

IV. **Each of the bolded terms is in one of the perfect tenses. Name which tense. (See page 53 for more information.)**

1. Present Perfect

2. Future Perfect

3. Past Perfect

V. Each of the bolded terms is in one of the progressive forms. Name which form. (See page 58 for more information.)

1. Past Perfect Progressive

2. Future Perfect Progessive

3. Future Progressive

4. Present Progressive

5. Past Progressive

VI. Determine if the sentence is in the active or passive voice. (See page 64 for more information.)

1. Passive

2. Passive

3. Active

4. Passive

VII. Determine if the bolded term is used as an adjective or adverb. (See page 70 for more information.)

1. Adverb

2. Adjective

3. Adjective

4. Adverb

VII. Determine whether the bolded term is a preposition or an adverb. (See page 81 for more information.)

1. Adverb

2. Preposition

3. Adverb

4. Preposition

IX. **Determine if the language below is a transitional phrase or a conjunctive adverb. (See page 85 for more information.)**

1. Transitional phrase

2. Conjunctive adverb

3. Conjunctive adverb

4. Transitional phrase

5. Conjunctive adverb

6. Transitional phrase

X. **Determine if the bolded language is an adjective clause or adverb clause. (See page 97 for more information.)**

1. Noun clause

2. Adjective clause

3. Adverb clause

XI. **Are these sentences grammatically correct? If not, why not? (See pages 62, 82, and 109 for more information.)**

1. If I was you, I would mail them a letter.

   Incorrect. It's the subjunctive mood, so it should be "If I *were* you . . ."

2. Rainy days in Tucson are as rare as Santa Fe.

   Incorrect. This is an incomplete comparison. It should be: Rainy days in Tucson are as rare as they are in Santa Fe.

3. The leaders paid attention not only to the people but they were also paying attention to the pets.

   Incorrect. It should be: The leaders not only paid attention to the people but also to the pets. The two elements connected by correlative conjunctions must be in parallel form.

XII. Which part of the sentence is the subject and which is the predicate? (See page 100 for more information.)

1. The bicycle veered away from the crowd.

   Subject: The bicycle. *Predicate:* veered away from the crowd.

2. Calico cats are always female.

   Subject: Calico cats. *Predicate:* are always female.

3. One of Mr. Miller's distant relatives was the notorious "Shoeless" Joe Jackson of the Chicago "Black Sox."

   Subject: One of Mr. Miller's distant relatives. *Predicate:* was the notorious "Shoeless" Joe Jackson of the Chicago "Black Sox."

4. Virginia Beach, a resort near the North Carolina border, has recently expanded its commercial base from tourism to fishing.

   Subject: Virginia Beach, a resort near the North Carolina border. *Predicate:* has recently expanded its commercial base from tourism to fishing.

XIII. True or false? The following are complete sentences. (See page 109 for more information.)

   1. Drank all the soda in the refrigerator.   *False*

   2. I leaped for joy.   *True*

   3. Feeling sad.   *False*

   4. When I woke him up early this morning.   *False*

   5. This is the right time.   *True*

SECTION II

Usage

COMMON ERRORS

L ANGUAGE changes constantly. This glossary provides information about contemporary English usage, focusing on key errors made by native speakers. It will show you how certain words and phrases are used and why certain usage is unacceptable.

"Informal" indicates that a word or phrase is often used in everyday speech but should generally be avoided in formal discourse. "Nonstandard" means that the word or phrase is not suitable for everyday speech and writing in standard American English and should never be used in formal discourse.

a/an   In both spoken and written English, *an* is used before words beginning with a vowel sound: He carried **an** umbrella. The Nobel prize is **an** honor, and when the consonants *f, h, l, m, n, r, s,* and *x* are pronounced by name: The renovations created **an** L-shaped room. Miles received **an** F in physics. Use *a* before words beginning with a consonant sound—What **a** fish! I bought **a** computer—and words that start with vowels but are pronounced as consonants: **A** union can be dissolved. They live in **a** one-room apartment. Also use *a* with words that start with consonant letters not listed above and with the vowel *u*: She earned **a** C in French. He made **a** U-turn.

For words that begin with *h,* if the initial *h* is not pronounced, the word is preceded by *an:* It will take **an** hour. Adjectives such as *historic, historical, heroic,* and *habitual* are commonly preceded by *an,* especially in British English, but the use of *a* is common in both writing and speech: She read **a** historical novel. When the *h* is strongly pronounced, as in a stressed first syllable, the word is preceded by *a*: I bought **a** history of Long Island.

above   *Above* can be used as an adjective (The **above** entry is incomplete) or as a noun (First, please read the **above**) in referring to what has been previously mentioned in a passage. Both uses are standard in formal writing.

agree to/agree with   *Agree to* means "to consent to, to accept" (usually a plan or idea). *Agree with* means "to be in accord with" (usually a person or group): I can't believe they will **agree to** the proposed merger when they don't **agree with** each other on anything.

ain't   The term is nonstandard for *am not*, *isn't*, or *aren't*. It is used informally for humorous effect or to evoke dialectal speech, usually in dialogue.

all right/alright   *All right* is always written as two words; *alright* is a misspelling: Betsy said that it was **all right** to use her car that afternoon.

almost/most   *Almost*, an adverb, means "nearly"; *most*, an adjective, means "the greatest part of" something. *Most* is not synonymous with *almost*, as the following example shows: During our vacation we shop at that store **almost** every day and buy **most** of the available snack foods.

In informal speech, *most* (as a shortened form of *almost*) is used as an adverb. It occurs before such pronouns as *all*, *anybody*, *anyone*, *everybody*, and *everyone*; the adjectives *all*, *any*, and *every*; and the adverbs *anywhere* and *everywhere*. For example: **Most** everyone around here is related. The use of *most* as an adverb is nonstandard and is uncommon in formal writing except when used to represent speech.

a.m., p.m.   These abbreviations for time are most frequently restricted to use with figures: The ceremony begins at 10 **a.m.** (not "ten-thirty a.m.")

among/between   *Among* is used to indicate relationships involving more than two people or things, while *between* is used to show relationships involving two people or things, or to compare one thing to a group to which it belongs: The three quarreled **among** themselves because she had to choose **between** two of them. *Between* is also used to express relationships of persons or things considered individually, no matter how many: **Between** holding public office, teaching, and raising a family, she has little free time.

and etc.   Since *etc.* means "and all the rest," *and etc.* is redundant; the *and* is not needed. Some writers prefer to use *and so forth* or *and the like* as a substitute for the abbreviation.

and/or   The combination *and/or* is used mainly in legal and business writing. Its use should be avoided in general writing, as in: He spends his weekends watching television **and/or** snacking. In such writing, either one or the other word is sufficient. If you mean "either," use *or*; if you mean "both," use *and*. To make a greater distinction, revise the phrasing: He spends his weekends watching television, snacking, **or both**.

and which/and who   *And* is unnecessary when *which* or *who* is used to open a relative clause. Use *and which* or *and who* only to open a second clause starting with the same relative pronoun: Elizabeth is my neighbor **who** goes shopping every morning **and who** calls me every afternoon to tell me about the sales.

a number/the number As a subject, *a number* is most often plural and *the number* is singular. **A number** of choices are available. **The number** of choices is limited. As with many agreement questions, this guideline is followed more often in formal discourse than in speech and informal writing.

anyplace   *Anyplace* is an informal expression for *anywhere*. It occurs in speech and informal writing but is best avoided in formal prose.

anyways/anyway; anywheres/anywhere   *Anyways* is nonstandard for *anyway*; *anywheres* is nonstandard for *anywhere*.

as   Do not use *as* in place of *whether*: We're not sure **whether** (not *as*) you should do that. Also avoid using *as* as a substitute for *because*, *since*, *while*, *whether*, or *who*, where its use may create confusion. In the following sentence, for example, *as* may mean "while" or "because": **As** they were driving to California they decided to see the Grand Canyon.

as/because/since   While all three words can function as subordinating conjunctions, they convey slightly different shades of meaning. *As* establishes a time relationship and can be used interchangeably with *when* or *while*. *Because* and *since*, in contrast, describe causes and effects: **As** we brought out the food, it began to drizzle. **Because** (**since**) Nancy goes skiing infrequently, she prefers to rent skis.

as/like   When *as* functions as a preposition, the distinction between *as* and *like* depends on meaning: *As* suggests that the subject is equivalent to the description: He was employed **as** a teacher. *Like*, in contrast, suggests similarity but not equivalence: Speakers **like** her excel in front of large groups.

at   Avoid using *at* with *where* in a question: Where are you seeing her (not *at*)? Whether used as an adverb or as a preposition, *where* contains the preposition *at* in its definition.

at this point in time   Although the phrase *at this point in time* is widely used (especially in politics), many people consider it verbose and stuffy. Instead, use *now* or *at this time*: We are not ready to discuss the new budget **now**.

awful/awfully Avoid using *awful* or *awfully* to mean "very" in formal discourse: We had an **awfully** busy day at the amusement park. Although the use of *awful* to mean "terrible" (rather than "inspiring awe") has permeated all levels of writing and speech, consider using in its place a word that more closely matches your intended meaning: We had an **unpleasant** (not *awful*) time because the park was hot, noisy, and crowded.

awhile/a while *Awhile* is an adverb and is always spelled as one word: We visited **awhile**. *A while* is a noun phrase (an article and a noun) and is used after a preposition: We rested for **a while**.

backward/backwards In formal discourse, *backward* is preferred: This stroke is easier if you use a **backward** motion (adjective). Counting **backward** from 100 can be an effective way to induce sleep (adverb).

bad/badly *Bad*, an adjective, is used to describe a noun or pronoun. *Badly*, an adverb, is used to describe a verb, adjective, or another adverb. Thus: She felt **bad** because her broken leg throbbed **badly**.

because/due to the fact that/since *Because* or *since* are preferred over the wordy phrase *due to the fact that*: He wrote the report longhand **because** (not *due to the fact that*) his computer was broken.

being as/being that Avoid both *being as* and *being that* in formal writing. Instead, use *since* or *because*. For example: **Since** you asked, I'll be glad to help.

better/had better The verb *had* is necessary in the phrase *had better* and should be retained in formal speech. She **had better** return the lawn mower today.

between you and I Although this phrase is heard occasionally in the speech of even educated people, it is incorrect. Pronouns that function as objects of prepositions should be in the objective case. Please keep this **between you and me**. I would appreciate it if you could keep this **between her and them**.

bi- Many words that refer to periods of time through the prefix *bi-* are potentially confusing. Ambiguity is avoided by using the prefix *semi-*, meaning "twice each" (semiweekly, semimonthly, semiannual) or by using the appropriate phrases (twice a week, twice each month, every two months; every two years).

borrow off/borrow from *Borrow off*, considered informal, should not be used in formal speech and writing; *borrow from* is the preferred expression.

bottom line This overworked term is frequently used as a synonym for *outcome* or *the final result*: The **bottom line** is that we have to reduce inventory to maintain profits. Careful writers and speakers avoid it for less shopworn descriptions.

bunch Use the noun *bunch* in formal writing only to refer to clusters of things grouped together, such as grapes or bananas: That **bunch** of grapes looks better than the other one. In formal writing, use *group* or *crowd* to refer to gatherings of people; *bunch* is used to refer to groups of people or items only in speech and informal writing.

burst, bursted/bust, busted *Burst* is a verb meaning "to come apart suddenly." The word *bursted* is not acceptable in either speech or writing. The verb *bust* and adjective *busted* are both informal or slang terms; as such, they should not be used in formal writing.

but however/but yet There is no reason to combine *but* with another conjunction: She said she was leaving, **yet** (not *but yet*) she poured another cup of coffee.

but that/but what As with the previous example, there is no reason to add the word *but* to either *that* or *what*: We don't doubt **that** (not *but that*) you will win this hand.

calculate/figure/reckon None of these words is an acceptable substitute for *expect* or *imagine* in formal writing, although they are all used in speech and informal prose.

can/may Traditionally, *may* is used in formal writing to convey permission; *can* to convey ability or capacity. In speech, however, the terms are used interchangeably to mean permission: **Can** (**May**) I borrow your hedge clippers? *Can* and *may* are frequently, but not always, interchangeable when used to mean possibility: A blizzard **can** (or **may**) occur any time during February. In negative constructions, *can't* is more common than *mayn't*, the latter being extremely rare and stilted: You **can't** eat that taco in the den.

cannot/can not *Cannot* is occasionally spelled *can not*. The one-word spelling is by far the more common. The contraction *can't* is used mainly in speech and informal writing.

can't help but *Can't help but*—as in: You **can't help but** like her— is a double negative. This idiom can be replaced by the informal *can't help* or the formal *cannot but* where each is appropriate: She **can't help** wishing that it was spring. I **cannot but** wish things had turned out differently. While *can't help but* is common in all types of speech, you should avoid using it in formal writing.

cause of . . . on account of/due to The phrases *on account of* and *due to* are unnecessary with *cause of:* One **cause of** physical and psychological problems is **due to** too much stress. Omit the phrases or revise the entire sentence. Change the sentence to: Too much stress **causes** physical and psychological problems.

center around/center on Although both phrases are often criticized for being illogical, they have been used in writing for more than a hundred years to express the notion of collecting or gathering as if around a center point. The phrase *revolve around* is often suggested as an alternative, and the prepositions *at*, *in*, and *on* are considered acceptable with *center* in the following sense: Their problems **centered on** their lack of expertise.

chair/chairperson *Chairperson* is used widely in academic and governmental circles as an alternative to *chairman* or *chairwoman*. While some reject the term *chairperson* as clumsy and unnecessary and use the term *chair* for any presiding officer, regardless of sex, *chairperson* is still standard in all types of writing and speech.

choose/chose *Choose* is a verb that means "to select one thing in preference to another": Why **choose** tomatoes when they are out of season? *Chose* is the past tense of *to choose*: I **chose** tomatoes over cucumbers at the salad bar.

conformity to/conformity with Although the word *conformity* can be followed by either *to* or *with*, *conformity to* is generally used when the idea of obedience is implied: The new commissioner issued a demand for **conformity to** health regulations. *Conformity with* is used to imply agreement or correspondence: This is an idea in **conformity with** previous planning.

consensus/consensus of The expression *consensus of* (consensus of opinion) is considered redundant, and the preferred usage is the single noun *consensus*, meaning "general agreement or concord": Since the **consensus** was overwhelming, the city planners moved ahead with the proposal. The phrase *general consensus* is also considered redundant. Increasingly, the word *consensus* is widely used attributively, as in the phrase *consensus politics*.

contact   The word is both a verb and a noun. As a verb, it is frequently used unprecisely to mean "to communicate" when a more exact word or phrase (*telephone*, *write to*, *consult*) would better communicate the idea. *Contact* as a noun meaning "a person through whom one can obtain information" is now standard usage: He is my **contact** in the state department.

couple/couple of   Both phrases are informally used to mean "two" or "several": I need a **couple** more cans of paint. I took **a couple of** aspirins for my headache. The expression *a couple of* is used in standard English, especially in referring to distance, money, or time: He is **a couple of feet** away. I have **a couple of thousand dollars** in the bank. The store will open in **a couple of weeks**. *Couple* may be treated as either a singular or plural noun.

criteria/criterion   *Criteria* is the plural of *criterion* (a standard for judgment). For example: Of all their **criteria** for evaluating job performance, customer satisfaction was the most important **criterion**.

data/datum   *Data* is the plural of *datum* (fact). Although *data* is often used as a singular, it should still be treated as plural in formal speech and writing: The **data pertain** (not *pertains*) to the first half of the experiment. To avoid awkward constructions, most writers prefer to use a more commonplace term such as *fact* or *figure* in place of *datum*.

decimate   The word *decimate* comes from a Latin term that meant "to select by lot and kill one person in ten of" (a rebellious military unit). The usual use of the word in English is "to destroy a large amount or proportion of": Disease **decimated** the population. Some people claim that *decimate* should only be used to mean "to destroy a tenth of," but in fact there is nothing wrong with the sense "to destroy a large amount or proportion of."

different from/different than   Although *different from* is the preferred usage (His attitude is **different from** mine), *different than* is widely accepted when a clause follows, especially when the word *from* would create an awkward sentence. Example: The stream followed a **different** course **than** the map showed.

differ from/differ with   *Differ from* means "to be unlike"; *differ with* means "to disagree with": The sisters **differ from** each other in appearance. We **differ with** you on this matter.

done   Using *done* as an adjective to mean "through, finished" is standard. Originally, *done* was used attributively (The pact between them was a **done** thing), but it has become more common as a complement: Are your pictures **done** yet? When we were **done** with the power saw, we removed the blade.

don't/does not   *Don't* is the contraction for *do not*, not for *does not*, as in I **don't** care, she **doesn't** (not *don't*) care. The use of *don't* as a contraction for *does not* is nonstandard.

double negatives   Double negatives are universally considered unacceptable: He **didn't have nothing** to do, for example. In standard speech and writing, *anything* would be used in place of *nothing*. There are certain uses of double negation, to express an affirmative, that are considered standard, however: We cannot sit here and do nothing, meaning "we must do something."

doubt that/doubt whether/doubt if   *Doubt that* is used to express conviction: I **doubt that** they intended to hurt your feelings. *Doubt whether* and *doubt if* are used to indicate uncertainty: I **doubt whether** (or **if**) anyone really listened to the speaker.

due to   In formal discourse, *due to* is acceptable only after a form of the verb *to be*: Her aching back was **due to** poor posture. *Due to* is not acceptable as a preposition meaning *because of* or *owing to*: **Because of** (not *due to*) poor weather, the bus was late.

each When *each* is used as a pronoun, it takes a singular verb (**Each** was born in Europe), although plurals are increasingly used in formal speech and writing in an attempt to avoid using *he* or *his* for sentences that include females or do not specify sex: Each of them had **their** (rather than *his*) own agenda. More and more, the same pattern of pronoun agreement is being used with the singular pronouns *anybody, anyone, everybody, everyone, no one, somebody,* and *someone.* When the pronoun *each* is followed by an *of*-phrase containing a plural noun or pronoun, usage guides suggest that the verb be singular, but the plural is used often even in formal writing: Each of the children **has** (or **have**) **had** a school physical.

When the adjective *each* follows a plural subject, the verb agrees with the subject: The rooms each **have** separate thermostats.

each and every Use *each* or *every* in place of the phrase *each and every,* generally considered wordy: **Each** of us enjoyed the concert. **Every** one of us stayed until the end of the performance.

each other/one another *Each other* is traditionally used to indicate two members; *one another* for three or more: The two children trade lunches with **each other**. The guests greeted **one another** fondly. In standard practice, though, these distinctions are not observed in either speech or writing.

enormity The word *enormity* means "outrageousness; atrociousness; monstrousness": the **enormity** of his crime. It is often used to mean "great size; enormousness": The **enormity** of the task overwhelmed her. Though this second use is common, many people consider it to be an error.

enthused/enthusiastic The word *enthused* is used informally to mean "showing enthusiasm." For formal writing and speech, use the adjective *enthusiastic*: The team was **enthusiastic** about the quarterback's winning play.

-ess/-or/-er   The suffix *-ess* has often been used to denote feminine nouns. While many such words are still in use, English is moving increasingly toward nouns that do not denote sex differences. The most widely observed guideline today is that if the sex of the performer is not relevant to the performance of the task or function, the neutral ending *-or* or *-er* should be used in place of *-ess*. Thus, words such as *ambassadress, ancestress, authoress, poetess, proprietress,* and *sculptress* are no longer used, and the airlines, for example, have replaced both *steward* and *stewardess* with *flight attendant*.

et al.   *Et al.*, the Latin abbreviation for *and other people*, is fully standard for use in a citation to refer to works with more than three authors: Harris **et al.**

etc.   Since *etc.* (et cetera) is the Latin abbreviation for *and other things*, it should not be used to refer to people. In general, it should be avoided in formal writing as imprecise. In its place, provide the entire list of items or use *and so on*.

-ette   English nouns whose *-ette* ending signifies a feminine role or identity are passing out of usage. *Suffragette* and *usherette*, for example, have been replaced by *suffragist* and *usher*, respectively.

everywheres/everywhere   *Everywheres* is a nonstandard term for *everywhere* and should be avoided in speech and writing.

except for the fact that/except that   Use *except that* in place of the verbose phrase *except for the fact that*: **Except that** (not *except for the fact that*) the button is missing, this is a lovely skirt.

fewer/less   Traditionally, *fewer*, a plural noun, has most often been used to refer to individual units that can be counted:

There are **fewer** buttons on this shirt. No **fewer** than forty of the fifty voters supported the measure. *Less*, a singular noun, is used to refer to uncountable quantities: She eats **less** every day. I have **less** patience than I used to.

Standard English does not usually reflect these distinctions, however. When followed by *than*, *less* is used as often as *fewer* to indicate plural countable nouns. There were no **less than** eight million people. No **less than** forty of the fifty voters supported the measure.

figuratively/literally *Figuratively* means "involving a figure of speech": The poet Robert Frost once **figuratively** described writing poetry without regular meter and rhyme as playing tennis with the net down. *Literally* means: "In the literal or strict sense": What does the word mean **literally**?

Literally is commonly used as an intensifier meaning "in effect, virtually": The state representative was **literally** buried alive in the caucus. This usage is often criticized and should be avoided in formal discourse.

fix The verb *fix*, meaning "to repair," is fully accepted in all areas of speech and writing. The noun *fix*, meaning "repair" or "adjustment," is used informally.

fixing to/intend to Use *intend to* in place of the informal or dialectal term *fixing to*: The community **intends to** (not *is fixing to*) raise money to help the victims of the recent fire.

flunk/fail Use the standard term *fail* in speech and writing; *flunk* is an informal substitute.

former/latter *Former* is used to refer to the first of two items; *latter*, the second: We enjoy both gardening and painting, the **former** during the summer and the **latter** during the winter. When dealing with three or more items, use *first* and *last* rather than *former* and *latter*: We enjoy gardening, painting, and skiing, but the **last** is very costly.

fortuitous   *Fortuitous* means "happening accidentally": A **fortuitous** meeting with a former acquaintance led to a change in plans. It is also used sometimes as a synonym for *lucky* or *fortunate*.

from whence   Although the phrase *from whence* is sometimes criticized on the grounds that *from* is redundant because it is included in the meaning of *whence*, the idiom is nonetheless standard in both speech and writing: She finally moved to Kansas, **from whence** she began to build a new life.

fulsome   Originally, *fulsome* meant "abundant," but for hundreds of years the word has been used to mean "offensive, disgusting, or excessively lavish." While the word still maintains the connotations of "excessive" or "offensive," it has also come to be used in the original sense as well: Compare the severe furniture of the living room to the **fulsome** decorations in the den.

fun   *Fun* should not be used as an adjective in formal writing. Instead, substitute a word such as *happy*, *pleasant*, or *entertaining*: They had a **pleasant** (not *fun*) afternoon at the park.

gentleman   Once used only to refer to men of high social rank, the term *gentleman* now also specifies a man of courtesy and consideration: He behaves like a **gentleman**. It is also used as a term of polite reference and address in the singular and plural: This **gentleman** is waiting to be served. Are we ready to begin, **gentlemen**?

get   The verb *get* is used in many slang and informal phrases as a substitute for forms of *to be*. For example: They won't **get** accepted with that attitude. In American English, an alternative past participle is *gotten,* especially in the sense of *received* and *acquired*: I **have gotten** (or **got**) all I ever wanted.

good/well *Good,* an adjective, should be used to describe someone or something: Joe is a **good** student. *Well,* when used as an adverb, should describe an action: She and Laura play **well** together on the swing set. *Well,* when used as an adjective after *look, feel,* or other linking verbs, often refers to good health: You're looking **well**.

good and/very Avoid using *good and* as a substitute for *very*: I was **very** (not *good and*) hungry.

graduate The passive form, once considered the only correct usage, is seldom used today: I was **graduated** from the Merchant Marine Academy last May. Although some critics condemn the use of *graduate* as a verb meaning "to receive a degree or diploma (from)," its use is common in both speech and writing: She **graduated** from high school in Cleveland.

great The word *great* has been overused in informal writing and speech as a synonym for *enthusiastic, good,* or *clever*: She was really **great** at making people feel at home.

had drank/had drunk According to some authorities, *had drank* is acceptable usage: I **had drank** a gallon of milk. *Had drunk,* though, is fully standard and the preferred usage.

had ought/ought *Had ought* is considered wordy; the preferred usage is *ought*: She **ought** (not *had ought*) to heed her mother's advice.

half/a half a/a half Use either *half* or *a half*; *a half a* is wordy: Please give me **a half** (not *a half a*) piece. I'd like **half** that slice, please.

hanged/hung Although both words are past-tense forms of *to hang, hanged* is used to refer to executions (Billy Budd was

hanged), and *hung* is used for all other meanings: The stockings were **hung** by the chimney with care.

has/have; has got/have got   The word *got* is unnecessary; simply use *has* or *have*: Jessica **has** a mild case of chicken pox.

have/of   Use *have* rather than *of* after helping verbs like *could, should, would, may,* and *might*: They should **have** (not *of*) let me know of their decision earlier.

he, she; he/she; s/he   The pronouns *he* and *she* refer to male and female antecedents, respectively. Traditionally, when an antecedent in singular form could be either female or male, *he* was always used to refer to either sex: A child is often apprehensive when **he** first begins school. Today, however, various approaches have been developed to avoid the all-purpose *he*. Many people find the construction *he/she* (*he or she*) awkward: A child is often apprehensive when **he/she** first begins school. The blended form *s/he* has not been widely adopted, probably because of confusion over pronunciation. Most people now favor either rephrasing the sentence entirely to omit the pronoun or reconstructing the sentence in the third-person plural: Children are often apprehensive when **they** first begin school.

hopefully   *Hopefully* originally meant "in a hopeful manner": The beggar looked up **hopefully**. It is now usually used to mean "it is to be hoped; I hope; let us hope": **Hopefully**, we'll get there on time. Although this sense is common and standard, many people consider it incorrect.

how come/why   *How come* is used informally in speech. In formal speech and writing, use *why*.

if/whether   Use *whether* rather than *if* to begin a subordinate clause when the clause states a choice: I don't know **whether** (not *if*) I should stay until the end or leave right after the opening ceremony.

impact Both the noun and verb *impact* are used to indicate forceful contact: I cannot overstate the **impact** of the new policy on productivity. Some speakers and writers avoid using *impact* as a verb to mean "to have an effect," as in: Our work here **impacts** on every division in the firm.

in Several phrases beginning with *in* are verbose and should be avoided in formal writing. Refer to the following table.

Replace the phrase	With
in this day and age	now
in spite of the fact that	although *or* even though
in the neighborhood of	approximately *or* about
in the event that	if

The following phrases can be omitted entirely:

in a very real sense	in reality
in number	in terms of
in nature	and in the case of

in/into *In* is used to indicate condition or location, "positioned within": She was **in** labor. The raccoon was **in** the woodpile. *Into*, in contrast, indicates movement or a change in condition "from the outside to the inside": The raccoon went **into** the shed. He went **into** cardiac arrest. *Into* is also used as a slang expression for *involved with* or *interested in*: They are really **into** health foods.

inferior than *Inferior to* and *worse than* are the generally preferred forms: This wine is **inferior to** (not *inferior than*) the burgundy we had last night.

in regards to/with regards to   Both terms are considered nonstandard terms for *regarding, in regard to, with regard to,* and *as regards*: **As regards** (not *in regards to*) your request of April 1, we have traced your shipment and it will be delivered tomorrow.

inside/outside; inside of/outside of   When the words *inside* and *outside* are used as prepositions, the word *of* is not included: Stay **inside** the house. The authorization is **outside** my department. *Inside of* is used informally to refer to time: I'll be there **inside of** an hour, but in formal speech or writing *within* is the preferred usage: The dump was cleaned up **within** a month.

insignia   *Insignia* was originally the plural of the Latin word *insigne*. The plural term *insignias* has been standard usage since the eighteenth century.

irregardless/regardless   *Regardless* is the standard term; avoid *irregardless* in both speech and writing.

is when/is where   Both phrases are nonstandard and are to be avoided in speech and writing.

its/it's/its'   *Its* is the possessive form of *it*: The shrub is losing **its** blossoms. *It's* is the contraction for *it is*: **It's** a nice day. The two are often confused because possessives are most frequently formed with *-'s. Its'* is nonstandard usage.

it's me/it's I   The traditional rule is that personal pronouns after the verb *to be* take the nominative case (*I, she, he, we, they*). Today, however, such usage as *it's me, that's him, it must be them* is almost universal in informal speech. The objective forms have also replaced the nominative forms in informal speech in such constructions as *me neither* and *who, them?* In formal discourse, however, the nominative forms are still used: it's **I**, that is **he**.

-ize/-wise   Use the suffix *-ize* to change a noun or adjective into a verb: **categorize**. Use the suffix *-wise* to change a noun or adjective into an adverb: **otherwise**.

kind of/sort of/type of   Avoid using either *kind of*, *sort of*, or *type of* as synonyms for *somewhat* in formal speech and writing. Instead, use *rather*: She was **rather** (not *kind of*) slender. It is acceptable to use the three terms only when the word *kind*, *sort*, or *type* is stressed: This **kind of** cheese is hard to digest. Do not add *a*: I don't know what **kind of** (not *kind of a*) cheese that is. When the word *kind*, *sort*, or *type* is not stressed, omit the phrase entirely: That's an **unusual** (not *unusual kind of*) car. She's a **pleasant** (not *pleasant sort of a*) person.

let's   *Let's* is often used as a word in its own right rather than as the contraction of *let us*. As such, it is often used in informal speech and writing with redundant or appositional pronouns: **Let's us** take in a movie. **Let's you and me** go for a walk. Usage guides suggest avoiding *let's us* in formal speech and writing, although both *let's you and me* and *let's you and I* occur in the everyday speech of educated speakers. While the former conforms to the traditional rules of grammar, the latter occurs more frequently.

like/such as   Use *like* to compare an example to the thing mentioned and *such as* to show that the example is representative of the thing mentioned: Molly wants to be a famous clothing designer **like** John Weitz, Liz Claiborne, and Yves St. Laurent. Molly has samples of many fine articles **such as** evening dresses, suits, and jackets.

   Many writers favor not separating *such* and *as* with an intervening word (samples of many fine articles **such as**) rather than: samples of **such** fine articles **as**.

lots/lots of Both terms are used in informal speech and writing as a substitute for *a great many*, *very many*, or *much*.

man The use of the term *man* as a synonym for *human being*, both by itself and in compounds (*mankind*), is declining. Terms such as *human being(s)*, *human race*, *humankind*, *humanity*, *people*, and, when necessary, *men and women* or *women and men* are widely accepted in formal usage.

-man/-person The use of the term *-man* as the last element in compound words referring to a person of either sex who performs some function (*anchorman*, *chairman*, *spokesman*) has declined in recent years. Now such compound words are widely used only if the word refers to a male. The sex-neutral word *person* is otherwise substituted for *man* (*anchorperson*, *chairperson*, *spokesperson*). In other instances, a form without a suffix (*anchor*, *chair*), or a word that does not denote gender (*speaker*), is used.

The compound words *freshman*, *lowerclassmen*, *underclassmen* are still generally used in schools, and *freshman* is used in the U.S. Congress as well. These terms are applied to members of both sexes. As a modifier, *freshman* is used with both singular and plural nouns: *freshman athlete*, *freshman legislators*. See also **chair/chairperson**.

me and *Me and* is considered nonstandard usage when part of a compound subject: **Donna and I** (not *Me and Donna*) decided to fly to Boston.

media *Media*, the plural of medium, is used with a plural verb: Increasingly, the radio and television **media seem** to be stressing sensational news.

mighty *Mighty* is used informally for *very* or *extremely*: He is a **mighty** big fighter.

more important/more importantly   Both phrases are acceptable in standard English: My donations of clothing were tax deductible; **more important(ly)**, the clothes were given to homeless people.

Ms. (or Ms)   The title *Ms.* is widely used in business and professional circles as an alternative to *Mrs.* and *Miss*, both of which reveal a woman's marital status. Some women prefer *Mrs.*, where appropriate, or the traditional *Miss*, which is still fully standard for an unmarried woman or a woman whose marital status is unknown. Since *Ms.* is not an abbreviation, some sources spell it without a period, others use a period to parallel *Mr.* It is correctly used before a woman's name but not before her husband's name: **Ms. Elizabeth Poff** or **Ms. Poff** (not *Ms. Ken Poff*).

much/many   Use *many* rather than *much* to modify plural nouns: They had **many** (not *much*) dogs. There were too **many** (not *much*) facts to absorb.

Muslim/Moslem   *Muslim* is now the preferred form for an adherent of Islam, though *Moslem*, the traditional form, is still in use.

mutual   One current meaning of *mutual* is "reciprocal": Employers and employees sometimes suffer from a **mutual** misunderstanding. Mutual can also mean "held in common, shared": Their **mutual** goal is clearly understood.

myself; herself; himself; yourself   The *-self* pronouns are intensive or reflexive, intensifying or referring to an antecedent: Kerri **herself** said so. Mike and I did it **ourselves**. Questions are raised when the *-self* forms are used instead of personal pronouns (I, me, etc.) as subjects, objects, or complements. This use of the *-self* forms is especially common in informal speech and writing: Many came to welcome my wife and **myself** back from China. All these forms are also used, alone or with other nouns or pronouns, after *as*, *than*, or *but* in all varieties of speech and writing: Letters have arrived for everyone but the counselors and **yourselves**. Although there is ample precedent in both British and American usage for the expanded uses of the *-self* constructions, the *-self* pronouns should be used in formal speech and writing only with the nouns and pronouns to which they refer: No one except **me** (not *myself*) saw the movie.

nauseous/nauseated   *Nauseated* is generally preferred in formal writing over *nauseous*: The wild ride on the roller coaster made Meghan feel **nauseated**.

neither . . . nor   When used as a correlative, *neither* is almost always followed by *nor*: **neither** Heather **nor** her father . . . The subjects connected by *neither . . . nor* take a singular verb when both subjects are singular (**Neither** Heather **nor** her father **is going** to watch the program) and a plural verb when both are plural (**Neither** the rabbits **nor** the sheep **have been** fed yet today). When a singular and a plural subject are joined by these correlatives, the verb should agree with the nearer noun or pronoun: **Neither** the mayor **nor** the council members **have** yielded. **Neither** the council members **nor** the mayor **has** yielded.

nohow   The word *nohow*, nonstandard usage for *in no way* or *in any way*, should be avoided in speech and writing.

none   *None* can be treated as either singular or plural depending on its meaning in a sentence. When the sense is "not any persons or things," the plural is more common: The rescue party searched for survivors, but **none were** found. When *none* is clearly intended to mean "not one" or "not any," it is followed by a singular verb: Of all the ailments I have diagnosed during my career, **none has been** stranger than yours.

no . . . nor/no . . . or   Use *no . . . or* in compound phrases: We had **no** milk **or** eggs in the house.

nothing like, nowhere near Both phrases are used in informal speech and writing, but they should be avoided in formal discourse. Instead, use *not nearly*: The congealed pudding found in the back of the refrigerator is **not nearly** as old as the stale bread on the second shelf.

nowheres/nowhere The word *nowheres*, nonstandard usage for *nowhere*, should be avoided in speech and writing.

of Avoid using *of* with descriptive adjectives after the adverbs *how* or *too* in formal speech and writing. This usage is largely restricted to informal discourse: How long **of** a ride will it be? It's too cold **of** a day for swimming.

off of/off *Off of* is redundant and awkward; use *off*: The cat jumped **off** the sofa.

OK/O.K./okay All three spellings are considered acceptable, but the phrases are generally reserved for informal speech and writing.

on account of/because of Since it is less wordy, *because of* is the preferred phrase: **Because of** her headache, they decided to go straight home.

on the one hand/on the other hand These two transitions should be used together: **On the one hand**, we hoped for fair weather; **on the other hand**, we knew the rain was needed for the crops. This usage, though, can be wordy. Effective substitutes include *in contrast*, *but*, *however*, and *yet*: We hoped for fair weather, **yet** we knew the rain was needed for the crops.

only The placement of *only* as a modifier is more a matter of style and clarity than of grammatical rule. In strict formal usage, *only* should be placed as close as possible before the word it modifies. In the following sentence, for example, the placement of the word *only* suggests that no one but the children was examined: The doctor examined **only** the children. In the next sentence, the placement of *only* says that no one but the doctor did the examining: **Only** the doctor examined the children. Nonetheless, in all types of speech and writing, people often place *only* before the verb regardless of what it modifies. In spoken discourse, speakers may convey their intended meaning by stressing the word or construction to which *only* applies.

owing to the fact that   *Because* is generally accepted as a less wordy substitute for *owing to the fact that.*

pair/pairs   When modified by a number, the plural of *pair* is commonly *pairs*, especially when referring to persons: The three **pairs** of costumed **children** led off the Halloween parade. The plural *pair* is used mainly in reference to inanimate objects or nonhumans: There are four **pair** (or **pairs**) of **shoelaces**. We have two **pair** (or **pairs**) of **rabbits**.

people/persons   In formal usage, *people* is most often used to refer to a general group, emphasizing anonymity: We the **people** of the United States . . . Use *persons* to indicate any unnamed individuals within the group: Will the **persons** who left their folders on the table please pick them up at their earliest convenience? Except when individuals are being emphasized, *people* is generally used rather than *persons*.

per; a/an   *Per,* meaning "for each," occurs mainly in technical or statistical contexts: This new engine averages fifty miles **per** hour. Americans eat fifty pounds of chicken **per** person **per** year. It is also frequently used in sports commentary: He scored an average of two runs **per** game. *A* or *an* is often considered more suitable in nontechnical use: The silk costs twenty dollars **a** yard. How many miles **an** hour can you walk?

percent/per cent   *Percent* was originally spelled *per cent*, an abbreviation of the Latin *per centum*. It almost always follows a number: I made **12 percent** interest by investing my money in that new account. In formal writing, use the word rather than the symbol (%). The use of the two-word form *per cent* is diminishing.

phenomena Like words such as *criteria* and *media, phenomena* is a plural form (of *phenomenon*), meaning "observable facts, occurrences, or circumstances": The official explained that the disturbing **phenomena** we had seen for the past three evenings were nothing more than routine aircraft maneuvers.

plenty As a noun, *plenty* is acceptable in standard usage: I have **plenty** of money. In informal speech and writing, *plenty* is often a substitute for *very*: She was traveling **plenty** fast down the freeway.

plus *Plus* is a preposition meaning "in addition to": My salary **plus** overtime is enough to allow us a gracious lifestyle. Recently, *plus* has been used as a conjunctive adverb in informal speech and writing: It's safe, **plus** it's economical. Many people object to this use.

practically Use *practically* as a synonym for *in effect*, or *virtually*. It is also considered correct to use it in place of *nearly* in all varieties of speech and writing.

previous to/prior to *Before* is generally preferred in place of either expression: **Before** (not *previous to* or *prior to*) repairing the tire, you should check to see if there are any other leaks.

providing/provided Both forms can serve as subordinating conjunctions meaning "on the condition that": **Provided** (**Providing**) that we get the contract in time, we will be able to begin work by the first of the month. While some critics feel that *provided* is more acceptable in formal discourse, both are correct.

rarely ever/rarely/hardly   The term *rarely ever* is used informally in speech and writing. For formal discourse, use either *rarely* or *hardly* in place of *rarely ever*: She **rarely** calls her mother. She **hardly** calls her mother.

real/really   In formal usage, *real* (an adjective meaning "genuine") should not be used in place of *really* (an adverb meaning "actually"): The platypus hardly looked **real**. How did it **really** happen?

reason is because/reason is since   Although both expressions are commonly used in informal speech and writing, formal usage requires a clause beginning with *that* after *reason is*: **The reason** the pool is empty **is that** (not *because* or *since*) the town recently imposed a water restriction. Another alternative is to recast the sentence: The pool is empty **because** the town recently imposed a water restriction.

regarding/in regard to/with regard to/relating to/relative to/with respect to/respecting   All the above expressions are formal substitutes for *about*, *concerning*, or *on*: Janet spoke **about** (not *regarding, relative to*, etc.) the PTA's plans for the September fund drive.

relate to   The phrase *relate to* is used informally to mean "understand" or "respond in a sympathetic manner": I can't **relate to** what you're talking about. It is rarely used in formal writing or speech.

repeat it/repeat it again   *Repeat it* is the expression to use to indicate someone should say something for a second time: I did not hear your name; please **repeat it**. *Repeat it again* indicates the answer is to be said a third time. In the majority of instances, *repeat it* is the desired phrase, *again* an unnecessary addition.

says/said   Use *said* rather than *says* after a verb in the past tense:

At the public meeting, he stood up and **said** (not *says*), "The bond issue cannot pass."

seldom ever/seldom *Seldom* is the preferred form in formal discourse: They **seldom** (not *seldom ever*) go to the beach.

shall/will Today, *shall* is used for first-person questions requesting consent or opinion. **Shall** we go for a drive? **Shall** I buy this dress or that? *Shall* can also be used in the first person to create an elevated tone: We **shall** call on you at six o'clock. It is sometimes used with the second or third person to state a speaker's resolution: You **shall** obey me.

Traditionally, *will* was used for the second and third persons: **Will** you attend the party? **Will** he and she go as well? It is now widely used in speech and writing as the future-tense helping verb for all three persons: I **will** drive, you **will** drive, they **will** drive.

should/would Rules similar to those for choosing between *shall* and *will* have long been advanced for *should* and *would*. In current American usage, use of *would* far outweighs that of *should*. *Should* is chiefly used to state obligation: I **should** repair the faucet. You **should** get the parts we need. *Would*, in contrast, is used to express a hypothetical situation or a wish: I **would** like to go. **Would** you?

since *Since* is an adverb meaning "from then until now": She was appointed in May and has been supervisor ever **since**. It is also used as an adverb meaning "between a particular past time and the present; subsequently": They had at first refused to cooperate, but have **since** agreed to volunteer. As a preposition, since means "continuously from": It has been rainy **since** June. It is also used as a preposition meaning "between a past time or event and the present": There have been many changes **since** the merger. As a conjunction, *since* means "in the period following the time when": He has called **since** he changed jobs. *Since* is also used as a synonym for *because*: **Since** you're here early, let's begin.

situation   The word *situation* is often added unnecessarily to a sentence: The **situation** is that we must get the painting done by the weekend. In such instances, consider revising the sentence to pare excess words: We must get the painting done by the weekend.

slow/slowly   Today *slow* is used chiefly in spoken imperative constructions with short verbs that express motion, such as *drive*, *walk*, *swim*, and *run*. For example: Drive **slow**. Don't walk so **slow**. *Slow* is also combined with present participles to form adjectives: He **was slow-moving**. It was a **slow-burning** fire. *Slowly* is found commonly in formal writing and is used in both speech and writing before a verb (He **slowly** walked through the hills) as well as after a verb: He walked **slowly** through the hills.

so   Many writers object to *so* being used as an intensifier, noting that in such usage it is often vague: They were **so** happy. *So* followed by *that* and a clause usually eliminates the vagueness: They were **so** happy **that** they had been invited to the exclusive party.

so/so that   *So that*, rather than *so*, is most often used in formal writing to avoid the possibility of ambiguity: He visited Aunt Lucia **so that** he could help her clean the basement.

some   *Some* is often used in informal speech and writing as an adjective meaning "exceptional, unusual" and as an adverb meaning "somewhat." In more formal instances, use *somewhat* in place of *some* as an adverb or a more precise word such as *remarkable* in place of *some* as an adjective: Those are **unusual** (not *some*) shoes. My sister and brother-in-law are going to have to rush **somewhat** (not *some*) to get here in time for dinner.

someplace/somewhere   *Someplace* should be used only in informal writing and speech; use *somewhere* for formal discourse.

somewheres   Somewheres is not accepted in formal writing or speech; use the standard *somewhere*: She would like to go **somewhere** (not *somewheres*) special to celebrate New Year's Eve.

split infinitive   There is a long-standing convention that prohibits placing a word between *to* and the verb: **To understand** fully another culture, you have to live among its people for many years. This convention is based on an analogy with Latin, in which an infinitive is only one word and therefore cannot be divided. Criticism of the split infinitive was particularly strong when the modeling of English on Latin was especially popular, as it was in the nineteenth century. Today many people note that a split infinitive sometimes creates a less awkward sentence: Many American companies expect **to more than double** their overseas investments in the next decade.

suppose to/supposed to; use to/used to   Both *suppose to* and *use to* are incorrect. The preferred usage is *supposed to* or *used to*: I was **supposed to** (not *suppose to*) get up early this morning to go hiking in the mountains. I **used to** (not *use to*) enjoy the seashore, but now I prefer the mountains.

sure/surely   When used as an adverb meaning *surely*, *sure* is considered inappropriate for formal discourse. A qualifier like *certainly* should be used instead of *sure*: My neighbors were **certainly** right about it. It is widely used, however, in speech and informal writing: They were **sure** right about that car.

sure and/sure to; try and/try to   *Sure to* and *try to* are the preferred forms for formal discourse: **Be sure to** (not *sure and*) come home early tonight. **Try to** (not *try and*) avoid the traffic on the interstate.

that The conjunction *that* is occasionally omitted, especially after verbs of thinking, saying, believing, and so forth: She said (*that*) they would come by train. The omission is most frequent in informal speech and writing, and almost always occurs when the dependent clause begins with a personal pronoun or a proper name.

that/which Traditionally, *that* is used to introduce a restrictive clause: They should buy the cookies **that** the neighbor's child is selling. *Which*, in contrast, is used to introduce nonrestrictive clauses: The cookies, **which** are covered in chocolate, would make a nice evening snack. This distinction is maintained far more often in formal writing than in everyday speech, where voice can often distinguish restrictive from nonrestrictive clauses.

that/which/who The relative pronoun *that* is used to refer to animals, things, and people. It can substitute in most cases for either *which* or *who(m)*: The hitchhiker **that** (or **whom**) we picked up was a student. In accepted usage, *who* is used only to refer to people. *Which* is used to refer to animals and inanimate objects: The pen, **which** you bought, is out of ink. The doctor, **who** participates in our insurance plan, is very nice.

them/those *Them* is nonstandard when used as an adjective: I enjoyed **those** (not *them*) apples very much.

they/their/them Although the word *they* is traditionally a third-person plural pronoun, many people now use it as a singular pronoun, in place of *he* or *she*: If anyone comes to the door, tell **them** I'm not at home. Some people disapprove of this use, but it is becoming very common in informal use. This is partly because there is no gender-neutral singular pronoun in English.

this here/these here/that there/them there   Each of these phrases is nonstandard: *this here* for *this; these here* for *these; that there* for *that; them there* for *those.*

thusly/thus   *Thusly* is a pointless synonym for *thus.* Speakers and writers often use *thusly* only for a deliberately humorous effect.

till/until/'til   *Till* and *until* are used interchangeably in speech and writing; *'til,* a shortened form of *until,* is rarely used.

time period   The expression *time period* is redundant, since *period* is a period of time: The local ambulance squad reported three emergency calls in a one-week **period** (not *time period*).

too   Be careful when using *too* as an intensifier in speech and writing: The dog is **too** mean. Adding an explanation of the excessive quality makes the sentence more logical: The dog is **too** mean to be trusted alone with children.

toward/towards   The two words are used interchangeably in both formal and informal speech and writing.

try and/try to   While *try to* is the preferred form for formal speech and writing, both phrases occur in speech and informal writing.

type/type of   In written English, *type of* is the preferred construction: This is an unusual **type of** flower. In informal speech and writing, it is acceptable to use *type* immediately before a noun: I like this **type** car.

used to could/used to be able to   The phrase *used to could* is nonstandard for *used to be able to*: I **used to be able to** (not *used to could*) touch my toes.

very   The adverb *very* is sometimes used unnecessarily, especially in modifying an absolute adjective: It was a **very** unique experience. In such instances, it clearly should be omitted. Further, *very* has become overworked and has lost much of its power. Use more precise modifiers such as *extremely* and *especially.*

want in/want out Both phrases are informal: *want in* for *want to enter*, *want out* for *want to leave*: The dog **wants to enter** (not *wants in*). The cat **wants to leave** (not *wants out*).

way/ways *Way* is the preferred usage for formal speech and writing; *ways* is used informally: They have a little **way** (not *ways*) to go before they reach the campground.

when/where *Where* and *when* are not interchangeable: Weekends are occasions **when** (not *where*) we have a chance to spend time with the family.

where at/where to Both phrases are generally considered to be too informal to be acceptable in good writing and formal speech: **Where** is John? (not *Where* is John *at?*) **Where** is Mike going? (not *Where* is Mike going *to?*)

where/that *Where* and *that* are not interchangeable: We see by the memo **that** (not *where*) overtime has been discontinued.

who/whoever; whom/whomever Traditionally, *who/whoever* is used as a subject (the nominative case) and *whom/whomever* as an object (the objective case). In informal speech and writing, however, since *who* and *whom* often occur at the beginning of a sentence, people usually select *who*, regardless of grammatical function. The case distinction remains important in formal speech and writing.

without/unless *Without* as a conjunction is a dialectal or regional use of *unless*.

with regards to/with regard to/as regards/regarding Use *with regard to*, *regarding*, or *as regards* in place of *with regards to* in formal speech and writing: **As regards** your inquiry, we have asked our shipping department to hold the merchandise until Monday.

would have   Do not use the phrase *would have* in place of *had* in clauses that begin with *if* and express a state contrary to fact: If the driver **had** (not *would have*) been wearing his seat belt, he would have escaped without injury.

would of/could of   There is no such expression as *would of* or *could of*: He **would have** (not *would of*) gone. *Of* is not a substitute for *-'ve*: She **would've** (not *would of*) left earlier.

you was   *You was* is nonstandard for *you were*: **You were** (not *you was*) late on Thursday.

COMMONLY
CONFUSED WORDS

WORDS are often confused if they have similar or identical forms or sounds. You may have the correct meaning in mind, but choosing the wrong word will change your expressed meaning. An *ingenuous* person is not the same as an *ingenious* person. Similarly, you may be using a word that is correct in a different context but does not express your intended meaning. To *infer* something is not the same as to *imply* it.

You may choose the wrong word because two words are identical or very similar in pronunciation but different in spelling. An example of a pair of words with the same pronunciation is *compliment, complement*. The confusion may arise from a small difference in spelling, as the pair *canvas, canvass*, or the homophones (words that sound alike) may be spelled quite differently, as the pairs *manor, manner* and *brake, break*. An example of a pair of words with similar but not identical pronunciation is *accept, except*; they are very different in usage and grammatical function.

Words may also be confused if they are spelled the same way but differ in meaning or in meaning and pronunciation, as the homophones *bear* "animal" and *bear* "carry, support" or the homographs (look-alike words) *row* (rō) "line" and *row* (rou) "fight."

Errors in word choice may also result if word groups overlap in meaning or usage. In informal contexts, *aggravate* may be used to mean "annoy" and *mad* may be used to mean "angry." *Leave* and *let* are interchangeable when followed by the word *alone* in the sense "to stop annoying or interfering with someone."

The following glossary lists words that are commonly confused and discusses their meanings and proper usage.

accept/except *Accept* is a verb meaning "to receive": Please **accept** a gift. *Except* is usually a preposition or a conjunction meaning "other than" or "but for": He was willing to **accept** an apology from everyone **except** me. When *except* is used as a verb, it means "to leave out": He was **excepted** from the new regulations.

accidentally/accidently The correct adverb is *accidentally*, from the root word *accidental*, not *accident*: Russell **accidentally** slipped on the icy sidewalk. *Accidently* is a misspelling.

ad/add An *ad* is an advertisement. Is the **ad** ready for the magazine? To *add* is to increase. Don't **add** another setting to the table.

adapt/adopt *Adapt* means "to adjust or modify to meet new needs": He **adapted** the novel for the screen. *Adopt* means "to take as one's own": She **adopted** the nickname in high school. They **adopted** a child from Russia. *Adopt* can also mean "to accept": The Senate **adopted** the report.

adoptive/adopted *Adoptive* refers to the parent: He resembles his **adoptive** father. *Adopted* refers to the child: Their **adopted** daughter wants to adopt a child herself.

adverse/averse Both words are adjectives, and both mean "opposed" or "hostile." *Averse*, however, is used to describe a subject's opposition to something: The minister was **averse** to the new trends developing in the country. *Adverse* describes something opposed to the subject: The **adverse** comments affected his self-esteem.

advice/advise *Advice*, a noun, means "suggestion or suggestions": Here's some good **advice**. *Advise*, a verb, means "to offer ideas or suggestions": Act as we **advise** you.

affect/effect Most often, *affect* is a verb, meaning "to influence," and *effect* is a noun meaning "the result of an action": His speech **affected** my mother very deeply, but had no **effect** on my sister at all. *Affect* is also used as a noun in psychology and psychiatry to mean "emotion": We can learn much about **affect** from performance. In this usage, it is pronounced with the stress on the first syllable. *Effect* is also used as a verb meaning "to bring about": His letter **effected** a change in their relationship.

aggravate/annoy In informal speech and writing, *aggravate* can be used as a synonym for *annoy*. However, in formal discourse the words mean different things and should be used in this way: Her back condition was **aggravated** by lifting the child, but the child's crying **annoyed** her more than the pain did.

aid/aide To *aid* is to help someone. She wanted to **aid** him in his struggle. An *aide* is an assistant. Tell her **aide** to get the copies.

aisle/isle *Aisle* means "a passageway between sections of seats": It was impossible to pass through the airplane **aisle** during the meal service. *Isle* means "island": I would like to be on a desert **isle** on such a dreary morning.

alley/ally An *alley* is a narrow back street. The cat snuck into the **alley**. An *ally* is a confederate. It's good to have an **ally** at your job.

all ready/already *All ready*, a pronoun and an adjective, means "entirely prepared"; *already*, an adverb, means "so soon" or "previously": I was **all ready** to leave when I noticed that it was **already** dinnertime.

allusion/illusion An *allusion* is a reference or hint: He made an **allusion** to the past. An *illusion* is a deceptive appearance: The canals on Mars are an **illusion**.

allude/elude Both words are verbs. *Allude* means "to mention briefly or accidentally": During our conversation, he **alluded** to his vacation plans. *Elude* means "to avoid or escape": The thief has successfully **eluded** capture for six months.

a lot/alot/allot *A lot* is always written as two words. It is used informally to mean "many": The unrelenting heat frustrated **a lot** of people. *Allot* is a verb meaning "to divide" or "to set aside": We **allotted** a portion of the yard for a garden. *Alot* is not a word; it is a misspelling of *a lot*.

altar/alter *Altar* is a noun meaning "a sacred place or platform": The couple approached the **altar** for the wedding ceremony. *Alter* is a verb meaning "to make different; to change": He **altered** his appearance by losing fifty pounds, growing a beard, and getting a new wardrobe.

alternately/alternatively *Alternately* is an adverb that means "in turn; one after the other": "We **alternately** stirred in the milk and the eggs." *Alternatively* is an adverb that means "on the other hand; one or the other": "You can go to China or, **alternatively,** you can go to Japan."

altogether/all together *Altogether* means "completely" or "totally"; *all together* means "all at one time" or "gathered together": It is **altogether** proper that we recite the Pledge **all together**.

ambiguous/ambivalent *Ambiguous* means "having several meanings." That gesture she made was **ambiguous**. *Ambivalent* means "uncertain, of two minds." Sarah was **ambivalent** about taking the kids to the beach.

among/between *Among* is a preposition that refers to three or more people or things. *Between* refers to two people or things. He had to decide **among** going to church, playing baseball, or staying home. *Between* is a preposition that refers to two people or things. It was **between** Jim and James.

amount/number *Amount* refers to quantity that cannot be counted: The **amount** of work accomplished before a major holiday is always negligible. *Number*, in contrast, refers to things that can be counted: He has held a **number** of jobs in the past five months. But some concepts, like time, can use either *amount* or *number*, depending how the elements are identified in the specific sentence: We were surprised by the **amount** of time it took us to settle into our new surroundings. The **number** of hours it took to repair the sink pleased us.

ante-/anti- The prefix *ante-* means "before": **antecedent, antechamber, antediluvian**; the prefix *anti-* means "against": **antigravity, antifreeze**. *Anti-* takes a hyphen before an *i* or a capital letter: **anti-Marxist, anti-inflationary**.

anxious/eager Traditionally, *anxious* means "nervous" or "worried" and consequently describes negative feelings. In addition, it is usually followed by the word *about*: I'm **anxious about** my exam. *Eager* means "looking forward" or "anticipating enthusiastically" and consequently describes positive feelings. It is usually followed by *to*: I'm **eager to** hear their new CD. Today, however, it is standard usage for *anxious* to mean "eager": They are **anxious to** see their new home.

anybody, any body/anyone, any one *Anybody* and *anyone* are pronouns; *any body* is a noun modified by *any* and *any one* is a pronoun or adjective modified by *any*. They are used as follows: Was **anybody** able to find **any body** in the debris? Will **anyone** help me? I have more cleaning than **any one** person can ever do.

any more/anymore *Any more* means "no more"; *anymore*, an adverb, means "nowadays" or "any longer": We don't want **any more** trouble. We won't go there **anymore**.

apt/likely *Apt* is standard in all speech and writing as a synonym for *likely* in suggesting chance without inclination: They are **apt** to call any moment now. *Likely,* meaning "probably," is frequently preceded by a qualifying word: The new school budget will **very likely** raise taxes. However, *likely* without the qualifying word is standard in all varieties of English: The new school budget will **likely** raise taxes.

ascent/assent *Ascent* is a noun that means "a move upward or a climb": Their **ascent** up Mount Rainier was especially dangerous because of the recent rock slides. *Assent* can be a noun or a verb. As a verb, *assent* means "to concur, to express agreement": The union representative **assented** to the agreement. As a noun, *assent* means "an agreement": The **assent** was not reached peacefully.

assistance/assistants *Assistance* is a noun that means "help, support": Please give us your **assistance** here for a moment. *Assistants* is a plural noun that means "helpers": Since the **assistants** were late, we found ourselves running behind schedule.

assure, ensure, insure *Assure* is a verb that means "to promise": The plumber **assured** us that the sink would not clog again. *Ensure* and *insure* are both verbs that mean "to make certain," although some writers use *insure* solely for legal and financial writing and *ensure* for more widespread usage: Since it is hard to **insure** yourself against mud slides, we did not buy the house on the hill. We left late to **ensure** that we would not get caught in traffic.

auger/augur An *auger* is a tool for boring holes. The carpenter had to borrow an **auger** to finish the job. To *augur* is to predict. Continuous dry spells **augur** poor crops for farmers.

bare/bear *Bare* is an adjective or a verb. As an adjective, *bare* means "naked, unadorned": The wall looked **bare** without the picture. As a verb, *bare* means "to reveal": He **bared** his soul. *Bear* is a noun or a verb. As a noun, *bear* refers to the animal: The teddy **bear** was named after Theodore Roosevelt. As a verb, *bear* means to carry: He **bears** a heavy burden.

before/prior to *Prior to* is used most often in formal contexts or in a legal sense: **Prior to** settling the claim, the Smiths spent a week calling the attorney general's office. Use *before* in almost all other cases: **Before** we go grocery shopping, we sort the coupons we have clipped from the newspaper.

beside/besides Although both words can function as prepositions, they have different shades of meaning: *beside* means "next to"; *besides* means "in addition to" or "except": **Besides**, Richard would prefer not to sit **beside** the dog. There is no one here **besides** John and me. *Besides* is also an adverb meaning "in addition": Other people **besides** you feel the same way about the dog.

bias/prejudice Generally, a distinction is made between *bias* and *prejudice*. Although both words imply "a preconceived opinion" or a "subjective point of view" in favor of something or against it, *prejudice* is generally used to express unfavorable feelings.

bimonthly/semimonthly *Bimonthly* is an adjective that means "every two months": "I made the pie for the **bimonthly** bridge game." *Bimonthly* is also a noun that means a publication issued every two months: "The magazine publisher issued several interesting **bimonthlies.**" *Semimonthly* is an adjective that means "happening twice a month": "We have **semimonthly** baseball games on the 1st and the 15th."

blonde/blond A *blonde* indicates a woman or girl with fair hair and skin. *Blond*, as an adjective, refers to either sex: I have three **blond** children. He is a cute **blond** boy. *Blonde*, as an adjective, still applies only to women: The **blonde** actress and her companion made the front page of the tabloid.

borrow/lend *Borrow* means "to take with the intention of returning": The book you **borrow** from the library today is due back in seven days. *Lend* means "to give with the intention of getting back": I will **lend** you the rake, but I need it back by Saturday. The two terms are not interchangeable.

brake/break The most common meaning of *brake* as a noun is "a device for slowing a vehicle": The car's new **brakes** held on the steep incline. *Brake* can also mean "a thicket" or "a species of fern." *Break*, a verb, means "to crack or make useless": Please be especially careful that you don't **break** that vase.

breath/breathe *Breath*, a noun, is the air taken in during respiration: Her **breath** looked like fog in the frosty morning air. *Breathe*, a verb, refers to the process of inhaling and exhaling air: "Please **breathe** deeply," the doctor said to the patient.

bring/take *Bring* is to carry toward the speaker: She **brings** it to me. *Take* is to carry away from the speaker: She **takes** it away.

buy/by *Buy*, a verb, means "to acquire goods at a price": We have to **buy** a new dresser. *By* can be a preposition, an adverb, or an adjective. As a preposition, *by* means "next to": I pass **by** the office building every day. As an adverb, *by* means "near, at hand": The office is close **by**. As an adjective, *by* means "situated to one side": They came down on a **by** passage.

callous/callus To be *callous* is to be unfeeling: He teased her in a **callous** manner. A callus is hardened skin: She developed a **callus** after her blister popped.

cannon/canon *Cannon* is a large gun: The sailors placed the **cannon** on deck. *Canon* is law: There is a **canon** that must be followed in this situation.

canvas/canvass *Canvas*, a noun, refers to a heavy cloth: The boat's sails are made of **canvas**. *Canvass*, a verb, means "to solicit votes": The candidate's representatives **canvass** the neighborhood seeking support.

capital/Capitol *Capital* is the city or town that is the seat of government: Paris is the **capital** of France. *Capitol* refers to the building in Washington, D.C., in which the U.S. Congress meets: When I was a child, we went for a visit to the **Capitol**. When used with a lowercase letter, *capitol* is the building of a state legislature. *Capital* also means "a sum of money": After the sale of their home, they had a great deal of **capital**. As an adjective, *capital* means "foremost" or "first-rate": He was a **capital** fellow.

censor/censure Both words are verbs, but they have different meanings. To *censor* is to remove something from public view on moral or other grounds, and to *censure* is to give a formal reprimand: The committee **censored** the offending passages from the book and **censured** the librarian for placing it on the shelves.

chafe/chaff *Chafe* is a verb that means "to wear or abrade by rubbing": That rough shirt **chafes** my skin. *Chaff* is the "husks of grains separated during threshing": You must always separate the wheat from the **chaff**.

chord/cord *Chord* is a noun that can mean a feeling or emotion: His speech struck a **chord**. It can also mean a series of notes sounded together: That sonata begins with a minor **chord**. *Cord* is a noun that means string or rope made of strands: He tied the package with strong **cord**.

cite/sight/site *To cite* means to "quote a passage": The scholar often **cited** passages from noted authorities to back up his opinions. *Sight* is a noun that means "vision": With her new glasses, her **sight** was once again perfect. *Site* is a noun that means "place or location": They picked out a beautiful **site** overlooking a lake for their new home.

climatic/climactic The word *climatic* comes from the word *climate* and refers to weather: This summer's brutal heat may indicate a **climatic** change. *Climactic*, in contrast, comes from the word *climax* and refers to a point of high drama: In the **climactic** last scene, the hideous creature takes over the world.

clothes/cloths *Clothes* are garments: For his birthday, John got some stylish new **clothes**. *Cloths* are pieces of fabric: Use these **cloths** to clean the car.

coarse/course *Coarse*, an adjective, means "rough or common": The horsehair fabric was too **coarse** to be made into a pillow. Although his manners are a little **coarse**, he has a heart of gold. *Course*, a noun, means "a path" or "a prescribed number of classes": They followed the bicycle **course** through the woods. My **courses** include English, math, and science.

complement/compliment Both words can function as either a noun or a verb. The noun *complement* means "that which completes or makes perfect": The rich chocolate mousse was a perfect **complement** to the light meal. The verb *complement* means "to complete": The oak door **complemented** the new siding and windows. The noun *compliment* means "an expression of praise or admiration": The mayor paid the visiting officials the **compliment** of escorting them around town personally. The verb *compliment* means "to pay a compliment to": Everyone **complimented** her after the presentation.

complementary/complimentary *Complementary* is an adjective that means "forming a complement, completing": The **complementary** colors suited the mood of the room. *Complimentary* is an adjective that means "expressing a compliment": The **complimentary** reviews ensured the play a long run. *Complimentary* also means "free": We thanked them for the **complimentary** tickets.

connote/denote *Connote* is a verb that means "to imply or suggest": The phrase "Wild West" **connotes** lawlessness. *Denote* is a verb that means "to indicate or refer to specifically": The symbol "X" **denotes** "poison."

continual/continuous Use *continual* to mean "intermittent, repeated often" and *continuous* to mean "uninterrupted, without stopping": We suffered **continual** losses of electricity during the hurricane. They had **continuous** phone service during the hurricane. *Continuous* and *continual* are never interchangeable with regard to spatial relationships: a **continuous** series of passages.

corps/corpse Both words are nouns. A *corps* is a group of people acting together; the word is often used in a military context: The officers' **corps** assembled before dawn for the drill. A *corpse* is a dead body: The **corpse** was in the morgue.

counsel/council *Counsel* is a verb meaning "to give advice": They **counsel** recovering gamblers. *Council* is a noun meaning "a group of advisers": The trade union **council** meets in Ward Hall every Thursday.

credible/creditable/credulous These three adjectives are often confused. *Credible* means "believable": The tale is unusual but seems **credible** to us. *Creditable* means "worthy": Sandra sang a **creditable** version of the song. *Credulous* means "gullible": The **credulous** boy believed that the movie was true.

cue/queue A *cue* is a hint, or a guiding suggestion: When the actor forgot his lines, they gave him a **cue**. A *queue* is a line: There is always a **queue** when I get to that theater.

demur/demure *Demur* is a verb meaning "to object": The board wanted her to be treasurer, but she **demurred**. *Demure* is an adjective meaning "modest" or "reserved": Her response to their compliments was a **demure** smile.

descent/dissent *Descent*, a noun, means "downward movement": Much to their surprise, their **descent** down the mountain was harder than their ascent had been. *Dissent*, a verb, means "to disagree": The town council strongly **dissented** with the proposed measure. *Dissent* as a noun means "difference in sentiment or opinion": **Dissent** over the new proposal caused a rift between colleagues.

desert/dessert *Desert* as a verb means "to abandon"; as a noun, "an arid region": People **deserted** in the **desert** rarely survive. *Dessert*, a noun, refers to the sweet served as the final course of a meal: My sister's favorite **dessert** is strawberry shortcake.

device/devise *Device* is a noun meaning "invention or contrivance": Do you think that **device** will really save us time? *Devise* is a verb meaning "to contrive or plan": Did he **devise** some **device** for repairing the ancient pump assembly?

die/dye *Die*, as a verb, means "to cease to live": The frog will **die** if released from the aquarium into the pond. *Dye* as a verb means "to color or stain something": I **dyed** the drapes to cover the stains.

discomfit/discomfort *Discomfit* is a verb meaning "to confuse or disconcert." He was **discomfited** by the question. *Discomfort* is a noun meaning the "lack of comfort." He experienced **discomfort** while wearing the itchy wool sweater.

discreet/discrete *Discreet* means "tactful"; *discrete*, "separate." For example: Do you have a **discreet** way of refusing the invitation? The mosaic is made of hundreds of **discrete** pieces of tile.

disinterested/uninterested *Disinterested* is used to mean "without prejudice, impartial" (He is a **disinterested** judge) and *uninterested* to mean "bored" or "lacking interest": They are completely **uninterested** in sports.

dominant/dominate *Dominant*, an adjective, means "ruling, controlling": Social scientists have long argued over the **dominant** motives for human behavior. *Dominate*, a verb, means "to control": Advice columnists often preach that no one can **dominate** you unless you allow them to.

dual/duel *Dual* means "of two, double": That boat has **dual** exhausts. A *duel* is a fight: They had a **duel** at dawn.

elicit/illicit *Elicit*, a verb, means "call forth"; *illicit*, an adjective, means "against the law": The assault **elicited** a protest against **illicit** handguns.

emigrate/immigrate *Emigrate* means "to leave one's own country to settle in another": She **emigrated from** France. *Immigrate* means "to enter a different country and settle there": My father **immigrated to** America when he was nine years old.

eminent/imminent *Eminent* means "distinguished": Marie Curie was an **eminent** scientist who won the Nobel prize twice. *Imminent* means "about to happen": The thundershower seemed **imminent**.

envelop/envelope *Envelop* is a verb that means "to surround": The music **envelops** him in a soothing atmosphere. *Envelope*, a noun, is a flat paper container, usually for a letter: Be sure to put a stamp on the **envelope** before you mail that letter.

equable/equitable *Equable* is an adjective meaning "free from many changes or variations": Southern California has an **equable** climate. *Equitable* is an adjective meaning "characterized by fairness": The judge is known for his evenhanded, **equitable** decisions.

especially/specially The two words are not interchangeable: *especially* means "particularly," *specially* means "for a specific reason." For example: I **especially** value my wedding ring; it was made **specially** for me.

ever so often/every so often *Ever so often* means "happening very often" and *every so often* means "happening occasionally."

everybody, every body/everyone, every one *Everybody* and *everyone* are indefinite pronouns: **Everybody** likes William, and **everyone** enjoys his company. *Every body* is a noun modified by *every* and *every one* is a pronoun modified by *every*; both refer to a person in a specific group and are usually followed by *of*: **Every body** of water in our area is polluted; **every one** of our ponds is covered in debris.

everyday/every day *Everyday* is an adjective that means "used daily, typical, ordinary"; *every day* is made up of a noun modified by the adjective *every* and means "each day": **Every day** they had to deal with the **everyday** business of life.

exam/examination *Exam* should be reserved for everyday speech and *examination* for formal writing: The SAT **examinations** are scheduled for this Saturday morning at 9:00.

exceptionable/exceptional *Exceptionable* is an adjective meaning "objectionable": His drinking at the party was **exceptionable**. *Exceptional* is an adjective meaning "unusual or extraordinary": That was an **exceptional** day we just had!

explicit/implicit *Explicit* means "stated plainly"; *implicit* means "understood, implied": You know we have an **implicit** understanding that you are not allowed to visit Web sites that contain **explicit** sex.

fair/fare *Fair* as an adjective means "free from bias," "ample," "unblemished," "of light hue," or "attractive." As an adverb, it means "favorably." It is used informally to mean "honest." *Fare* as a noun means "the price charged for transporting a person" or "food."

farther/further Traditionally, *farther* is used to indicate physical distance: Is it much **farther** to the hotel? *Further* is used to refer to additional time, amount, or abstract ideas: Your mother does not want to talk about this any **further**.

figuratively/literally *Figuratively* is an adverb that means "metaphorically or symbolically": When they saw the big dog, they **figuratively** jumped out of their skins. *Literally* is an adverb that means "actually": I'm telling you the truth when say I **literally** jumped up and clicked my heels together. It also means "according to the exact meaning of the words": I took her words **literally**.

flaunt/flout *Flaunt* means "to show off"; *flout*, "to ignore or treat with disdain." For example: They **flouted** convention when they **flaunted** their wealth.

flounder/founder *Flounder* means "to struggle with clumsy movements": We **floundered** in the mud. *Founder* means "to sink": The ship **foundered**.

forego/forgo *Forego* is a verb meaning "to go before." The moon's rising **foregoes** the tide's change. *Forgo* is a verb meaning "to restrain from or do without." I'll **forgo** dessert this evening, thank you.

formally/formerly Both words are adverbs. *Formally* means "in a formal manner": The minister addressed the king and queen **formally**. *Formerly* means "previously": **Formerly**, he worked as a chauffeur; now, he is employed as a guard.

forth/fourth *Forth* is an adverb meaning "going forward or away": From that day **forth**, they lived happily ever after. *Fourth* is most often used as an adjective that means "next after the third": Wyatt was the **fourth** in line.

gambit/gamut *Gambit* is "any maneuver by which one seeks an advantage": His **gambit** was to begin the speech with a flattering reference to his boss's wife. *Gamut* is "the entire range or scale": He went through the **gamut** of emotions during his divorce.

gibe/jibe/jive The word *gibe* means "to taunt; deride; jeer." The word *jibe* means "to be in agreement with; accord; correspond": The facts of the case didn't **jibe**. The word *jive* is slang and means "to tease; fool; kid."

gourmet/gourmand A *gourmet* is a connoisseur of fine food and drink. He knows more about food than most French **gourmets**. A *gourmand* is someone who loves good food and wine, sometimes to excess. Bill is a **gourmand**; he doesn't care if it's French wine, as long as there's a lot of it.

gorilla/guerrilla *Gorilla*, a noun, refers to a large ape. The silverback **gorilla** was majestic. *Guerrilla*, a noun, refers to one of a band of irregular soldiers. The **guerrillas** attacked the base at dawn.

hanged/hung *Hanged* is the past tense and past participle of hang when the meaning is to execute by suspending by the neck: "The sheriff **hanged** the man at dawn." *Hung* is the past tense and participle of hang when the meaning is to suspend from above with no support from below: "The curator **hung** the paintings for the exhibition."

healthy/healthful *Healthy* means "possessing health"; *healthful* means "bringing about health": They believed that they were **healthy** people because they ate **healthful** food.

historic/historical The word *historic* means "important in history": a **historic** speech; a **historic** battlefield. The word *historical* means "being a part of, or inspired by, history": **historical** records; a **historical** novel.

home in/hone in The expression *home in* means "to approach or focus on (an objective)." It comes from the language of guided missiles, where *homing in* refers to locking onto a target. The expression *hone in* is an error.

human/humane Both words are adjectives. *Human* means "pertaining to humanity": The subject of the documentary is the **human** race. *Humane* means "tender, compassionate, or sympathetic": Many of her patients believed that her **humane** care speeded their recovery.

idea/ideal *Idea* means "thought," while *ideal* means "a model of perfection" or "goal." The two words are not interchangeable. They should be used as follows: The **idea** behind the blood drive is that our **ideals** often move us to help others.

i.e./e.g. *E.g.* means "for example." The laws were incredibly strict (**e.g.,** you couldn't eat ice cream on the street). The abbreviation *i.e.* means "that is" or "in other words." Clark Kent (**i.e.,** Superman) was in love with Lois Lane.

imply/infer *Imply* means "to suggest without stating": The message on Karen's postcard **implies** that her vacation has not turned out as she wished. *Infer* means "to reach a conclusion based on understood evidence": From her message I **infer** that she wishes she had stayed home. When used in this manner, the two words describe two sides of the same process.

incredible/incredulous *Incredible* means "cannot be believed"; *incredulous* means "unbelieving": The teacher was **incredulous** when she heard the pupil's **incredible** story about the fate of his term project.

individual/person/party *Individual* should be used to stress uniqueness or to refer to a single human being as contrasted to a group of people: The rights of the **individual** should not supersede the rights of a group. *Person* is the preferred word in other contexts: What **person** wouldn't want to have a chance to sail around the world? *Party* is used to refer to a group: Send the **party** of five this way, please. *Party* is also used to refer to an individual mentioned in a legal document.

ingenious/ingenuous *Ingenious* means "resourceful, clever": My sister is **ingenious** when it comes to turning leftovers into something delicious. *Ingenuous* means "frank, artless": The child's **ingenuous** manner is surprising considering her fame.

insolate/insulate *Insolate* is a verb meaning "to expose to the sun's rays": The treatment for the skin disease called for him to **insolate** himself. *Insulate* is a verb that means "to cover with a material that prevents passage of heat, electricity or sound": We have to **insulate** the house or we'll end up paying a fortune in heating bills.

it's/its *It's* is a contraction for "It is": **It's** not March yet. *Its* is the possessive form of "it": The coat has lost **its** gloss.

later/latter *Later* is used to refer to time; *latter*, the second of two items named: It is **later** than you think. Of the two shirts I just purchased, I prefer the **latter**.

lay/lie *Lay* is a transitive verb that means "to put down" or "to place." It takes a direct object: Please **lay** the soup spoon next to the teaspoon. *Lie* is an intransitive verb that means "to be in a horizontal position" or "be situated." It does not take a direct object: The puppy **lies** down where the old dog had always **lain**. The hotel **lies** on the outskirts of town. The confusion arises over *lay*, which is the present tense of the verb *lay* and the past tense of the verb *lie*.

To lie (recline)

Present: Spot **lies** (**is lying**) down.

Future: Spot **will lie** down.

Past: Spot **lay** down.

Perfect: Spot **has** (**had, will have**) **lain** down.

To lay (put down)

Present: He **lays** (**is laying**) his dice down.

Future: He **will lay** his dice down.

Past: He **laid** his dice down.

Perfect: He **has** (**had, will have**) **laid** his dice down.

Although *lie* and *lay* are used interchangeably by many people, phrases such as the following are considered nonstandard and should be avoided: **Lay** down, dears. The dog **laid** in the sun. Abandoned cars were **laying** in the junkyard. The reports **have laid** in the mailbox for a week.

lead/led *Lead* as a verb means "to take or conduct on the way": I plan to **lead** a quiet afternoon. *Led* is the past tense: He **led** his followers through the dangerous underbrush. *Lead*, as a noun, means "a type of metal": Pipes are made of **lead**.

learn/teach *Learn* is to acquire knowledge: He **learned** fast. *Teach* is to impart knowledge: She **taught** well. The two words describe two sides of the same process and are not interchangeable.

leave/let *Leave* and *let* are interchangeable only when followed by the word *alone*: **Leave** him alone. **Let** him alone. In other instances, *leave* means "to depart" or "permit to remain in the same place": If you **leave**, please turn off the copier. **Leave** the extra paper on the shelf. *Let* means "to allow": **Let** him work with the assistant, if he wants.

lessen/lesson *Lessen* is a verb meaning "to decrease": To **lessen** the pain of a burn, apply ice to the injured area. *Lesson* is most often used as a noun meaning "material assigned for study": Today, the **lesson** will be on electricity.

lightening/lightning *Lightening* is a form of the verb that means "to brighten": The cheerful new drapes and bunches of flowers went a long way in **lightening** the room's somber mood. *Lightning* is most often used as a noun to mean "flashes of light generated during a storm": The thunder and **lightning** frightened the child.

loath/loathe *Loath* means reluctant. He was **loath** to sell the diamond. *Loathe* means to hate. I **loathed** everything she did and said.

loose/lose *Loose* as an adjective means "free and unattached": The dog was **loose** again. *Loose* can also be a verb meaning "let loose": The hunters **loose** the dogs as soon as the ducks fall. *Lose* is a verb meaning "to part with unintentionally": He will **lose** his keys if he leaves them on the countertop.

mad/angry Traditionally, *mad* has been used to mean "insane"; *angry* has been used to mean "full of ire." While *mad* can be used to mean "enraged, angry," in informal usage, you should replace *mad* with *angry* in formal discourse: The president is **angry** at Congress for overriding his veto.

masterful/masterly *Masterful* is an adjective whose first definition is "imperious or dominating." He was a **masterful** commander who did not tolerate any dissent. *Masterly* is an adjective that means "like or befitting a master." That was a **masterly** performance.

maybe/may be *Maybe*, an adverb, means "perhaps": **Maybe** the newspapers can be recycled with the plastic and glass. *May be*, a verb, means "could be": It **may be** too difficult, however.

miner/minor A *miner* is a person who works in a mine: The **miners** went down deep into the earth. A *minor* is a person underage: We don't serve beer to **minors.**

moral/morale As a noun, *moral* means "ethical lesson": Each of Aesop's fables has a clear **moral**. *Morale* means "state of mind" or "spirit": Her **morale** was lifted by her colleague's good wishes.

orient/orientate The two words both mean "to adjust to or familiarize with new surroundings; place in a particular position." There is no reason to prefer or reject either word; however, some people object to *orientate*, so *orient* is a safer choice in a conservative writing situation.

passed/past *Passed* is a form of the verb meaning "to go by": Bernie **passed** the same buildings on his way to work each day. *Past* can function as a noun, adjective, adverb, or preposition. As a noun, *past* means "the history of a nation, person, etc.": The lessons of the **past** should not be forgotten. As an adjective, *past* means "gone by or elapsed in time": John is worried about his **past** deeds. As an adverb, *past* means "so as to pass by": The fire engine raced **past** the parked cars. As a preposition, *past* means "beyond in time": It's **past** noon already.

patience/patients *Patience*, a noun, means "endurance": Antonella's **patience** makes her an ideal babysitter. *Patients* are people under medical treatment: The **patients** must remain in the hospital for another week.

peace/piece *Peace* is "freedom from discord": The negotiators hoped that the new treaty would bring about lasting **peace**. *Piece* is "a portion of a whole" or "a short musical arrangement": I would like just a small **piece** of cake, please. The **piece** in E flat is especially beautiful.

pedal/peddle A *pedal* is a foot lever: Don't put your foot on the **pedal!** To *peddle* is to sell: He tried to **peddle** that merchandise everywhere.

percent/percentage *Percent* is used with a number, *percentage* with a modifier. *Percentage* is used most often after an adjective: A high **percentage** of your earnings this year is tax deductible.

personal/personnel *Personal* means "private": Your question is an unacceptable intrusion into my **personal** affairs. *Personnel* refers to employees: Attention all **personnel!** The use of *personnel* as a plural has become standard in business and government: The **personnel were** dispatched to the Chicago office.

plain/plane *Plain* as an adjective means "easily understood," "undistinguished," or "unadorned": His meaning was **plain** to all. The **plain** dress suited the gravity of the occasion. As an adverb, *plain* means "clearly and simply": She's just **plain** foolish. As a noun, *plain* is a flat area of land: The vast **plain** seemed to go on forever. As a noun, *plane* has a number of different meanings. It most commonly refers to an *airplane*, but is also used in mathematics and fine arts and to refer to a tool used to shave wood.

practicable/practical *Practicable* means "capable of being done": My decorating plans were too difficult to be **practicable**. *Practical* means "pertaining to practice or action": It was just not **practical** to paint the floor white.

precede/proceed Both words are verbs, but they have different meanings. *Precede* means "to go before": Morning **precedes** afternoon. *Proceed* means "to move forward": **Proceed** to the exit in an orderly fashion.

precipitate/precipitous *Precipitate* means "to hasten the occurrence of." That bill is going to **precipitate** an international crisis. *Precipitous* means "characterized by precipices, or cliffs." That is a **precipitous** mountain.

presence/presents *Presence* is used chiefly to mean "attendance, close proximity": Your **presence** at the ceremony will be greatly appreciated. *Presents* are gifts. Thank you for giving us such generous **presents**.

principal/principle *Principal* can be a noun or an adjective. As a noun, *principal* means "chief or head official" (The **principal** decided to close school early on Tuesday) or "sum of capital": Invest only the interest, never the **principal**. As an adjective, *principal* means "first or highest": The **principal** ingredient is sugar. *Principle* is a noun only, meaning "rule" or "general truth": Regardless of what others said, she stood by her **principles**.

quiet/quite *Quiet*, as an adjective, means "free from noise": When the master of ceremonies spoke, the room became **quiet**. *Quite*, an adverb, means "completely, wholly": By the late afternoon, the children were **quite** exhausted.

quotation/quote *Quotation*, a noun, means "a passage quoted from a speech or book": The speaker read a **quotation** of twenty-five lines to the audience. *Quote*, a verb, means "to repeat a passage from a speech, etc.": Marci often **quotes** from popular novels. *Quote* and *quotation* are often used interchangeably in speech; in formal writing, however, a distinction is still observed between the two words.

rack/wrack *Rack* is a "framework of bars, wires or pegs on which articles are arranged or deposited." I put the pepper on the spice **rack**. *Wrack* is "damage or destruction." The storm produced **wrack** and ruin.

rain/reign/rein As a noun, *rain* means "water that falls from the atmosphere to earth." As a verb, *rain* means "to send down, to give abundantly": The crushed piñata **rained** candy on the eager children. As a noun, *reign* means "royal rule," as a verb, "to have supreme control": The monarch's **reign** was marked by social unrest. As a noun, *rein* means "a leather strap used to guide an animal," as a verb, "to control or guide": He used the **rein** to control the frisky colt.

raise/rise/raze *Raise*, a transitive verb, means "to elevate": How can I **raise** the price of my house? *Rise*, an intransitive verb, means "to go up, to get up": Will housing costs **rise** this year? *Raze* is a transitive verb meaning "to tear down, demolish": The wrecking crew was ready to **raze** the condemned building.

respectful/respective *Respectful* means "showing (or full of) respect": If you are **respectful** toward others, they will treat you with consideration as well. *Respective* means "in the order given": The **respective** remarks were made by executive board members Joshua Whittles, Kevin McCarthy, and Warren Richmond.

reverend/reverent As an adjective (usually capitalized), *Reverend* is an epithet of respect given to a member of the clergy: The **Reverend** Mr. Williams gave the sermon. As a noun, a reverend is "a member of the clergy": In our church, the **reverend** opens the service with a prayer. *Reverent* is an adjective meaning "showing deep respect": The speaker addressed the princess with a **reverent** greeting.

right/rite/write *Right* as an adjective means "proper, correct" and "as opposed to left," as a noun it means "claims or titles," as an adverb it means "in a straight line, directly," as a verb it means "to restore to an upright position." *Rite* is a noun meaning "a solemn ritual": The religious leader performed the necessary **rites.** *Write* is a verb meaning "to form characters on a surface": The child liked to **write** her name over and over.

seasonal/seasonable *Seasonal* is an adjective that means "pertaining to or dependent on the seasons of the year." His work as a gardener was **seasonal.** *Seasonable* means "suitable to or characteristic of the season." The weather wasn't especially harsh; it was, in fact, **seasonable.**

sensual/sensuous *Sensual* carries sexual overtones: The massage was a **sensual** experience. *Sensuous* means "pertaining to the senses": The **sensuous** aroma of freshly baked bread wafted through the house.

set/sit *Set*, a transitive verb, describes something a person does to an object: She **set** the book down on the table. *Sit*, an intransitive verb, describes a person or thing resting: Carlos **sits** on the straight-backed chair.

somebody/some body *Somebody* is an indefinite pronoun: **Somebody** recommended this restaurant. *Some body* is a noun modified by an adjective: I have a new spray that will give my limp hair **some body.**

someone/some one *Someone* is an indefinite pronoun: **Someone** who ate here said the pasta was delicious. *Some one* is a pronoun or adjective modified by *some*: Please pick **some one** magazine that you would like to read.

sometime/sometimes/some time Traditionally, these three words have carried different meanings. *Sometime* means "at an unspecified time in the future": Why not plan to visit Niagara

Falls **sometime**? *Sometimes* means "occasionally": I visit my former college roommate **sometimes**. *Some time* means "a span of time": I need **some time** to make up my mind about what you have said.

stanch/staunch *Stanch* is a verb that means "to stop the flow of something. The bandage **stanched** the bleeding. *Staunch* is an adjective that means "firm or steadfast in principle." He is **staunch** in his stand against bigotry.

stationary/stationery These two words sound alike, but they have very different meanings. *Stationary* means "staying in one place": From this distance, the satellite appeared to be **stationary**. *Stationery* means "writing paper": A hotel often provides **stationery** with its name preprinted.

straight/strait *Straight* is most often used as an adjective meaning "unbending": The path cut **straight** through the woods. *Strait*, a noun, is "a narrow passage of water connecting two large bodies of water" or "distress, dilemma": He was in dire financial **straits**.

subsequently/consequently *Subsequently* means "occurring later, afterward": We went to a new French restaurant for dinner; **subsequently**, we heard that everyone who had eaten the Caesar salad became ill. *Consequently* means "therefore, as a result": The temperature was above 90 degrees for a week; **consequently** all the tomatoes burst on the vine.

taught/taut *Taught* is the past tense of *to teach*: My English teachers **taught** especially well. *Taut* means "tightly drawn": Pull the knot **taut** or it will not hold.

than/then *Than*, a conjunction, is used in comparisons: Robert is taller **than** Michael. *Then*, an adverb, is used to indicate time: We knew **then** that there was little to be gained by further discussion.

their/there/they're These three words sound alike, but they have very different meanings. *Their*, the possessive form of *they*, means "belonging to them": **Their** house is new. *There* can point out place (**There** is the picture I was telling you about) or call attention to someone or something: **There** is a mouse behind you! *They're* is a contraction for *they are*: **They're** not at home right now.

threw/thru/through *Threw*, the past tense of the verb *throw*, means "to hurl an object": He **threw** the ball at the batter. *Through* means "from one end to the other" or "by way of": They walked **through** the museum all afternoon. *Through* should be used in formal writing in place of *thru*, an informal spelling.

to/too/two Although the words sound alike, they are different parts of speech and have different meanings. *To* is a preposition indicating direction or part of an infinitive; *too* is an adverb meaning "also" or "in extreme"; and *two* is a number: I have **to** go **to** the store **to** buy **two** items. Do you want **to** come **too**?

tortuous/torturous *Tortuous* is an adjective meaning "full of twists and turns." That was an especially **tortuous** road. *Torturous* is an adjective meaning pertaining to or involving torture. The prisoners worked in the **torturous** heat.

track/tract *Track*, as a noun, is a path or course: The railroad **track** in the Omaha station has recently been electrified. *Track*, as a verb, is "to follow": Sophisticated guidance control systems are used to **track** the space shuttles. *Tract* is "an expanse of land" or "a brief treatise": Jonathan Swift wrote many **tracts** on the political problems of his day.

unexceptional/unexceptionable Both *unexceptional* and *unexceptionable* are adjectives, but they have different meanings and are not interchangeable. *Unexceptional* means "commonplace, ordinary": Despite the glowing reviews the new restaurant had received, we found it offered **unexceptional** meals and service. *Unexceptionable* means "not offering any basis for exception or objection, beyond criticism": We could not dispute his argument because it was **unexceptionable.**

usage/use *Usage* is a noun that refers to the generally accepted way of doing something. The word refers especially to the conventions of language: "Most unique" is considered incorrect **usage.** *Use* can be either a noun or a verb. As a noun, *use* means "the act of employing or putting into service": In the adult education course, I learned the correct **use** of tools. *Usage* is often misused in place of the noun *use*: Effective **use** (not *usage*) of your time results in greater personal satisfaction.

use/utilize/utilization *Utilize* means "to make use of": They should **utilize** the new profit-sharing plan to decrease taxable income. *Utilization* is the noun form of *utilize*. In most instances, however, *use* is preferred to either *utilize* or *utilization* as less overly formal and stilted: They should **use** the new profit-sharing plan to decrease taxable income.

venal/venial *Venal* is an adjective that means corruptible. He was a **venal** judge. *Venial* is an adjective that means a slight flaw or offense. What he did wasn't that serious; it was a **venial** offense.

which/witch *Which* is a pronoun meaning "what one": **Which** desk is yours? *Witch* is a noun meaning "a person who practices magic": The superstitious villagers accused her of being a **witch.**

who's/whose *Who's* is the contraction for *who is* or *who has*: **Who's** the person in charge here? **Who's** got the money? *Whose* is the possessive form of *who*: **Whose** book is this?

wreak/wreck *Wreak* is a verb meaning "to inflict or execute (punishment, etc.)": They **wreaked** havoc on the enemy. *Wreck* as a noun means "anything reduced to a ruin": That car is an absolute **wreck**. It can be a verb as well: Don't **wreck** the computer the first time you use it.

your/you're *Your* is the possessive form of *you*: **Your** book is overdue at the library. *You're* is the contraction of *you are*: **You're** just the person we need for this job.

AVOIDING INSENSITIVE
and
OFFENSIVE LANGUAGE

THIS essay is intended as a general guide to language that can, intentionally or not, cause offense or perpetuate discriminatory values and practices by emphasizing the differences between people or implying that one group is superior to another. Its purpose is to make readers aware of the possible consequences of the words they choose. Before looking at the words themselves, it is important to note that offensive or insensitive speech is not limited to a specific group of words. One can be hurtful and insulting by using any type of vocabulary, if that is one's intent. While in most cases it is easy to avoid blatantly offensive slurs and comments, more subtle bias that is an inherent part of our language or that is the habit of a lifetime is much harder to change.

Several factors complicate the issue. A group may disagree within itself as to what is acceptable and what is not. Many seemingly inoffensive terms develop negative connotations over time and become dated or go out of style as awareness changes. A "within the group" rule often applies, which allows a member of a group to use terms freely that would be considered offensive if used by a nonmember of the group.

What is considered acceptable shifts constantly as people become more aware of language and its power. The rapid changes of the last few decades have left many people puzzled and afraid of unintentionally insulting someone. At the same time, these changes have angered others, who decry what they see as extremes of "political correctness" in rules and locutions that alter language to the point of obscuring, even destroying, its meaning. The abandonment of traditional usages has also upset many people. But while it is true that some of the more extreme attempts to avoid offending language have resulted in ludicrous obfuscation, it is also true that heightened sensitivity in language is a statement of respect, indicates precision of thought, and is a positive move toward rectifying the unequal social status between one group and another.

Suggestions for avoiding language that reinforces stereotypes or excludes certain groups of people are given in the following pages. In each case the suggested terms are given on the right. While these suggestions can reflect trends, they cannot dictate or predict the preferences of each individual.

SEXISM

Sexism is the most difficult bias to avoid, in part because of the convention of using *man* or *men* and *he* or *his* to refer to people of either sex. Other, more disrespectful conventions include giving descriptions of women in terms of age and appearance while describing men in terms of accomplishment, and neglecting to use parallel terms to refer to men and women. Some suggestions for avoiding sexism in language are given below.

REPLACING *MAN* OR *MEN*

Man may refer to a male or to a human in general. This ambiguity is often thought to be slighting of women.

mankind, man	human beings, humans, humankind, humanity, people, human race, human species, Homo sapiens, society, men and women

a man who	someone who, anyone who
man-made	synthetic, artificial
man in the street	average person, ordinary person

USING GENDER-NEUTRAL TERMS FOR OCCUPATIONS, POSITIONS, ROLES, ETC.

Terms that specify or imply a particular sex can unnecessarily perpetuate certain stereotypes when used generically.

anchorman	Anchor
bellman, bellboy	bellhop
businessman	business executive, manager, business owner, retailer, etc.
chairman	chair, chairperson
cleaning lady, girl, maid	housecleaner, housekeeper, cleaning person, office cleaner
clergyman	member of the clergy, minister, rabbi, priest, pastor, etc.
clergymen	the clergy
congressman	representative, member of Congress, legislator
fireman	firefighter
forefather	ancestor
girl/gal Friday	assistant
housewife	homemaker
insurance man	insurance agent
layman	layperson, nonspecialist, nonprofessional

mailman, postman	mail carrier, letter carrier
policeman	police officer, law enforcement officer
salesman, saleswoman, saleslady, salesgirl	salesperson, sales representative, sales associate, clerk
spokesman	spokesperson, representative,
stewardess, steward	flight attendant
weatherman	weather reporter, weathercaster, meteorologist
workman	worker
actress	actor

AVOIDING THE GENERIC USE OF THE PERSONAL PRONOUNS *HE, HIS,* AND *HIM*

Like *man*, the word *he* can be used both generically and referring to males. The generic use can be seen to exclude women.

When a driver approaches a red light, he must prepare to stop.	When drivers approach a red light, they must prepare to stop.
	When a driver approaches a red light, he or she must prepare to stop.
	When approaching a red light, a driver must prepare to stop.
	A driver must prepare to stop when approaching a red light.
Man's natural rights are the foundation of all his civil rights.	The natural rights of human beings are the foundation of all their civil rights.

REFERRING TO MEMBERS OF BOTH SEXES WITH PARALLEL NAMES, TITLES, OR DESCRIPTIONS

Don't be inconsistent unless you are trying to make a specific point.

men and ladies	men and women, ladies and gentlemen
10 men and 13 females	10 men and 13 women
Betty Schmidt, an attractive 49-year-old physcian, and her husband, Alan Schmidt, a noted editor	Betty Schmidt, a physician, and her husband, Alan Schmidt, a noted editor
Mr. David Kim and Mrs. Betty Harrow	Mr. David Kim and Ms. Betty Harrow (unless Mrs. is her known preference)
man and wife	husband and wife
Dear Sir:	Dear Sir/Madam: Dear Madam or Sir: To whom it may concern:
Mrs. Smith and President Jones	Governor Smith and President Jones

RACE, ETHNICITY, AND NATIONAL ORIGIN

Some words and phrases that refer to racial and ethnic groups are clearly offensive. Other words (e.g., *Indian, Oriental, colored*) are outdated or inaccurate. *Hispanic* is generally accepted as a broad term for Spanish-speaking people of the Western Hemisphere, but more specific terms (*Latino, Mexican American, Cuban Ameri-*

can) are also acceptable and in some cases preferred. *Mixed race* and *multiracial* are acceptable terms for people who identify with more than one race.

Negro, colored, Afro-American	African-American (generally preferred to Afro-American)
Oriental, Asiatic	Asian, or more specific designations such as Pacific Islander, Chinese American, Korean
Indian	Indian properly refers to people who live in or hail from India. American Indian, Native American, or more specific designations (Chinook, Hopi), are usually preferred when referring to the native peoples of the Western Hemisphere.
Eskimo	Inuit, Alaska natives
native (noun)	native peoples, early inhabitants, aboriginal peoples (but not aborigines)

AGE

The concept of aging is changing as people are living longer and more active lives. Be aware of word choices that reinforce stereotypes (*decrepit, senile*) and avoid mentioning age unless it is relevant to the subject at hand. As with other groups, preferred terms for referring to older people are changing, and individual preferences may vary.

elderly, aged, old, geriatric, the elderly, the aged	older person, senior citizen, older people, senior citizens, seniors

SEXUAL ORIENTATION

The term *homosexual* to describe a man or a woman is increasingly replaced by the terms *gay* for men and *lesbian* for women. Among homosexuals, certain terms (such as *queer* and *dyke*) that are usually considered offensive have been gaining currency in recent years, particularly among radicals and in the academic community. However, it is still prudent to avoid these terms in standard contexts. The term *life partner* is frequently used when referring to one member of a committed gay relationship as well as to members of heterosexual relationships. *Sexual orientation* has replaced *sexual preference*, which implies choice. In some contexts, *same-sex* is appropriate: *same-sex marriage, same-sex parents.*

AVOIDING DEPERSONALIZATION OF PERSONS WITH DISABILITIES OR ILLNESSES

Terminology that emphasizes the person rather than the disability is generally preferred when referring to a person with a physical or mental impairment or disability. *Handicap* is used to refer to the environmental barrier that affects the person. (Stairs handicap a person who uses a wheelchair.) While words such as *crazy, demented*, and *insane* are used in facetious or informal contexts, these terms are no longer in technical use and are not used to describe people with clinical diagnoses of mental illness. The euphemisms *challenged, differently abled*, and *special* are preferred by some people, but are often ridiculed and are best avoided.

Mongoloid	person with Down syndrome
wheelchair-bound	a person who uses a wheelchair

AIDS sufferer, person afflicted with AIDS, AIDS victim	person with AIDS, P.W.A., HIV+ (someone who tests positive for HIV but does not yet show symptoms of AIDS)
polio victim	has/had polio
the handicapped, the disabled, cripple	persons with disabilities, person with a disability, person who uses crutches or other more specific description
deaf-mute, deaf and dumb	deaf person

AVOIDING PATRONIZING OR DEMEANING EXPRESSIONS

These are expressions that can offend, regardless of intention.

girls (when referring to adult women), the fair sex	women
sweetie, dear, dearie, honey	(usually not appropriate with strangers or in public situations)
old maid, spinster, bachelorette	single woman, woman, divorced woman (but only if one would specify "divorced man" in the same context)
the little woman, old lady, ball and chain	wife
boy (when referring to or addressing an adult man)	man, sir

AVOIDING LANGUAGE THAT EXCLUDES OR UNNECESSARILY EMPHASIZES DIFFERENCES

Expressions that can offend, regardless of intention. References to age, sex, religion, race, and the like should only be included if they are relevant.

lawyers and their wives	lawyers and their spouses
a secretary and her boss	a secretary and boss, a secretary and his or her boss
a good female surgeon	a good surgeon
the male nurse	the nurse
Arab man denies assault charge	man denies assault charge
the articulate black student	the articulate student
Marie Curie was a great woman scientist	Marie Curie was a great scientist (unless the intent is to compare her only with other women in the sciences)
Christian name	given name, personal name, first name
Mr. Johnson, the black representative, met with the President today to discuss civil-rights legislation.	Mr. Johnson, a member of the Congressional Black Caucus, met with the President today to discuss civil-rights legislation.

SECTION QUIZ

NOW that you've read the section on Usage, see how much you've learned by taking the quiz below.

I.   **Choose the correct word for each sentence.**

1. Bill had to choose **among/between** Charles, Stan, and Arthur for the prize.

2. Writers **like/as** him are always in demand.

3. We sat down for **a while/awhile**.

4. He felt **bad/badly** because his thumb hurt **bad/badly**.

5. There are three **criterion/criteria** for picking a winner.

6. You're looking **good/well**.

7. He was **hanged/hung** by the sheriff at noon.

8. The tree is losing **it's/its** leaves.

9. Don't walk so **slow/slowly**.

10. The cake, **that/which** is smothered with icing, is on the table.

II. **The following words are commonly confused. Choose the correct word for each sentence.**

1. She was **accepted/excepted** from physical education class.

2. Is the **ad/add** working to sell the product?

3. The dean was **adverse/averse** to the students' desire to stay late.

4. His eulogy **affected/effected** the people deeply.

5. I asked my **aid/aide** to bring me some paper.

6. I would love to have an **ally/alley** in this political fight.

7. A mirage is nothing but an optical **allusion/illusion.**

8. The couple went to the **altar/alter** to exchange their vows.

9. Bill was **ambiguous/ambivalent** about going to play golf.

10. His **assent/ascent** up Mt. Everest was hard because of the storm.

11. Weather like this doesn't **augur/auger** well for putting out the fires.

12. His **breath/breathe** looked like smoke in the cold.

13. He developed a **callous/callus** on his hand after playing tennis.

14. What he said to me really struck a **chord/cord.**

15. The writer often **sited/cited** passages from Shakespeare.

16. Make sure you buy the **course/coarse** salt, not the fine type.

17. The **corps/corpse** is at the funeral home.

18. They pushed the buzzer on **cue/queue.**

19. The floor is made up of thousands of **discreet/discrete** pieces of tile.

20. The sky was dark, and the thunderstorm seemed **imminent/eminent.**

21. She went through a **gambit/gamut** of emotions during the trial.

22. My mother is **ingenuous/ingenious** when it comes to fixing broken toys.

23. To **lessen/lesson** the pain of a bee sting, apply ice.

24. Sally's **patience/patients** make her perfect for babysitting.

25. The **principal/principle** decided to close school because of snow.

26. You can always find **stationary/stationery** in the room of a good hotel.

27. The politician wrote so many **tracts/tracks** about the war that they started to ignore him.

28. The army **wreaked/wrecked** havoc on the enemy.

III. **Provide the gender-neutral terms for the following words.**

1. anchorman

2. bellboy

3. chairman

4. cleaning lady

5. congressman

6. housewife

7. mailman

8. salesman

9. stewardess

10. actress

IV. **The paragraph below contains a number of usage errors. See if you can find them all. The corrected version, with the errors italicized and explanations in parentheses, follows.**

A married couple decided to take a vacation to Spain. From the beginning, however, things went bad. The husband, Jeff, asked for an isle seat and instead got a window seat. He demanded to see the stewardess, but she was too busy to help. Jeff sat in his seat and sulked, already in a foul mood. He had several criterion for a good airline, and one of them was prompt service. His wife, Susan, was enthused about the trip. She was going to have fun irregardless of little things that went wrong. She had made a commitment to herself to have a great time, no matter what. She'd had her fare share of troubles on vacations, but unlike Jeff, she was the eternal optimist.

Nine hours later, they were in Madrid. They only had fifty dollars among them, so they had to find a bank immediately. Jeff spotted a ATM, but couldn't figure out the directions, as they were in Spanish. Fortunately, Susan remembered her high school Spanish, and they were able to get some cash. Despite Jeff's initial bad mood, the rest of the vacation went very well and they both had lots of fun.

ANSWERS

To learn more about the subjects covered in this quiz, refer back to the page numbers listed below.

I. **Choose the correct word for each sentence. (See page 153 for more information.)**

1. among
2. like

3. a while

4. bad, badly

5. criteria

6. well

7. hanged

8. its

9. slow

10. which

II. **The following words are commonly confused. Choose the correct word for each sentence. (See page 186 for more information.)**

1. excepted

2. ad

3. averse

4. affected

5. aide

6. ally

7. illusion

8. altar

9. ambivalent

10. ascent

11. augur

12. breath

13. callus

14. chord

15. cited

16. coarse

17. corpse

18. cue

19. discrete

20. imminent

21. gamut

22. ingenious

23. lessen

24. patience

25. principal

26. stationery

27. tracts

28. wreaked

III. **Provide the gender-neutral terms for the following words. (See page 216 for more information.)**

1. anchor

2. bellhop

3. chair, chairperson

4. housekeeper

5. representative

6. homemaker

7. mail carrier

8. salesperson

9. flight attendant

10. actor

IV. Key to errors in the paragraph:

A couple decided to take a vacation to Spain. From the beginning, however, things went *bad* (should be *badly,* an adverb). The husband, Jeff, asked for an *isle* (should be *aisle; isle* means "island") seat and instead got a window seat. He demanded to see the *stewardess* (should say *flight attendant*), but she was too busy to help. Jeff sat in his seat and sulked, already in a bad mood. He had several *criterion* (should be *criteria,* which is the plural) for a good airline, and one of them was prompt service. His wife, Susan, was *enthused* (should be *enthusiastic; enthused* is only for very informal speech) about the trip. She was going to have fun *irregardless* (should be *regardless*) of little things that went wrong. She had made a commitment to herself to have a great time, no matter what. She'd had her *fare* (should be *fair*) share of troubles on vacations, but unlike Jeff, she was the eternal optimist.

Nine hours later, they were in Madrid. They only had fifty dollars *among* (should be *between,* which indicates two people) them, so they had to find a bank immediately. Jeff spotted *a* (should be *an*) ATM, but couldn't figure out the directions *as* (should be *since,* the preferred word) they were in Spanish. Fortunately, Susan remembered her high school Spanish, and they were able to get some cash. Despite Jeff's initial bad mood, the rest of the vacation went very well and they both had lots of fun.

SECTION III

Spelling

SPELLING RULES

Correct spelling is an important part of correct usage. English spellings present some difficulties because so many words are not spelled the way they sound. The following rules can serve as general guidelines. Remember that no spelling rule should be followed blindly because every rule has its exceptions.

1. **Silent *E* Dropped.** Silent *e* at the end of a word is usually dropped before a suffix beginning with a vowel: *abide, abiding; recite, recital.*

   Exceptions: Words ending in *ce* or *ge* retain the *e* before a suffix beginning with *a* or *o* to keep the soft sound of the consonant: *notice, noticeable; courage, courageous.*

2. **Silent *E* Kept.** A silent *e* following a consonant (or another *e*) is usually retained before a suffix beginning with a consonant: *late, lateness; spite, spiteful.*

   Exceptions: *fledgling, acknowledgment, judgment, wholly,* and a few similar words.

3. **Final Consonant Doubled.** A final consonant following a single vowel in one-syllable words, or in a syllable that will take the main accent when combined with a suffix, is doubled before a suffix beginning with a vowel: *begin, beginning; occur, occurred; bat, batted.*

   Exceptions: *h* and *x* in final position; *transferable, gaseous,* and a few others.

4. **Final Consonant Single.** A final consonant following another consonant, a double vowel or diphthong, or that is not in a

stressed syllable, is not doubled before a suffix beginning with a vowel: *part, parting; remark, remarkable.*

Exceptions: an unaccented syllable does not prevent doubling of the final consonant, especially in British usage: *traveller* for *traveler.*

5. **Double Consonants Remain.** Double consonants are usually retained before a suffix except when a final *l* is to be followed by *-ly* or *-less.* To avoid a triple *l,* one *l* is dropped: *full, fully.*

Exceptions: Usage is divided, with some preferring *skilful* over *skillful, instalment* over *installment,* etc.

6. **Final Y.** If the *y* follows a consonant, change *y* to *i* before all endings except *-ing.* Do not change it before *-ing* or if it follows a vowel: *bury, buried, burying; try, tries;* but *attorney, attorneys.*

Exceptions: *day, daily; gay, gaily; lay, laid; say, said.*

7. **Final IE to Y.** Words ending in *-ie* change to *-y* before *-ing*: *die, dying; lie, lying*

8. **Double and Triple E Reduced.** Words ending in double *e* drop one *e* before an ending beginning in *e,* to avoid a triple *e.* Words ending in silent *e* usually drop the *e* before endings beginning in *e* to avoid forming a syllable. Other words ending in a vowel sound commonly retain the letters indicating the sound. *Free + -ed = freed.*

9. **EI or IE.** Words having the sound of *ē* are commonly spelled *ie* following all letters but *c;* with a preceding *c,* the common spelling is *ei.* Examples: *believe, achieve, besiege;* but

conceit, ceiling, receive, conceive. When the sound is *ā*, the common spelling is *ei* regardless of the preceding letter. Examples: *eight, weight, deign.*

Exceptions: *either, neither, seize, financier*; some words in which *e* and *i* are pronounced separately, such as *notoriety*.

10. **Words Ending in C.** Before an ending beginning with *e, i,* or *y*, words ending in *c* commonly add *k* to keep the *c* hard: *panic, panicky.*

11. **Compounds.** Some compounds written as a unit bring together unusual combinations of letters. They are seldom changed on this account: *bookkeeper, roommate.*

Exceptions: A few words are regularly clipped when compounded, such as *full* in *awful, cupful,* etc.

WORDS COMMONLY MISSPELLED

aberrant	according	acquitted	advise
abscess	accordion	across	affect
absence	accumulate	address	affidavit
absorption	accustom	adequate	against
abundance	achievement	adherent	aggravate
accede	acknowledge	adjourn	aggression
accept	acknowledg-	admittance	aging
acceptance	ment	adolescence	aisle
accessible	acoustics	adolescent	alien
accidentally	acquaintance	advantageous	alleged
acclaim	acquiesce	adverse	allegiance
accommodate	acquire	advertisement	all right
accomplish	acquittal	advice	allusion

almost	approximate	barbecue	buoyant
already	apropos	barbiturate	bureau
altar	arctic	barrette	bureaucracy
alter	arguing	basically	burglary
although	argument	basis	business
altogether	arouse	beggar	cafeteria
always	arrangement	beginning	caffeine
amateur	arthritis	belief	calendar
analysis	article	believable	calisthenics
analytical	artificial	believe	camaraderie
analyze	ascend	beneficial	camouflage
anesthetic	asinine	beneficiary	campaign
annual	asked	benefit	cancel
anoint	assassin	benefited	cancellation
anonymous	assent	bias	candidate
answer	assess	biscuit	cantaloupe
Antarctic	assistant	blizzard	canvas
antecedent	assure	bludgeon	capacity
anticipation	asthma	bologna	cappuccino
antihistamine	atheist	bookkeeping	carburetor
anxiety	athlete	bouillon	career
anxious	athletic	boulevard	careful
apartment	attendance	boundaries	Caribbean
aperitif	attorneys	braggadocio	carriage
apocryphal	author	breathe	carrying
apostasy	authoritative	brief	casserole
apparatus	auxiliary	brilliant	category
apparent	averse	broccoli	caterpillar
appearance	bachelor	bronchial	cavalry
appetite	balance	brutality	ceiling
appreciate	balloon	bulletin	cellar
appropriate	bankruptcy	buoy	cemetery

census
certain
challenge
chandelier
changeable
changing
characteristic
chief
choir
choose
chose
cigarette
cinnamon
circuit
civilized
climate
climbed
cloth
clothes
clothing
codeine
collateral
collectible
colloquial
colonel
colossal
column
coming
commemorate
commission
commitment
committed

committee
comparative
comparison
competent
competition
competitive
complaint
completely
concede
conceivable
conceive
condemn
condescend
conferred
confidential
congratulate
conscience
conscientious
conscious
consensus
consequently
consistent
consummate
continuous
control
controlled
controversial
controversy
convalesce
convenience
convenient
coolly

copyright
cornucopia
corollary
corpse
corporation
correlate
correspondence
correspondent
counselor
counterfeit
courageous
courteous
courtesy
crisis
criticism
criticize
culinary
curiosity
curriculum
cylinder
debt
debtor
deceive
decide
decision
decisive
defendant
deferred
definite
definitely
definition
dependent

de rigueur
descend
descendant
describe
description
desiccate
desirable
despair
desperate
destroy
develop
development
diabetes
diaphragm
dictionary
difference
different
dilemma
dining
diocese
diphtheria
disappear
disappearance
disappoint
disastrous
discipline
disease
dispensable
dissatisfied
dissident
dissipate
distinguish

divide

divine

doesn't

dominant

dormitory

drunkenness

duly

dumbbell

during

easier

easily

ecstasy

effervescent

efficacy

efficiency

efficient

eighth

eightieth

electrician

eligibility

eligible

eliminate

ellipsis

embarrass

emperor

encouragement

encouraging

endurance

enemy

energetic

enforceable

enthusiasm

entirely

environment

equipped

equivalent

erroneous

especially

esteemed

exacerbate

exaggerate

exceed

excel

excellence

excellent

except

exceptionally

excessive

executive

exercise

exhaust

exhibition

exhilarate

existence

expense

experience

experiment

explanation

exquisite

extemporane-
ous

extraordinary

extremely

exuberance

facilities

facsimile

fallacious

fallacy

familiar

fascinate

fascinating

fascism

feasible

February

fictitious

fiend

fierce

fiery

fiftieth

finagle

finally

financial

financially

fluorescent

fluorine

foliage

forcible

forehead

foreign

forfeit

formally

formerly

forte

fortieth

fortunately

forty

fourth

friend

frieze

fuel

fulfill

fundamental

furniture

galoshes

gauge

genealogy

generally

genius

gibe

gnash

government

governor

graffiti

grammar

grateful

grievance

grievous

guarantee

guard

guardian

guerilla

guidance

handkerchief

haphazard

happily

harass

harebrained

hazard

height	inalienable	introduce	liqueur
heinous	incident	inveigle	literature
hemorrhage	incidentally	irrelevant	livelihood
hemorrhoid	inconvenience	irresistible	loneliness
hereditary	incredible	island	loose
heroes	indelible	jealous	lose
hesitancy	independent	jeopardize	losing
hierarchy	indestructible	journal	lovable
hindrance	indictment	judgment	lovely
hoarse	indigestible	judicial	luxury
hoping	indispensable	khaki	magazine
hors d'oeuvres	inevitable	kindergarten	maintain
huge	inferred	knowledge	maintenance
humorous	influential	laboratory	manageable
hundredth	information	laid	management
hurrying	initial	larynx	maneuver
hydraulic	initiative	later	manufacturer
hygiene	innocuous	latter	maraschino
hygienist	innuendo	leery	marital
hypocrisy	inoculation	legitimate	marriage
hypocrite	inscrutable	leisure	marriageable
icicle	installation	length	mathematics
ideally	insurance	liable	mayonnaise
identification	instantaneous	liaison	meant
idiosyncrasy	intellectual	libel	medicine
ignorance	intelligence	library	medieval
imaginary	intercede	license	memento
immediately	interest	lieutenant	mileage
immense	interfere	lightning	millennium
implement	intermittent	likelihood	millionaire
impostor	interrupt	likely	miniature
impresario	intimate	liquefy	minuet

minutes	nowadays	pamphlet	perspiration
miscellaneous	nuisance	paradise	persuade
mischievous	nuptial	parakeet	persuasion
missile	obbligato	parallel	persuasive
misspell	obedience	paralysis	petition
mistletoe	obstacle	paralyze	philosophy
moccasin	occasion	paraphernalia	physical
molasses	occasionally	pari-mutuel	physician
molecule	occurred	parliament	piccolo
monotonous	occurrence	partial	piece
mortgage	offense	participate	pilgrimage
mosquito	official	particularly	pitiful
murmur	omission	pasteurize	plaited
muscle	omit	pastime	planning
mutual	omitted	pavilion	plateau
mysterious	oneself	peaceable	plausible
naïve	ophthalmology	peasant	playwright
narrative	opinion	peculiar	pleasant
naturally	opponent	penetrate	plebeian
necessarily	opportunity	penicillin	pneumonia
necessary	oppression	perceive	poinsettia
necessity	optimism	perform	politician
neighbor	optimist	performance	pomegranate
neither	orchestra	peril	portray
neutron	ordinarily	permanent	possess
nickel	origin	permissible	possession
niece	original	permitted	possessive
ninetieth	outrageous	perpendicular	possibility
ninety	overrun	perseverance	possible
ninth	paean	persistent	practically
noticeable	pageant	personal	practice
notoriety	paid	personnel	prairie

precede

precedence

precisely

predecessor

preference

preferred

prejudice

preparatory

prescription

prevalent

primitive

principal

principle

prior

privilege

probability

probably

procedure

proceed

profession

professor

proffer

prominent

pronounce

pronunciation

propaganda

propagate

protégé(e)

psychiatry

psychology

publicly

pursuant

pursue

pursuit

putrefy

quantity

quarantine

questionnaire

queue

quizzes

rarefy

realistically

realize

recede

receipt

receivable

receive

recipe

reciprocal

recognize

recommend

reference

referred

reign

relegate

relevant

relieve

religious

remembrance

reminisce

reminiscence

remiss

remittance

renaissance

rendezvous

repetition

replaceable

representative

requisition

resemblance

reservoir

resistance

responsibility

restaurant

restaurateur

resuscitate

reticence

reveille

rheumatism

rhyme

rhythm

riddance

ridiculous

rococo

roommate

sacrifice

sacrilegious

safety

salary

sandwich

sarsaparilla

sassafras

satellite

satisfaction

scarcity

scary

scene

scenery

schedule

scheme

scholarly

scissors

secede

secrecy

secretary

seize

seizure

sense

sentence

separate

separately

sergeant

serviceable

seventieth

several

severely

sheikh

shepherd

sheriff

shining

shoulder

shrapnel

siege

sieve

significance

silhouette

similar

simile

simultaneity
simultaneous
sincerely
sixtieth
skiing
socially
society
solemn
soliloquy
sophomore
sorority
souvenir
sovereign
spaghetti
spatial
special
specifically
specimen
speech
sponsor
spontaneous
statistics
statute
stevedore
stiletto
stopped
stopping
strategy
strength
strenuous
strictly
stubbornness

studying
stupefy
submitted
subordinate
substantial
subtle
subtly
succeed
success
successful
succession
successive
sufficient
superintendent
supersede
supplement
suppress
surprise
surround
surveillance
susceptible
suspicion
suspicious
sustenance
syllable
symmetrical
sympathize
sympathy
synchronous
synonym
synonymous
syphilis

systematically
tangible
tariff
technical
technique
temperament
temperature
temporarily
tendency
tentative
terrestrial
theory
therefore
thirtieth
thorough
thought
thousandth
through
till
titillate
together
tomorrow
tonight
tournament
tourniquet
tragedy
tragically
transferred
transient
tries
truly
twelfth

twentieth
typical
tyranny
unanimous
undoubtedly
unique
unison
unmanageable
unnecessary
until
upholsterer
usable
usage
using
usually
utilize
vacancy
vacuum
vague
valuable
variety
vegetable
veil
vengeance
vermilion
veterinarian
vichyssoise
vigilant
village
villain
violence
visible

vision	weird	wield	wrought
virtue	wherever	withdrawal	xylophone
volume	whether	woolen	yacht
warrant	whim	wretched	yield
warriors	wholly	writing	zealous
weather	whose	written	zucchini
Wednesday	witch	wrote	

USING A SPELL-CHECKER

A spell-checker is a computer program that checks or verifies the spelling of words in an electronic document. While it can be a valuable tool for writers, it cannot be relied upon to catch all types of spelling errors. It is most useful in finding misspellings that produce "nonwords"—words with transposed, wrong, or missing letters. For example, it will reject *ther* (for *there*) and *teh* (for *the*). However, it cannot distinguish between words that sound or look alike but differ in meaning. It will accept *to* or *too* regardless of whether the context is correct, and it will accept typos such as *on* (for *of*) or *form* (for *from*). It is important, therefore, not to rely too heavily on spell-checkers and to go over your writing carefully to avoid such mistakes.

RULES OF WORD DIVISION

It is often necessary to divide a word at the end of a line. Words must always be divided between syllables. Consult a dictionary if you are not sure where the syllable division occurs. The following rules should be followed to avoid confusing the reader.

1. Do not divide a one-syllable word. This includes past tenses like *walked* and *dreamed*, which should never be split before the *-ed* ending.

2. Do not divide a word so that a single letter is left at the end of a line, as in *a-bout*, or so that a single letter starts the following line, as in *cit-y*.

3. Hyphenated compounds should preferably be divided only after the hyphen. If the first portion of the compound is a single letter, however, as in *D-day*, the word should not be divided.

4. Word segments like *-ceous, -scious, -sial, -tion, -tious* should not be divided.

5. The portion of a word left at the end of a line should not encourage a misleading pronunciation, as would be the case if *acetate*, a three-syllable word, were divided after the first *e*.

SECTION QUIZ

NOW that you've read the section on Spelling, see how much you've learned by taking the quiz below.

You will be given two choices for the spelling of each of the following words. Pick the correct choice.

1. aberant/aberrant

2. abcess/abscess

3. acede/accede

4. accesible/accessible

5. accommodate/accommadate

6. accordion/acorrdion

7. achievment/achievement

8. acknowledgment/acknowledgement

9. acquaintance/acquaintence

10. acquiese/acquiesce

11. acquittal/aquittal

12. adress/address

13. ajourn/adjourn

14. adolesence/adolescence

15. allegance/allegiance

16. anasthetic/anesthetic

17. antehistamine/antihistamine

18. barbacue/barbecue

19. begger/beggar

20. believeble/believable

21. benefit/benefet

22. cantalope/cantaloupe

23. Caribbean/Carribean

24. caterpillar/catepillar

25. contraversial/controversial

26. decieve/deceive

27. dilemma/dilema

28. dissapear/disappear

29. disipate/dissipate

30. dumbell/dumbbell

31. excelent/excellent

32. exhilerate/exhilarate

33. fesible/feasible

34. florescent/fluorescent

35. fullfill/fulfill

36. guidence/guidance

37. hankerchief/handkerchief

38. higherarchy/hierarchy

39. hygene/hygiene

40. imaginary/imagenary

41. incidentally/incidently

42. insurence/insurance

43. intermittent/intermitent

44. judgement/judgment

45. larynix/larynx

46. luxery/luxury

47. manuver/maneuver

48. marrage/marriage

49. mayonnase/mayonnaise

50. molecule/molacule

51. murmer/murmur

52. obsticle/obstacle

53. omitt/omit

54. opression/oppression

55. overun/overrun

56. paralell/parallel

57. pavillion/pavilion

58. posess/possess

59. preferance/preference

60. proceedure/procedure

61. questionaire/questionnaire

62. recieve/receive

63. rememberance/remembrance

64. repetition/repetiton

65. resevoir/reservoir

66. rhthym/rhythm

67. salery/salary

68. sattelite/satellite

69. sargeant/sergeant

70. shrapenel/shrapnel

71. silouette/silhouette
72. sincerly/sincerely
73. sophmore/sophomore
74. stupify/stupefy
75. sucess/success
76. supicion/suspicion
77. tariff/tarif
78. temperment/temperament
79. tentitive/tentative
80. tommorow/tomorrow
81. twelfth/twelth
82. until/untill
83. vaccum/vacuum
84. viel/veil
85. vetanarian/veterinarian
86. vigilent/vigilant
87. wierd/weird
88. wreched/wretched
89. yeild/yield
90. zuccini/zucchini

ANSWERS

To learn more about the subjects covered in this quiz, refer back to pages 233–244.

1. aberrant
2. abscess
3. accede
4. accessible

5. accommodate

6. accordion

7. achievement

8. acknowledgement

9. acquaintance

10. acquiesce

11. acquittal

12. address

13. adjourn

14. adolescence

15. allegiance

16. anesthetic

17. antihistamine

18. barbecue

19. beggar

20. believable

21. benefit

22. cantaloupe

23. Caribbean

24. caterpillar

25. controversial

26. deceive

27. dilemma

28. disappear

29. dissipate

30. dumbbell

31. excellent

32. exhilarate

33. feasible

34. fluorescent

35. fulfill

36. guidance

37. handkerchief

38. hierarchy

39. hygiene

40. imaginary

41. incidentally

42. insurance

43. intermittent

44. judgment

45. larynx

46. luxury

47. maneuver

48. marriage

49. mayonnaise

50. molecule

51. murmur

52. obstacle

53. omit

54. oppression

55. overrun

56. parallel

57. pavilion

58. possess

59. preference

60. procedure

61. questionnaire

62. receive

63. remembrance

64. repetition

65. reservoir

66. rhythm

67. salary

68. satellite

69. sergeant

70. shrapnel

71. silhouette

72. sincerely

73. sophomore

74. stupefy

75. success

76. suspicion

77. tariff

78. temperament

79. tentative

80. tomorrow

81. twelfth

82. until

83. vacuum

84. veil

85. veterinarian

86. vigilant

87. weird

88. wretched

89. yield

90. zucchini

Punctuation

[.] PERIOD

A *PERIOD* IS USED:
after a statement,

> Some of us still support the mayor.
>
> Others think he should retire.

after an indirect question,

> She asked what time the train leaves.

after a mild command,

> Would you close the door, please.
>
> Read the next two chapters by Tuesday.

and after a question used as a statement.

> It's hot today, isn't it.

A period is used after many abbreviations.

> i.e., e.g., etc., Mr., Mrs., Ms., Dr., Inc., U.S., M.D., Sept., Pa., D.C.

A period is *not* used in acronyms, in U.S. Postal Service state abbreviations, with initials used in place of personal names, or after metric abbreviations.

> UNICEF, UNESCO, NASA, NATO, IRA, AIDS, OPEC, NAFTA
>
> NY, PA, CA, ME, MD
>
> FDR, JFK, LBJ
>
> 50 km, 3 kg, 100 mm

A period is used within decimal numbers and amounts of money.

A sales tax of 7.5 percent is leveled on all clothing in this state.

He spent $44.50 on the shirt, $36.09 on the pants, and $22.00 on the tie.

[?] QUESTION MARK

Sentences that ask a question should be followed by a *question mark*.

Who invited him to the party?

"Is something the matter?" she asked.

What constitutional principle did John Marshall establish in *Marbury v. Madison*? in *McCullough v. Maryland*? in *Fletcher v. Peck*?

You can get us in free?

A question mark is also used to indicate doubt about information.

Socrates was born in 470 (?) B.C.E.

The code dates back to a.d. 500 (?).

A question mark is *not* used after an indirect question or after a polite command phrased as a question.

I wonder why.

She asked if the application had been mailed.

Won't you sit down.

Why don't you take off your coat.

[!] EXCLAMATION POINT

An *exclamation point* is used to end a sentence, clause, phrase, or single word that expresses a command or a strong emotion, such as surprise or admiration.

Go away!

What a week this has been!

Note: Avoid overusing exclamation points in writing. They are effective only when used sparingly.

[,] COMMA

The *comma* is the most frequently used mark of punctuation within a sentence. The main use of a comma is to clarify the structure and meaning of a sentence. The secondary use of a comma is to indicate emphasis, pauses, and stress. Adding unnecessary commas or omitting necessary ones can confuse a reader and obscure the meaning of a sentence.

Independent clauses may be grouped into sentences by using the coordinating conjunctions *and, but, yet, for, or, nor,* and *so.* The first clause is usually followed by a comma. If the subject of both clauses is the same, the comma is generally omitted.

We tried to reason with him, but he had already made up his mind.

Joe is finishing high school this year, and Jennifer is a junior at Harvard.

Take six cooking apples and put them into a flameproof dish.

Introductory words, phrases, clauses, and transitional expressions are set off by a comma.

> Your honor, I object.
>
> Theoretically, she will have to get the permission of the chairman.
>
> Thoroughly chilled, he decided to set out for home.
>
> Yes, we are prepared for any motion that the prosecution may make.
>
> However, it is important to understand everyone's point of view.
>
> Born to wealthy parents, he was able to pursue his career without financial worries.
>
> After the first few years of marriage, most couples realize that there are certain matters upon which they will never agree.
>
> Since the team was in last place, it was not surprising that only fifteen hundred fans showed up for the final game of the season.

When the introductory phrase is short, the comma is often omitted. Be certain that the sentence is clear as it stands.

> In this article I will demonstrate that we have chosen the wrong policy.
>
> At the present time the number of cigarette smokers is declining.

Conjunctive adverbs, transitional expressions, and parenthetical expressions that occur in the middle of the sentence require two commas to set them off.

> It is important, however, to understand everyone's point of view.
>
> Most new employees, after the first month, settle easily into the company's routine.

We can, I hope, agree on a budget for next year.

You may, if you insist, demand a retraction.

If a sentence can be read without pauses before and after the modifier, the commas may be omitted.

We can therefore conclude that the defendant is innocent of the charges.

The applicant must understand before sending in the forms that the deposit fee is not refundable.

A phrase or clause is called *restrictive* if omitting it would change the meaning of the sentence. Such a phrase or clause "restricts" or limits the meaning of the word or words it applies to, and therefore cannot be omitted. Restrictive phrases and clauses are not set off by commas.

The Elizabethan composers Byrd, Gibbons, and Dowland influenced her greatly.

The novel that she wrote in 1996 won a literary award.

The only state that is in the Hawaii-Aleutian time zone is Hawaii.

The city where I live is Seattle.

When a phrase or clause is not essential to the meaning of the sentence, it is called *nonrestrictive*. Such phrases and clauses are set off by commas.

She was much influenced by Elizabethan composers, especially Byrd, Gibbons, and Dowland.

Her most recent novel, written in 1996, won a literary award.

Hawaii, which is the fiftieth state, is in the Hawaii-Aleutian time zone.

Seattle, the city where I live, is close to both the sea and the mountains.

Conjunctive adverbs can be placed anywhere in a sentence depending on where you want the emphasis. They are always set off by commas.

However, it is important to understand everyone's point of view.

It is important, however, to understand everyone's point of view.

It is important to understand everyone's point of view, however.

Appositives are words that give additional information about the preceding or following word or expression. Many appositives are nonrestrictive and are thus set off from the rest of the sentence with commas. Be careful not to set off restrictive appositives, which are necessary for the meaning of the sentence.

March, the month of crocuses, can still bring snow and ice.

Mr. Case, a member of the committee, refused to comment.

His favorite author, Stephen King, entered the auditorium.

My friend Mary spoke at the convention.

The crowd fell silent as the author Stephen King entered the auditorium.

A comma is used to separate words, phrases, and clauses that are part of a series of three or more items, with a word like *and* or *or* usually occurring between the last two items.

The chief agricultural products of Denmark are butter, eggs, potatoes, beets, wheat, barley, and oats.

England, Scotland, and Wales share the island of Great Britain.

Cabbage is especially good with corned beef, game, or smoked meats.

Environmentally conscious businesses use recycled paper, photocopy on both sides of a sheet, and use ceramic cups.

Note: Some writers omit the final comma when punctuating a series, and newspapers and magazines sometimes follow this practice. Book publishers and educators, however, usually follow the practice recommended above.

In a series of adjectives, commas must be used when each adjective is considered separately, not as a modifier of other adjectives.

the beautiful, expensive dress

the happy, smiling children

the hungry, meowing cat

Do not use commas to separate adjectives that are so closely related that they appear to form a single element with the noun they modify. Adjectives that refer to the number, age, size, color, or location of the noun often fall within this category. To determine whether or not to use the comma in these instances, insert the word *and*. If *and* cannot replace the comma without creating an awkward sentence, it is safe to conclude that a comma is not necessary.

twenty happy little children

several dingy old Western mining towns

beautiful tall golden aspens

a dozen long white dresses

When dates and addresses are used in sentences, they are followed by a comma. When only the month and year are given, the comma is usually omitted.

> All contributions should be sent to the recording secretary at 4232 Grand Boulevard, Silver Spring, MD 70042, as soon as possible.

> She was born on Tuesday, December 20, 1901, in a log cabin near Casey Creek, Kentucky.

> We took our first trip to Alaska in August 1988.

Use a comma when it is necessary to prevent misreading. The comma tells the reader to stop briefly before reading on. Words may run together in confusing ways unless you use a comma to separate them. Use a comma in such sentences even though no rule requires one.

> Soon after, she quit the job for good.

> The people who can, usually contribute some money to the local holiday drive.

> After she ate, the cat washed herself and went to sleep.

[;] SEMICOLON

A *semicolon* is used to separate parts of a sentence—such as independent clauses, items in a series, and explanations or summaries—from the main clause. It makes a stronger break in the sentence than a comma does. In choosing among the three punctuation marks that separate main clauses—the comma, the semicolon, and the colon—a writer needs to decide on the relationship between ideas.

Separate independent clauses not joined by a coordinating conjunction are separated by a semicolon.

The house burned down; it was the last shattering blow.

We have made several attempts to reach you by telephone; not a single call has been returned.

When separate independent clauses are joined by a conjunctive adverb such as *however, nevertheless, otherwise, therefore, besides, hence, indeed, instead, nonetheless, still, then,* or *thus,* a semicolon is used after the first clause.

The funds are inadequate; therefore, the project will close down.

Enrollments exceed all expectations; however, there is a teacher shortage.

He knew that tickets for the performance would be scarce; therefore, he arrived at the concert hall two hours early.

Long or possibly ambiguous items in a series, especially when those items already include commas, are separated by a semicolon.

In the next year, they plan to open stores in Sewickley, Pennsylvania; Belleville, Illinois; Breckenridge, Colorado; and Martinez, California.

Academically talented students were selected on the basis of grades; tests of vocabulary, memory, reading, inductive reasoning, math, and perceptual speed and accuracy; and teacher recommendations.

A semicolon is used before *i.e., e.g., that is, for example,* etc., when the next part of the sentence is a complete clause.

On the advice of his broker, he chose to invest in major industries; i.e., he invested in steel, automobiles, and oil.

She organizes her work well; for example, she puts correspondence in folders of different colors to indicate degrees of urgency.

[:] COLON

As a mark of introduction, the *colon* tells the reader that the first statement is going to be explained by the second or that a quotation or series will follow.

A colon is used to introduce a long formal statement or a quotation.

This I believe: All people are created equal and must enjoy equally the rights that are inalienably theirs.

Fagles's translation of the *Iliad* begins: "Rage—Goddess, sing the rage of Peleus' son Achilles, murderous, doomed, that cost the Achaeans countless losses, . . ."

When one independent clause is followed by another that explains or exemplifies it, they can be separated by a colon. The second clause may or may not begin with a capital letter.

They cannot pay their monthly bills because their money is tied up in their stocks and bonds: they are paper-rich and cash-poor.

There's only one solution: we must reduce next year's budget.

The negotiators finally agreed on a basic principle: neither side would seek to resupply the troops during the cease-fire.

The conference addresses a basic question: How can we take the steps needed to protect the environment without stalling economic growth?

A colon is used to introduce a series or list.

There were originally five Marx brothers: Groucho, Chico, Harpo, Zeppo, and Gummo.

The senior citizens demanded the following: better police protection, more convenient medical facilities, and a new recreational center.

A colon is used to follow the salutation in a formal letter.

Dear Mr. Guerro:

Dear Ms. McFadden:

Dear Valued Customer:

The parts of a citation are separated by a colon.

Genesis 3:2

Journal of Astrophysics 43:2

A colon is placed between the title and the subtitle of a book.

In 1988 Brooks published *Gilded Twilight: The Later Years of Melville and Twain.*

A colon is used to separate hours from minutes in indicating time.

1:30 p.m.

12:30 a.m.

In a bibliographical citation, a colon may separate the place of publication from the name of the publisher.

> New York: Random House, Inc.

Do not use a colon to introduce a list that is the object of the verb.

> The senior citizens' demands included better police protection, more convenient medical facilities, and a new recreational center.

Do not use a colon to introduce a list after the verb *to be* or to introduce a list following a preposition:

> The courses she is taking are French, medieval history, Greek, and the nineteenth-century novel.

> I have had enough of mosquitoes, leaking tents, wet blankets, and whining children.

> The committee consisted of nine teachers, twelve parents, and six business leaders.

[—] DASH

A *dash* is used to show sudden changes in thought or to set off certain sentence elements. Like the exclamation point, dashes are dramatic and thus should be used sparingly in formal writing. Do not confuse the dash with the hyphen. (See page 279 on the hyphen.)

The dash may be used to mark an abrupt change in thought or shift in tone.

> He won the game—but I'm getting ahead of the story.

> She told me—does she really mean it?—that she will inform us of any changes in advance.

Where commas might cause confusion, a dash may be used to set off appositives.

> The premier's promise of changes—land reform and higher wages—was not easily fulfilled.

> The qualities Renoir valued in his painting—rich shadows, muted colors, graceful figures—were abundant in the ballet dancers he used as subjects.

A dash may be used to add emphasis to parenthetical material or to mark an emphatic separation between that material and the rest of the sentence.

> Her influence—she was a powerful figure in the community—was a deterrent to effective opposition.

> The car he was driving—a gleaming red convertible—was the most impressive thing about him.

Halting or hesitant speech may be indicated by a dash. Also note the use of the dash to attribute this section of writing to its author.

> "Well—er—it's hard to explain," he faltered.

> Madame de Vionnett instantly rallied.

> "And you know—though it might occur to one—it isn't in the least that he's ashamed of her.

> She's really—in a way—extremely good looking."

> —Henry James

Interrupted speech may also be indicated by a dash.

"Harvey, don't climb up that—." It was too late.

If they discovered the truth—he did not want to think of the consequences.

A dash may replace an offensive word or part of one.

"You're full of—!" he shouted.

Where's that son of a b—?

[· · ·] ELLIPSIS

The *ellipsis* mark consists of three spaced periods (. . .).

It is sometimes convenient to omit part of a quotation. When this is done, the omission must be marked with points of ellipsis, usually with spaces between them. When the omission comes in the middle of a sentence, three points are used. When the omission includes the end of one or more sentences, four points are used.

Lewis Thomas offers the following advice:

If something is to be quoted, the exact words must be used. If part of it must be left out . . . insert three dots to indicate the omission, but it is unethical to do this if it means connecting two thoughts which the original author did not intend to have tied together.

Ellipsis may also be used to indicate breaks in thought in quoted speech (compare with **dash**).

"I don't know where he is. . . ."

"If only she hadn't died so soon. . . ."

Note: If the sentence is complete, the period is added, resulting in four spaced periods. If the sentence is incomplete, use only three dots for the ellipsis.

[( )] PARENTHESES

Parentheses are used to enclose nonessential material within a sentence. This can include facts, explanations, digressions, and examples that may be helpful but are not necessary for the sentence. Do not put a comma before a parenthesis.

Faulkner's stories (but not his novels) were required reading for the course.

The community didn't feel (and why should they?) that there was adequate police protection.

Many workers (including those in the mail room) distrust the new shipping regulations.

Parentheses are also used to enclose part of a sentence that would be confusing if enclosed by commas.

The authors he advised (none other than Hemingway, Lewis, and Cather) would have been delighted to honor him today.

An explanatory item that is not part of the statement is enclosed in parentheses.

He wrote to *The Paris* (Illinois) *News.*

Parentheses are used to enclose numbers or letters that designate each item in a series.

The project is (1) too time-consuming, (2) too expensive, and (3) poorly staffed.

Parentheses are used to indicate an abbreviation that will be used in the remainder of the paragraph.

The Federal Trade Commission (FTC) has issued regulations on the advertising of many products.

If a full sentence is enclosed within the parentheses, the period comes before the closing parenthesis.

Seven U.S. presidents were born in Virginia. (The other southern states were the birthplaces of only one or two presidents each.) Ohio also produced seven, and Massachusetts and New York, four each.

If the parenthetical element is a fragment of a sentence, the period goes outside the closing parenthesis.

Two U.S. presidents were born in Vermont (Chester Alan Arthur and Calvin Coolidge), and one was born in New Hampshire (Franklin Pierce).

[[ ]] BRACKETS

When writers insert something within a quoted passage, the insertion should be set off with *brackets*. Insertions are sometimes used to supply words that explain, clarify, or correct the contents of a direct quotation.

According to the *Globe* critic, "This [*Man and Superman*] is one of Shaw's greatest plays."

"Young as they are," he writes, "these students are afflicted with cynicism, world-weariness, and *a total disregard for tradition and authority*." [Emphasis is mine.]

"As a result of the Gemini V mission [the flight by astronauts Cooper and Conrad in August 1965], we have proof that human beings can withstand the eight days in space required for a round-trip to the moon."

Lewis Thomas warns that it is "unethical to [omit words in a quotation] . . . if it means connecting two thoughts which the original author did not intend to have tied together."

Writers can make clear that an error in the quotation has been carried over from the original by using the Latin word *sic*, meaning "thus."

"George Washington lived during the seventeenth [*sic*] century."

"The governor of Missisipi [*sic*] addressed the student body."

Brackets are used to enclose comments made in a verbatim transcript.

Sen. Eaton: The steady rise in taxes must be halted. [Applause]

Brackets are used to substitute for parentheses with material already enclosed in parentheses.

[1]See "Rene Descartes" (M.C. Beardsley, *The European Philosophers from Descartes to Nietzsche* [New York, 1960]).

The publication date, inserted by the editor, of an item appearing in an earlier issue of a periodical is enclosed in brackets.

Dear Sir: Your excellent article on China [April 15] brings to mind my recent experience . . .

When traveling in India [*Travel Monthly*, March 2001], one should recall the words of . . .

[""] QUOTATION MARKS

Use quotation marks:

1. To distinguish spoken words from other matter, as in reporting dialogue.

   "God bless us every one!" said Tiny Tim.

2. To mark single words, sentences, paragraphs, or poetic stanzas that are quoted verbatim from the original.

   Portia's speech on "the quality of mercy" is one of the most quoted passages from Shakespeare.

   It was Shaw who wrote: "All great truths begin as blasphemies."

3. To enclose a quotation within a quotation, in which case single quotation marks are used.

   Reading Jill's letter, Pat said, "Listen to this! 'I've just received notice that I made dean's list.' Isn't that great?"

4. To enclose titles of newspaper and magazine articles, essays, stories, poems (if they are not long or major works), and chapters of books. The quotation marks distinguish such literary pieces from the books or periodicals (these are italicized) in which they appear.

Our anthology contains such widely assorted pieces as Bacon's essay "Of Studies," Poe's "The Gold Bug," Keats's "Ode to a Nightingale," and an article on literary criticism from *The American Scholar.*

5. To enclose titles of short musical compositions and songs, as distinguished from symphonies and operas, which are italicized.

   Our national anthem is "The Star-Spangled Banner."

   Even the youngsters laughed at the "Figaro" aria from *The Barber of Seville.*

6. To enclose titles of works of art, such as paintings, drawings, photographs, and sculpture; especially when italics are not available.

   Most people recognize Da Vinci's "Mona Lisa" (or "La Gióconda") or Rodin's "The Thinker."

7. To enclose titles of radio and television programs or series.

   "The Six O'Clock News"

   "Star Trek"

8. To enclose titles of plays *only* if they are referred to as part of a larger collection. Referred to as single volumes, they are italicized.

   "The Wild Duck" is the Ibsen play included in this edition of *Modern European Plays.*

9. To enclose names of ships and airplanes, especially when italics are not available.

Lindbergh flew across the Atlantic in the "Spirit of St. Louis."

My parents sailed to Europe on the "Queen Elizabeth."

10. To emphasize a word or phrase that is itself the subject of discussion. Italics may also be used for this purpose.

The words "imply" and "infer" are not synonymous.

Such Freudian terms as "ego," "superego," "id," and "libido" are not used by all therapists.

11. To draw attention to an uncommon word or phrase, a technical term, or a usage very different in style (dialect, extreme slang) from the context. This practice should be used with discretion.

Teachers need not be dismayed when students smirk at "uncool" traditions.

In glassblowing, the molten glass is called "metal."

12. To suggest ironic use of a word or phrase.

The radio blasting forth John's favorite "music" is to his grandfather an instrument of torture.

Doris's skiing "vacation" consisted of three weeks with her leg in a cast.

Note: The placement of quotation marks next to commas, periods, etc., is determined by certain arbitrary rules and varies with the different marks of punctuation.

1. Use quotation marks both before and after a quoted word, phrase, or longer passage.

2. Use a comma between the quoted matter and such phrases as "according to the speaker," "he said," "she replied," and "they asked" whenever these phrases introduce a quotation, are used parenthetically, or follow a quotation that, in its original form, would end with a period.

John asked, "Why not this week?"

According to the Declaration of Independence, "all men are created equal."

"Well," announced Peggy's father, "we are all going on vacation."

"The merger is imminent," replied the new chairperson.

3. Whenever a phrase such as "he said," "she replied," or "he asked" follows a question or an exclamation, use the corresponding punctuation before the closing quotation mark.

"Why can't we go to the movies this week?" asked Arlene.

"We simply can't buy you a car. And that's final!" replied the boy's mother.

4. Always place the closing quotation mark *before* a colon or semicolon.

She remembered that the girls had always called Gail "the brain"; she began to wonder if the reputation endured.

There were several reasons why Tom was acknowledged as "the champ": physical strength, intellectual superiority, and qualities of leadership.

5. Place the closing quotation mark *after* a question mark or exclamation point only when the latter is part of the quoted passage.

"Hurry, please, before it's too late!" she cried.

"Is there any hope of recovering the property?" he asked.

In all other cases, place the quotation mark *before* the exclamation point or question mark.

Did Pangloss really mean it when he said, "This is the best of all possible worlds"?

How absurd of him to say "This is the best of all possible worlds"!

6. If a quotation consists of two or more consecutive paragraphs, use quotation marks at the beginning of each paragraph, but place them at the end of the last paragraph only.

ITALICS/UNDERLINING

Italics are used to emphasize or set apart specific words and phrases. In handwritten papers, underlining indicates italics.

The titles of newspapers, magazines, and books are italicized.

Her job requires her to read the *New York Times*, the *Wall Street Journal*, and the *Washington Post* every day.

"Song of Myself" is the first poem in Whitman's *Leaves of Grass*.

Every year *Consumer Reports* runs "Best Buy Gifts" in the November issue.

Italics are used for the titles of plays and movies, radio and television programs, and for the titles of works of art and long musical works.

Shakespeare's *Hamlet*

The Playboy of the Western World

the movie *High Noon*

Huston's *The Maltese Falcon*

Leonardo da Vinci's *Last Supper*

Sesame Street

Handel's *Messiah*

Don Giovanni by Mozart

Porgy and Bess

Italics are used for the names of ships and planes.

the aircraft carrier *Intrepid*

Lindbergh's *The Spirit of St. Louis*

Words and phrases from a foreign language are italicized. Accompanying translations are often enclosed in quotation marks. Words of foreign origin that have become familiar in an English context should not be italicized.

As a group, these artists appear to be in the avant-garde. They are not, however, to be thought of as *enfants terribles*, or "terrible children," people whose work is so outrageous as to shock or embarrass.

Italics are used for words used as words and letters used as letters.

I can never remember how to spell *broccoli.*

Be sure to pronounce the final *e* in *Nike.*

Italics are used to show that words are to be emphasized.

The boss is *very* hard to get along with today.

Joan loaned the tape to Robert, and *he* gave it to Sally.

[/] FORWARD SLASH (ALSO CALLED "SOLIDUS" OR "VIRGULE")

A *forward slash* is used to separate lines of poetry within the text.

William Blake's stanza on anger in "A Poison Tree" seems as appropriate today as when it was first written: "I was angry with my friend: / I told my wrath, my wrath did end. / I was angry with my foe: / I told it not, my wrath did grow."

A forward slash is used in dates and fractions.

winter 1998/99

the fiscal year 2000/01

$3/4 + 2/3$

$x/y - y/x$

Options and alternatives are separated by a forward slash.

I have never seen the advantage of pass/fail courses.

['] APOSTROPHE

An *apostrophe* is used in contractions to show where letters or numerals have been omitted.

I'm

he's

didn't

won't

let's

Ma'am

four o'clock

readin', 'ritin', an' 'rithmetic

the class of '99

An apostrophe is used when making letters or numbers plural.

GI's

V.I.P.'s

figure 8's

The handwriting is very hard to read: the *n*'s and *u*'s look alike.

The number of PhD's awarded to U.S. citizens declined in the 1980's.

Note: The apostrophe may be omitted in dates: 1980s.

The apostrophe is used with nouns to show possession.

The company's management resisted the union's demands.

An apostrophe plus *s* is added to all words—singular or plural—that do not end in -*s* to show possession.

> the little boy's hat
>
> the front office's idea
>
> children's literature
>
> a week's vacation
>
> somebody else's fault
>
> the mice's tails

Just an apostrophe is added at the end of plural words that end in -*s* to show possession.

> the little boys' hats
>
> the farmers' demands
>
> the Joneses' yard
>
> two weeks' vacation
>
> the oil companies' profits
>
> for old times' sake

Style guides disagree on how to treat singular nouns that end in -*s*. Perhaps the best practice is to follow your own pronunciation. If the possessive form has an extra syllable, then add an apostrophe and *s*; otherwise just add an apostrophe.

> Tess's bad luck
>
> Socrates' worldview
>
> for goodness' sake
>
> Williams's poems
>
> Dickens' (or Dickens's) novels

the class's attitude

Ulysses' voyage

Marx's philosophy

The possessive of compound words or two or more proper names is formed by adding an apostrophe plus *s* to the last word of the compound.

sister-in-law's job

editor-in-chief's pen

Japan and Germany's agreement

Lewis and Clark's expedition

the University of South Carolina's mascot

one another's books

anyone else's property

> *Note:* Never use an apostrophe with a possessive personal pronoun. These personal pronouns are already possessive and therefore have no need for an apostrophe: *my, mine, your, yours, her, hers, its, our, ours, their,* and *theirs.*

[-] HYPHEN

Although a *hyphen* and a dash may appear to be the same at first glance, they are two very different marks of punctuation. The dash is more than twice as long as the hyphen. The hyphen is used to group words and parts of words together, while the dash is used to clarify sentence structure. A dash is formed by typing two successive hyphens (--) on a word processor that does not have a dash character.

A hyphen is used at the end of a line of text when part of a word must be carried over to the next line.

. . . insta-

bility

Hyphens are sometimes used to form compound words.

twenty-five

three-fourths

forty-one sixty-fourths

mother-in-law

president-elect

double-breasted

self-confidence

ex-wife

hands-on

the nineteen-eighties

In certain situations, hyphens are used between prefixes and root words to prevent confusion in pronunciation or to avoid confusing a word with another whose spelling is identical. If you are uncertain about a particular word, consult a dictionary.

catlike vs. bull-like

antibiotic vs. anti-intellectual

semiliterate vs. semi-invalid

recover vs. re-cover

coop vs. co-op

recreation vs. re-creation

When the root word of a compound is a proper noun or proper adjective, a hyphen is used to separate the prefix.

anti-American

neo-Nazi

non-European

pro-French

Hyphens are used to combine the elements of a compound modifier when used before the noun it modifies.

hand-to-hand combat

a well-dressed woman

a double-parked car

an out-of-work actor

an up-to-date dictionary

These modifiers are usually not hyphenated when they follow the noun, unless the compound is so common that it has become fixed.

They fought hand to hand.

She is always very well dressed.

The car was double parked.

She is out of work.

The dictionary is up-to-date.

When two modifiers are joined together, common elements are often not repeated.

This textbook covers both macro- and microeconomics.

The study included fourth-, eighth-, and twelfth-grade students.

CAPITALIZATION

The important words in titles are *capitalized*. This includes the first and last words and all other words except articles, prepositions, and coordinating conjunctions, such as *and, but,* and *or.* The second element of a hyphenated compound is also not capitalized unless it is a proper noun or adjective.

Gone With the Wind

With Malice toward None

The Universe Within

Sports-related Injuries

The Brain: A User's Manual

A World to Lose

The Great War, 1914-1918

Twentieth-Century Views

Proper nouns—names of specific people, places, organizations, groups, events, etc.—are capitalized, as are the proper adjectives derived from them.

Martin Luther King, Jr.

United States Coast Guard

New Orleans

Canada

Latinos

Spanish Civil War

Canadian

Jeffersonian

When proper nouns and adjectives have taken on a specialized meaning, they are often no longer capitalized.

My brother ordered a turkey sandwich with russian dressing.

The shop specializes in china and plaster of paris ornaments.

The address was written in india ink on a manila envelope.

Titles of people are capitalized when they are used before a name or when they are used in place of a name to refer to the specific person who holds the title. They are not capitalized when they refer to the office rather than to the person.

Queen Victoria reigned from 1837 to 1901. The Queen's husband, Prince Albert, died in 1861. Some of England's greatest novels were written while she was queen.

President Lincoln was assassinated in 1865. The President and his wife were attending a performance at Ford's Theater. During the years he was president, the South seceded from the Union, and the Civil War began.

Kinship terms are capitalized when they are used before a name or alone in place of a name. They are not capitalized when they are preceded by modifiers.

I'm expecting Aunt Alice to drop by this weekend.

I forgot to call Mother on her birthday.

I forgot to call my mother on her birthday.

Geographical features are capitalized when they are part of the official name. In the plural, they are capitalized when they precede names, but not when they follow.

The Sonoran Desert is in southern Arizona.

The Arizona desert is beautiful in the spring.

In recent years, Lakes Erie and Ontario have been cleaned up.

The Hudson and Mohawk rivers are both in New York State.

Points of the compass are capitalized only when they are used as the name of a section of the country.

We've been driving east for over two hours.

We visited the South last summer and the Southwest the year before.

He was born in southwestern Nebraska.

PRONUNCIATION

Pronunciation is more or less standardized, but of course there are exceptions. Sometimes a word may have two approved pronunciations. Take *either*. It can be pronounced with the first "e" as in *bee*. Or it can be pronounced with the first "e" sounding like an "i," as in *tiger*. Both are correct, but most people seem to prefer the strong *e*.

In addition, our language is not always pronounced the way it's written, as it is in some foreign languages. This is a common complaint of nonnative speakers who are learning English. For example, the word *coax* seems like it should be pronounced *co-ax*. But instead it is pronounced *c-oks*. This can be quite frustrating.

Your dictionary is your greatest aid when trying to learn the pronunciation of English words. Most words have more than one syllable, and so the question of emphasis comes into play. In multisyllable words, one, or some, syllables are stressed and others are not. If, for example, you take the word *reverberation,* when you look it up (if you don't know this already), you'll discover that it has five syllables and that the stress is on the fourth syllable.

To prepare you for consulting the dictionary, you can review this pronunciation key:

PRONUNCIATION KEY

STRESS. The symbol (ʹ), as in **mother** (muthʹer), and **red′ wine′**, marks primary stress; any syllable immediately followed by (ʹ) is pronounced with greater emphasis than syllables not marked (ʹ). The symbol (ʹ), as used following the second syllables of **grand- mother** (grandʹ muthʹer), and **ice′ wa′ter**, marks secondary stress; a syllable marked for secondary stress is pronounced with less emphasis than one marked (ʹ) but with more than those bearing no stress mark.

a	act, bat, marry	f	fit, differ, puff	l	low, mellow, all, bottle	ou	out, loud, cow	û(r)	urge, burn, cur
ā	age, paid, say	g	give, trigger, beg			p	pot, supper, stop	v	voice, river, live
â(r)	air, dare, Mary			m	my, summer, him			w	witch, away
ä	ah, part, balm	h	hit, behave, hear						
b	back, cabin, cab					r	read, hurry, near	y	yes, onion
ch	child, teacher, beach	hw	which, nowhere	n	now, sinner, on, button	s	see, passing, miss	z	zoo, lazy, those
		i	if, big, mirror, furniture			sh	shoe, fashion, push	zh	treasure, mirage
d	do, madder, bed	ī	ice, bite, pirate, deny	ng	sing, Washington				
e	edge, set merry			o	ox, bomb, wasp	t	ten, matter, bit	ə	occurs in unac- cented syllables to indicate the sound of the reduced vowel in:
ē	equal, seat, bee, mighty	j	just, tragic, fudge	ō	over, boat, no	th	thin, ether, path		
				ô	order, ball, raw	t͟h	that, either, smooth		
ėr	ear, mere	k	keep, token, make	oi	oil, joint, joy	u	up, sun		
				o͝o	book, tour				
				o͞o	ooze, fool, too				

occurs between ī and r and between ou and r to show triph- thongal quality, as in **fire** (fī^ər), **hour** (ou^ər).

alone
system
easily
gallop
circus

ABBREVIATIONS

In standard academic, scientific, business, or other formal writing, abbreviations are generally avoided unless they are the commonly required ones and are specifically known and accepted terms within a particular discipline or trade.

Some abbreviations that are acceptable in journalistic or business writing may not be appropriate in extremely formal announcement or invitations in which even dates may be spelled out.

Abbreviations are often used in ordering and billing, catalogs, tabulations, telephone books, classified advertising, recordkeeping, scorekeeping, and similar cases where brevity is essential.

In some cases, the decision to use an abbreviation is a matter of individual preference. It is usually prudent to use the spelled-out form the first time the term is used in a piece of writing. Thereafter, one should be consistent in using either the written-out or the abbreviated form. As in all writing, it is most important to maintain consistency of usage within any single written document, whether it be a letter or a treatise.

Use abbreviations in writing:

1. The following titles and forms of address whenever they precede a proper name: *Mr., Mrs., Ms., Dr., Mme., M.* Do not spell out these titles even in the most formal contexts.

Mlle. Modiste	Dr. Jekyll
Mr. Hyde	Mme. Marie Curie
Ms. O'Hara	Mrs. Lopez

2. Titles of the clergy, government officials, officers of organizations, and military personnel, except in an extremely formal context and provided that the title is followed by a first name or initial as well as a surname. If the title is followed only by a surname, it should be spelled out.

Gen. George Armstrong Custer	General Custer
Sgt. Leon Greene	Sergeant Greene
Prof. Barbara Page	Professor Page
Gov. Mario Cuomo	Governor Cuomo
Rev. John McDermott	The Reverend John Mc-Dermott *or* The Reverend Dr. (or Mr.) McDermott
Hon.	The Honorable Harvey Douglas *or* The Honorable Mr. Douglas

Note above that in very formal writing, the title *Honorable* or *Reverend* is spelled out and is preceded by *The*. When the first name or initial is omitted the title *Mr.* or *Dr.* is substituted.

3. *Jr.* or *Sr.* following a name. These abbreviations should be added only when the names preceding them include a first name or initial.

4. *Esq.* following a name. Not a common usage in the United States, this abbreviation should not be used with any other title.

   James Grant, Esq. (*not* Mr. James Grant, Esq.)

5. Academic degrees: *BA* (Bachelor of Arts); *MA* (Master of Arts); *MS* (Master of Science); *PhD* (Doctor of Philosophy); *MD* (Doctor of Medicine), etc. When a person's name is followed by a scholastic degree or by the abbreviations of religious or fraternal orders (e.g., BPOE), it should not be preceded by *Mr., Miss, Dr.*, or any other title.

6. The terms used to describe business firms (*Co., Corp., Inc., Bro.* or *Bros., Ltd., R.R.* or *Ry.*) only when these abbreviations are part of the legally authorized name. In all other

cases (except for brevity in tables, listings, etc.), *Company, Corporation, Incorporated, Brothers, Limited, Railroad,* and *Railway* should be spelled out.

7. Except in formal writing, the names of states, territories, or possessions that immediately follow the name of a city, mountain, airport, or other specific geographic location. Check the dictionary for all such abbreviations. In addressing mail, authorized postal abbreviations (e.g., CA) should be used.

    Detroit, Mich.
    San Juan, P.R.

8. Certain expressions derived from Latin and more common in their abbreviated forms.

    i.e. (*id est*), that is
    e.g. (*exempli gratia*), for example
    et al. (*et alii*), and others
    etc. (et cetera), and so forth

Do not abbreviate:

1. Names of countries except:

    U.S. (United States) when preceding the name of an American ship. The abbreviation *U.S.* may also be used in tables, footnotes, etc., or, in all but the most formal writing, as an attributive modifier: *U.S. Congress, U.S. Post Office, U.S. economic policies,* etc.

2. The days of the week or the months of the year except in the most informal situations or in tables.

3. Weights and measures except in lists of items, technical writing, etc.

I had hoped to lose ten pounds.
We used ten yards of cloth

Do not use a period after the following abbreviations or shortened forms:

1. After a contraction, which is not to be confused with an abbreviation. Contractions contain apostrophes that indicate omitted letters; they never end with a period.

   sec't'y or sec'y   sec.
   Nat'l   natl.

2. After chemical symbols.

   H_2O NaCl

3. After *percent*.

4. After specific military terms.

   USA   United States Army
   USMC   United States Marine Corps
   USN   United States Navy
   USNR   United States Naval Reserve
   USCG   United States Coast Guard
   USNG   United States National Guard
   MP   military police
   SP   shore patrol
   POW   prisoner of war
   APO   Army post office

5. After the initials of certain governmental agencies or call letters of television and radio stations.

   NATO, UNICEF, CIA, CARE, POEC, KCTS Seattle, WQXR New York.

6. After letters that are used as symbols rather than initials.

Let us assume that A and B are playing opposite C and D.

7. After listed items (as in catalogs, outlines, or syllabi), if none of the items is a complete sentence. If the list includes only one complete sentence, use a period after this and all other items on the list, including those which are not complete sentences. Consistency is essential: a period after each item or no end punctuation whatever.

8. After points of the compass.

NE	SW
ESE	E by NE

RULES FOR USING NUMBERS

In general, numbers that can be stated in only one or two words are spelled out.

There were twelve girls and twenty-six boys present.

The sweater cost sixty dollars.

He gave one-tenth of his income to charity.

Other numbers are usually shown in figures.

There are 392 members in the association.

The radio cost him $136.50

The population of Chicago in 1980 was 3,005,072.

Any numeral at the beginning of a sentence is usually spelled out. If this is awkwardly long or difficult to read, rewrite the sentence to avoid beginning with a numeral.

> Three hundred and sixty students attended the dance.
>
> Twenty-six million votes were cast for him.
>
> Six thousand dollars was stolen from the safe.

It is important to be consistent in the treatment of numbers when they appear in the same series or in the same sentence or paragraph. When they are in close sequence, do not spell out some and use figures for others.

> The three chairs are 36, 72, and 122 years old.
>
> He spent $800 on rent, $90 on food, and $265 on clothes.

Use figures (generally) for dates, decades, pages, dimensions, decimals, percentages, measures, statistical data, exact amounts of money, designations of time when followed by A.M. or P.M., and addresses.

June 24, 1945	2.5 cm	£12.95
the 1920's	0.9631	96.8°
124 B.C.	23 percent	86%
p. 263	75 pounds	8:30 A.M.
p. xxvi	93 miles	3:20 P.M.
2' x 4'	$369.27	4262 B Street

Spell out ordinal numbers whenever possible.

sixteenth century	Fifth Avenue
Eighty-second Congress	Third Republic
Third Assembly District	Twenty-third Psalm

A common rule for the styling of numbers that is used by many magazines, newspapers, and editorial departments is to spell out only numbers from one through ten and larger round or approximate numbers.

SECTION QUIZ

NOW that you've read the section on Punctuation, see how much you've learned by taking the quiz below.

I. **Insert commas wherever necessary in the following sentences.**

1. Bill is finishing his graduate studies and Sally is going into the Navy.

2. Ideally she'll want to go to Paris to model.

3. However it is important to see the best possible alternatives.

4. We can I trust agree on the details.

5. Given an early education in economics he wasn't about to give up his postion.

6. His most recent painting finished in 1999 was never sold.

7. Germany France and Spain are all part of Europe.

8. He was born on Wednesday July 11 1978 in a children's hospital in Eugene Oregon.

9. After she ate the cat curled up and went to sleep.

II. **Insert a semicolon or a colon wherever necessary in the following sentences.**

1. The house burned down it was the last shattering blow.

2. This I believe All people are created equal.

3. In the next few weeks they plan to begin racing in Louisville, Kentucky Carson City, Nevada and Escondido, California.

4. There is only one answer everyone must stop using salt.

III. **Match the punctuation mark with its name.**

!	dash
:	hyphen
. . .	question mark
" "	exclamation mark
-	parentheses
—	apostrophe
'	elipsis
?	semicolon
.	quotation marks
;	brackets
( )	colon
[ ]	period

IV. **The following paragraph contains a number of errors. Can you spot them all?**

Mrs Davis couldnt remember whether she was supposed to buy carrots or celery for dinner. She looked at the clock. It was 12 Pm. She had some errands to do before she could go to the supermarket. "Ive got enough money-I think," she said a loud. 'But maybe I should go to the bank first. Then Ill just buy both vegetables and not worry about it.' She

went to the garage, got into her car with her shopping basket and put it into gear. She drove to the bank parked the car
walked inside and took out some money from her account.
Then she did her errands and drove quick to the supermarket. She was home in time to see her favorite tv show.

ANSWERS

To learn more about the subjects covered in this quiz, refer back to
the page numbers listed below.

I. **Insert commas wherever necessary in the following sentences. (See page 255 for more info.)**

1. Bill is finishing his graduate studies, and Sally is going into the Navy.

2. Ideally, she'll want to go to Paris to model.

3. However, it is important to see the best possible alternatives.

4. We can, I trust, agree on the details.

5. Given an early education in economics, he wasn't about to give up his postion.

6. His most recent painting, finished in 1999, was never sold.

7. Germany, France, and Spain are all part of Europe.

8. He was born on Wednesday, July 11, 1978, in a children's hospital in Eugene, Oregon.

9. After she ate, the cat curled up and went to sleep.

II. Insert a semicolon or a colon wherever necessary in the following sentences. (See pages 260–264 for more info.)

1. The house burned down; it was the last shattering blow.

2. This I believe: All people are created equal.

3. In the next few weeks they plan to begin racing in Louisville, Kentucky; Carson City, Nevada; and Escondido, California.

4. There is only one answer: everyone must stop using salt.

III. Match the punctuation mark with its name.

!   exclamation mark

:   colon

. . .   elipsis

" "   quotation marks

-   hyphen

—   dash

'   apostrophe

?   question mark

.   period

;   semicolon

( )   parentheses

[ ]   brackets

ANSWERS TO QUIZ IV:

Mrs (should be *Mrs.* Davis) couldnt (should be *couldn't*) re-member whether she was supposed to buy carrots or celery for dinner. She looked at the clock. It was 12 Pm (should be *P.M.*). She had some errands to do before she could go to the supermarket. "Ive (should be *I've*) got enough money- (should be a dash: *enough money—I think*) I think," she said a loud (should be *aloud*). ' (should be quotation mark (") at beginning and end of this sentence) But maybe I should go to the bank first. Then Ill (should be *I'll*) just buy both vegetables and not worry about it.' She went to the garage, got into her car with her shopping basket and put it (should be *put the car* to avoid ambiguity) into gear. She drove to the bank parked the car walked inside and took out some money from her account (should have commas following *bank, car, inside*). Then she did her errands and drove quick (should be *quickly*) to the supermarket. She was home in time to see her favorite tv (should be *TV*) show.

SECTION V

Writing

GETTING STARTED

THE rules of usage, punctuation, and grammar are just cold facts unless they're employed toward clear, comprehensive, and effective writing. Writing consists of two parts—determining what to say, and then saying it clearly and concisely. It sounds simple enough, but in practice can be difficult. One easy way to efficiently accomplish this goal is to make a rudimentary outline of your essay. Not only will it help organize your thoughts, but it will serve as a guidepost and save you time as you write.

Don't let the task of writing intimidate you. Anything you write, you can change, alter, rearrange, or toss. Also, remember that every writer can seek help, either through a book like this, or friends, or mentors, or all of the above. So, don't be shy about reaching out.

The critical thing is to get a draft down. You can't improve on something if there's nothing there! Here are a few things to keep in mind as you write:

- **Showing is much more effective than telling.** For example, which statement is stronger, "The river was foul," or "The scum of oil floated on the river, along with old tires, used diapers, and old plastic bottles"? It's the latter, because the reader can come to the conclusion that the river was "foul" on their own. Instead of saying, "The woman was very beautiful," why not say something like, "She was the kind of woman who when she walked into a room made even married men reconsider."

- **Let the facts speak for themselves.** Sometimes, it's better to keep your opinion out of your prose. "How anyone cannot be swayed by the fact that 50,000 teenagers begin smoking every year is beyond me," dissipates the strength of the simple statement that every year 50,000 teenagers start smoking. That fact is strong and stark enough to do the job of shocking and convincing the reader.

- **Avoid common grammatical mistakes.** We've covered these in earlier sections of the book, but it might be helpful to review the section on "Shifts," (page 126) so that you avoid shifts in tense, voice, mood, and perspective. The section on parallelism (page 137) is also helpful, as it is very easy to shift from one form to another. Instead of writing, "William was hot, cranky, and needed food," it's better—and clearer—to write, "William was hot, cranky, and hungry."

- **Spelling and punctuation *do* matter.** You can consult previous sections of this book for help. We also recommend having a good dictionary handy.

- **Revising is a necessary part of writing.** For some people, the idea is pure drudgery, but look at it this way—revising is an opportunity to make your prose better. You can revise each day after you write. When you're finished for the day, read it over from the beginning and see what jumps out at you. Clunky phrasing will reveal itself, as will weak metaphors, limp analogies, tired exposition, and mediocre word choices. A more substantial revision can occur once the work is completed. If you wait at least a day or two after you have finished your writing, the passage of time lets your mind refresh itself and see the work from a new perspective.

WRITING A TERM PAPER

L ET'S break it down in terms of writing a term paper:
A term paper, or any research paper, calls upon the writer to focus on an assigned or chosen topic, gather and interpret source materials, marshal arguments, and organize, document, and expess ideas forcefully.

A term paper may be a factual inquiry, an anlysis of causes and effects, or an account or interpretation of events, ideas, or themes. It may explain or analyze a phenomenon or describe an experience. But whether it is basically informative, argumentative, or narrative, it should always be (1) clear of purpose, (2) unslanted (not omitting contrary evidence), (3) concise and to the point, and (4) well documented, with sources acknowledged in footnotes and/or a bibliography.

Begin the assignment as early as possible, to allow time for proper research, for rethinking the subject or approach, and for reorganizing and revising the paper.

THE SUBJECT

The subject and scope of the term paper should be neither too ambitious nor too narrow or technical in scope. Do not pose a question whose answer is too obvious or address an issue whose solution is self-evident. First make sure that adequate information on the topic is conveniently available. If there is a choice of topics, make a preliminary visit to the library for exploratory reading and research before making the final choice.

Remember that the term paper has not only a subject but a thesis. Your thoughts and conclusions, not those of other writers, are the essence of the paper. These personal thoughts and conclusions, however, must be well oranized and supported by the research.

LIBRARY RESEARCH

The student who knows how to use the library and all its resources will avoid many problems in researching. Although the primary sources and direct information (as from interviews) are valuable for certain topics, it is usually the books, journals, microfilm, etc., available in the reference room of the library that form the backbone of the term paper.

Particularly useful souces, in addition to books on the subject, are (1) encyclopedias; (2) the *Readers' Guide to Periodical Literature* (for leads to pertinent magazine and journal articles); (3) book bibliographies and cross-references that lead to other usable sources; and, with some subjects, (4) government agencies and private organizations and their publications. Make a preliminary list of sources that promise to be helpful; the paper's final bibliography will come from this list. Many librarians will do online research for you (often for a fee), giving you access to material in electronic databases.

While reading, take systematic notes, organizing and explaining various aspects of the topic. Taking notes on index cards will facilitate the sorting and rearranging of information. If you prefer using a notebook, write on one side only of each page so that the pages can be pulled out and rearranged later. Some students enter their notes into a computer, so that they may take advantage of electronic or word-processing programs to organize their data.

While taking notes, record not only factual information but also relevant quotations, questions that come to mind, and personal observations and ideas. It is also helpful to summarize various points as you go along—in your own words, not those of the authors consulted. This will make the actual writing of the paper easier and lessen the risk of inadvertent plagiarism. Research sources (with title, author, page number, and all necessary bibliographic information) for both quotations and paraphrases should be written down carefully on first reading, to avoid having to recheck later.

INTERNET RESEARCH

Internet research can be divided into two parts: the research that you can do on your home computer, and the research that you can do on a public library database (which includes online versions of books that have been indexed and can be searched by subject, keyword, name, etc.).

The Internet at home can be a huge resource. There are many institutions whose official Web sites contain trusted, factual information. The main portal for U.S. government Web sites is *www.usa.gov*, and it can lead you to scores of Web sites—from libraries to museums to information on the military and farming and the environment, and so on. Each of these Web sites has substantial resources and documents you can download for free. The United Nations (*www.un.org*) is another great resource. In addition, more and more scientists are posting their research on the Internet, often through nonprofit organizations (The World Wildlife Fund and The Union of Concerned Scientists are two examples).

Armed with a vast array of Internet sources from the comfort of your home computer, you may feel reluctant to make the trip to the library to seek more facts. However, keep in mind that sometimes it is difficult to distinguish between what is a vetted, scholarly resource and what is not. The very useful Wikipedia, used by millions, describes itself as "the free encyclopedia that anyone can edit." Researchers, beware. If you are writing a paper, you need to quote reliable sources.

OUTLINE

An outline helps the writer not only to plan the overall paper but also to organize and develop individual sections and ideas. Based on the research notes and sequentially arranged, the outline helps to crystallize the major and supporting points to be made and the step-by-step presentation required. Preparing the outline will also help you decide how best to organize the material: chronologically, by category, or in some other logical way.

Many students make a sketchy outline early in their research stage, then revise and expand it as the research continues. A topic outline, indicating the sequence of ideas and subtopics, may later be expanded into a paragraph outline, which expresses these points as complete, final units and which may grow into the final term paper.

WRITING

Before beginning the actual writing, have a clear idea of the intended approach of the paper. How formal is it to be? Should it be completely objective and factual, somewhat argumentative, or strong and impassioned?

Beginning the actual writing often seems the hardest part of the term paper. Begin at all costs, even if not satisfied with the opening sentence or paragraph; this can be improved later. (Some find it easier to start in the middle of the paper or even with the conclusion, and to write the beginning later.)

There are four standard openings with which to begin a term paper: a summary sentence, a defining statement, a quotation, or a posed question. As you write, remember: (1) The thesis should be made clear to the reader at the very beginning of the paper. What are you setting out to discuss or prove? (2) The purport of each paragraph should be made clear by a topic, or key, sentence, usually the first sentence of the paragraph. (3) Depending on the nature of the paper, first-person references—such as "I" and "me"—should be avoided or minimized.

Do not expect to write a good term paper in just one draft. A second and third draft will almost always be necessary. In the first draft concentrate on substance and organization. Grammar, sentence construction, and spelling can be corrected later. Leave nothing of substance out of the first draft: it will be easier to shorten the paper later than to add to it. (See the earlier sections of this book for proper manuscript preparation, footnotes and bibliography, etc.)

After the first draft has been read and reread, it should be rewritten and reorganized as much as necessary. Use of scissors and tape or glue can be helpful in reordering or inserting material; a word processor or computer can ease this part of the process.

The final manuscript should be as perfect as you can make it in all ways: in organization, clarity, and style; in grammar, punctuation, and spelling; and in exactness of quotations, footnotes, and bibliography. It should be clear and to the point, and free of pretentious words, of overly long sentences, and of digressions. Footnotes or parenthetical acknowledgments should be scrupulously incorporated wherever there is a debt to another source for a specific idea or quotation, or to another writer's statement of "fact" that is clearly debatable or controversial. On the other hand, do not quote or footnote excessively: a term paper is meant to be a documented presentation of your themes or ideas, not a dense, pedantic recitation of material from other sources. It is the use of research material, the process of reasoning, personal insights, and writing skills that are the essence of the term paper.

Once you have done your research, you will need to cite your sources. Below is the proper method for using footnotes and bibliographies.

FOOTNOTES

Footnotes serve a variety of purposes: to indicate the source of a fact, opinion, or quotation; to provide additional or explanatory material that, although relevant, would interrupt the flow of the main text; and to cross-refer the reader to another part of the text. Excessive use of footnotes, however, is usually distracting; it is the sign, generally, of spurious scholarship or of pedantry.

Material in the text to which footnotes are to be keyed should be numbered with superscript Arabic numerals ([1], [2], [3], [4], etc.). These numerals are usually placed without intervening space at the close of a sentence, quotation, or paragraph, unless doing so would cause confusion or ambiguity (in which case the numeral is placed within the sentence, after the specific word, phrase, or name to which it refers).

Footnote numbers should continue consecutively throughout an article or chapter, with the numbering beginning again in each chapter.

Some writers prefer to use special symbols (*, †, ‡, §, ||, ¶, etc.) instead of superscript numerals. Because this system of symbols is limited and confusing, it is preferably avoided.

Footnotes are placed at the bottom of the page under a straight line that extends from the left to the right margins. (Some style manuals suggest that this line extend only two or three inches in from the left margin.) One line of space is left blank above this separation line and two lines of space are left blank below it. The footnote, which begins with the appropriate superscript number without a space after it, is usually typed single-space. The first line of the footnote is the same indentation used throughout the text itself; subsequent lines are typed to the same margins as the text itself. Avoid carrying footnotes onto a following page if at all possible.

BOOKS: FIRST FOOTNOTE REFERENCES

When a book is first mentioned in a footnote, the bibliographical information should be as complete as possible. The information should appear in the following order:

1. **Author's name or authors' names.** Normal word order is used. The given name or initials are given first, using the form in which the name is generally encountered, the surname being followed by a comma.

2. **Title of the chapter or part.** When reference is made to an article in a collection, symposium, or the like, the title of the article appears within quotation marks, the final quotation mark being preceded by a comma.

3. **Title of the book.** The title is underlined (to indicate italics) and followed by a comma unless the next information is in parentheses; in such a case, the comma follows the closing parentheses. If the title is exceptionally long, it may be shortened by omissions (indicated by three ellipsis points in each case). The title should be given as it is shown on the title page of the book cited.

4. **Editor's or translator's name.** The name of the editor or translator, given in its full and normal form, is preceded by "ed." or "trans." It is followed by a comma unless the next material is in parentheses.

5. **Edition used.** If the edition is other than the first one, the edition is identified in Arabic numerals, followed by a comma unless the next material is in parentheses.

6. **Series title.** The name of the series is shown without underlining or quotation marks. It is followed by the specific number of the work in the series, preceded and followed by commas. If the next material is in parentheses, the second comma is placed after the closing parenthesis.

7. **Number of volumes.** If there is more than one volume in the work and it appears relevant to indicate this fact, the number is shown in Arabic numerals.

8. **Place of publication.** This information, plus the name of the publisher and date of publication, is shown within one set of parentheses. The place of publication is usually found on the title page: if more than one city is shown, it is necessary only to show the publisher's main place of activity. If the city is not well known or might be confused with another of the same name, add the state or nation. The place of publication is followed by a colon.

9. **Name of the publisher.** The name of the company, institution, etc., that published the work is shown next, followed by a comma.

10. **Date of publication.** The date of publication is usually found on the copyright page or title page. If no date is shown on either, write "n.d." (without quotation marks) to indicate "no date." The parentheses containing the place of publication, publisher's name, and date of publication is followed by a comma. When several dates are shown on a copyright page only the earliest need be given. But the date of the latest *edition* is always pertinent.

11. **Volume number.** If there are two or more volumes in the work, give the volume number in capital Roman numerals, enclosed by commas. If this information is followed by the page number, omit "Vol." and give the volume number only, followed by a comma.

12. **Page number or numbers.** The page number (preceded by "p.") is shown in Arabic numerals (unless the original uses Roman numerals), followed by a period. However, if the volume number has been given, the "p." may be omitted. In the case of a reference to several sequential pages, "pp." rather than "p." is used.

ARTICLES IN PERIODICALS: FIRST FOOTNOTE REFERENCES

When a magazine or newspaper article is referred to in a footnote for the first time, the bibliographical information is given in the following order:

1. **Author's name or authors' names.** The name is given in normal order and usual form, followed by a comma.

2. **Title of the article.** The title is given in full, enclosed by quotation marks, with a comma preceding the closing quotation mark.

3. **Name of the periodical.** The name of the periodical, underlined to indicate italics, is followed by a comma. If there is a familiar abbreviation of the name of the periodical, it may be used.

4. **Volume number.** The volume number in capital Roman numerals is followed by a comma unless the next item is within parentheses.

5. **Issue number or name.** If the pagination of each issue is separate and the issue is not designated by month, give the issue number or name.

6. **Year and month.** The month (if necessary) and year of the volume are enclosed by parentheses followed by a comma.

7. **Page number or numbers.** The page number (preceded by "p.") or numbers (preceded by "pp.") are given in Arabic numerals (unless the original text uses Roman numerals) and terminated with a period. However, if the volume number has been given, the "p." may be omitted.

SUBSEQUENT FOOTNOTE REFERENCES

After the first footnote reference to a book, article, or the like, it is unnecessary to repeat all the bibliographical information in each reference to the same work.

If a footnote reference is the same work as the preceding footnote, use "ibid." (Latin: *ibidem* "in the same place") in place of all bibliographical information. If a different volume or page of the same work is to be indicated, this information follows "ibid." and a comma.

If "ibid." might be used if it were not for the intervention of references to other works, some writers use either "op cit." (Latin: *opere citato* "in the work cited") or "loc. cit." (*loco citato* "in the cited place") after the author's surname to avoid restatement of all the bibliographical data when the volume (and, with "loc. cit.," page) is the same as that of the first footnote reference to the work.

Many writers prefer to avoid "op. cit." and "loc. cit." as well as "ibid." by simply giving the author's surname, followed by the year of publication and page number, in parentheses in the body of the text. The page number may be preceded by either a comma or a colon.

(Taylor 1880, 944)

(Dilworth 1986:328–333)

When the author's name is part of the text, the year and page number form the parenthetical reference.

This information can be found in Lazarsfeld et al. (1944:61), and is substantiated by . . .

COMMON ABBREVIATIONS IN FOOTNOTES

The following abbreviations are commonly encountered in footnotes:

anon.	anonymous
ch. (chs.)	chapter (chapters)
chap. (chaps.)	chapter (chapters)
col.	column
comp.	compiled
ed.	editor; edition
esp.	especially
f. (ff.)	and the following page (pages)
n.d.	no date
no. (nos.)	number (numbers)
n.s.	new series
p. (pp.)	page (pages)
pass.	(*passim*) throughout

repr.	reprint; reprinted
rev.	revised
ser.	series
supp., suppl.	supplement
tr., trans.	translator; translation
vol. (vols.)	volume (volumes)

SAMPLE FOOTNOTES: FIRST REFERENCE

A book by one author, first edition:

[4]Telford Taylor, *Munich: The Price of Peace* (New York: Vintage Books, 1980), p. 944.

A book by one author, revised or later edition:

[2]James B. Dilworth, *Production and Operations Management,* 3d ed. (New York: Random House, 1986), pp. 328–333.

A book by two or more authors:

[2]Mary Luisa and Jack Denton Scott, *The Complete Rice Cookbook* (New York: Times Books, 1985), p. 68.

[3]P. F. Lazarsfeld, B. Berelson, and H. Gaudet, *The People's Choice* (New York: Duell, Sloan, and Pearce, 1944), p. 61–3.

A book having one or more editors:

[4]Peter Russell, ed., *An Examination of Ezra Pound* (Norfolk, Conn.: New Directions, 1950), pp. 14–23.

[5]William Van O'Connor and Edward Stone, eds., *A Casebook on Ezra Pound* (New York: Thomas Y. Crowell, 1959), p. 137.

A book having an author and an editor:

[3]Thomas Robert Malthus, *On Population,* ed. Gertrude Himmelfarb (New York: The Modern Library, 1960), p. xxvii.

A book having a translator:

[4]Andrei Amalrik, *Notes of a Revolutionary,* trans. Guy Daniels (New York: Alfred A. Knopf, 1982), p. 193.

A book in several volumes:

[1]Dennis Sherman, ed., *Western Civilization: Images and Interpretations* (New York: Alfred A. Knopf, 1983), II, pp. 104–106.

A book in a series:

[3]Arthur S. Link, *Woodrow Wilson and the Progressive Era, 1910–1917,* New American Nation Series (New York: Harper, 1954), pp.16–31.

An article in an edited collection of contributions:

[2]Herbert H. Rowen, "Kingship and Republicanism in the Seventeenth Century: Some Reconsiderations," in *From the Renaissance to the Counter-Reformation,* ed. by Charles H. Carter (New York: Random House, 1965), p. 430.

An unsigned article in an encyclopedia:

[3]"Rivers and Lakes," *The Random House Encyclopedia,* 1983, p. 258.

A signed article in an encyclopedia:

[2]Edgar Frederick Carritt, "Aesthetics," *Encyclopedia Britannica*, 1956, I, 265–267.

An unsigned article in a periodical:

[3]"About the MLA Convention," *PMLA*, CI (November, 1986), pp. 932–937.

A signed article in a periodical:

[12]Roger I. Glass, "New Prospects for Epidemiologic Investigations," *Science*, Vol. 234, No. 4779 (Nov. 21, 1986), pp. 951–955.

A bulletin report or pamphlet:

[13]United Nations, *Measures for the Economic Development of Under-Developed Countries* (New York: United Nations, 1951), pp. 8–9.

[14]*Education: An Answer to Poverty*, The Office of Education and the Office of Economic Opportunity (Washington, D.C.: Government Printing Office, 1965), pp. 68–70.

An unpublished thesis or dissertation:

[3]L. S. Yorick, "The Myth of Anchises in Shakespeare's *Hamlet* (unpublished Ph.D. dissertation, Department of English, University of Chicago), p. 9.

A private communication:

[10]Information in a letter to the author from Professor John R. Perry, University of Chicago, September 14, 1987.

SAMPLE FOOTNOTES: SUBSEQUENT REFERENCES

General:

[17]Taylor, p. 947.

[18]Dilworth, pp. 118–32.

[19]Luisa and Scott, p. 112.

(Alternative) Same work and page as in footnote immediately preceding:

[20]Ibid.

(Alternative) Same work and page as in footnote immediately preceding but different page:

[3]Ibid., p. 321.

(Alternative) Same work as previously cited but not in footnote immediately preceding:

[6]Taylor, op. cit., p. 31.

(Alternative) Same work (same page) as previously cited but not in footnote immediately preceding:

[6]Taylor, loc. cit.

BIBLIOGRAPHIES

Although bibliographies may be organized by subject, types of publications cited, chronological sequence, or alphabetical order, alphabetical arrangement by author is, by far, most common. Within the list, a given author's works may be arranged chronologically.

The bibliography should by typed so that the first line of each item begins flush with the left margin and succeeding lines are indented several spaces. The material is usually single-spaced (but double-spaced between items).

The context of bibliographical entries is the same as that of footnotes with only these major differences:

1. **Author's name.** The surname comes first, followed by a comma; then the given name, followed by a period.

2. **Title.** The title is closed by a period.

3. **Publication data.** The place of publication, name of the publisher, and date of publication are not enclosed by parentheses; a period is placed after the date.

SAMPLE ENTRIES

"Controversies in Education: The American High School." *Phi Delta Kappan*, XL (November, 1958), pp. 3–126.

Gide, André. *The André Gide Reader.* Edited by David Littlejohn. New York: Alfred A. Knopf, 1971.

Baum, Andrew, Jeffrey D. Fisher, and Jerome E. Singer. *Social Psychology*. New York: Random House, 1985.

Johnson, E. L. "Cooperation in Higher Education." *Liberal Education*, XLVIII (December 1962).

Russell, Peter (ed.). *An Examination of Ezra Pound.* Norfolk, Conn.:
    New Directions, 1950.

Schwartz, Harry. *Russia's Soviet Economy.* 2d ed. Englewood Cliffs,
    N.J.: Prentice-Hall, 1954.

White, Newman Ivey. *Shelley.* 2 vols. New York: Alfred A. Knopf,
    1940.

When writing for a specific publication or publisher, the author should ask whether there is a preferred house style or style manual to be followed. Among the widely used style manuals are *The Chicago Manual of Style* (published by the University of Chicago Press) and *The MLA Style Sheet* (published by the Modern Language Association).

CITING INTERNET SOURCES

Since the Internet is now one of the chief sources for information, it follows that rules have been formulated for citing Internet sources. Here are some broad categories:

Scholarly Project

The Influence of Biblical Literature on the Idea of Manifest Destiny.
    Ed. Steven Willensky.

April 1998. Stanford U. 2 August 1999 <http://www.stanford.edu/
    ~letrs/iblimd/>.

Information Database

Ginsberg: *Silk Trade Information on the Internet.* 29 March 2003.
    Lib. of Congress, Washington. 22 March 2004 <http://ginsberg.
    loc.gov/>.

Personal Site

Billings, Warren. Home page. 17 May 2006. 15 May 2006 <http://
www.cass.umontreal.ca:9134/~warren/>.

Book

Crowther, Brock. "Life in 18th Century Australian Prisons." *The
Prison Project*. Ed. Stacey Johnson. July 2005. Illinois U. 1 May
2006 <http://www.illinois.edu/~letrs/pp/crowther/ap.html>.

Poem

Frost, Robert. "The Road Not Taken." *Collected Poems*. Ed. William
Johnson. June 2003. Adelphi U. 3 June 2003 <http://www.adelphi.
edu/~letrs/cp/frost.html#p9>.

Article in a Journal

Carson, Rachel. "The Struggle With Obesity." *Modern Medicine*. 2.4
(2003): 3 pars. 4 May 2003 <http://www.unc.edu/mm/02–4/
carson.html>.

Article in a Magazine

Christian, Marcie. "Why Can't Daddy Read?" *Harper's* 3 June 2004.
3 June 2004 <http://www.time.com/wcdr/3472.asp>.

Work from a Library Subscription Service

Miller, Tony. "Corruption in Modern Baseball." *American Journal of
Criminology* 35 (2004): 573–98. Gale. Roanoke County Lib. System, NC. 3 June 2006 <http://www.galegroup.com/>.

Prefixes, Suffixes, and Roots

COMMON PREFIXES AND THEIR MEANINGS

a- **1.** place or state (*ashore, asleep*). **2.** not (*atypical*). **3.** without (*amoral*).

ab- off, away (*abnormal*).

ad- toward (*adhere, adjoin*).

ambi- both (*ambiance, ambiguous, ambivalence*).

ambul- to walk (*ambulatory, amble*).

amphi- both (*amphibian, amphibious*); on two sides (*amphitheater*).

ante- **1.** happening before (*antebellum*). **2.** in front of (*anteroom*).

anti- **1.** against (*antislavery*). **2.** preventing or counteracting (*anticoagulant, anti-freeze*). **3.** destroying or disabling (*antiaircraft, antipersonnel*). **4.** rival of (*Antichrist, antipope*). **5.** identical in some respects (*anticlimax, antihero, antipartical*).

aqua- water (*aquarium*).

audi- to hear (*auditory, audible*).

auto- self (*autograph*).

bene- good (*beneficial, benevolent*).

bi- twice, two (*bicentennial, bigamy, bipartisan, bisect*).

bio- life (*biodegradable, biology*).

centi- hundred (*centipede*); hundredth (*centimeter*).

chron- time (*chronology, chronicle*).

circum- round, around (*circuit, circumvent, circus*).

co- 1. joint (*costar*). 2. auxiliary, helping (*copilot*).

com- (or **con-**) with, together with (*combine, compare, confer, convene*).

con- with, together (*convene, converge*).

contra- against, opposite, opposing (*contraception, contradict, contrary*).

counter- against (*counterattack, counterclockwise*).

de- 1. motion down or away (*deplane, descend*). 2. reversing or undoing the effects of an action (*deflate, dehumanize*). 3. removal of something (*decaffeinate*). 4. finishing or completeness of an action (*defunct, despoil*).

deci- ten (*decibel*).

demi- half (*demigod*).

demo- people (*democracy*).

di- two (*diptych*); double (*dioxide*).

dia- through or across (*diameter, diaphanous*); completely (*diagnosis*).

dict- speak (*dictate, diction*).

dis- 1. opposite of (*disagreement*). 2. not (*disapprove, dishonest, disobey*). 3. reverse; remove (*disconnect, discontinue, dissolve*).

dyna- power (*dynamic, dynasty*).

dys- ill, bad (*dysfunctional, dyslexia, dyspepsia*).

en-[1] 1. to cause (person or thing) to be in (the place or state mentioned); keep or place in (*enrich, entomb*). 2. to restrict completely (*encircle*).

en-[2] in (*enthusiasm*).

epi- 1. on, at (*epicenter*). 2. outer (*epidermis*). 3. additional (*episode*).

equi- equal (*equidistant, equilibrium*).

eu- good, well (*eulogy, euphemism, euphoria*).

ex- 1. out or out of (*exclude, exhale, exit*). 2. former (*ex-member*).

extra- outside of (*extragalactic*) or beyond (*extrasensory*).

fore- 1. before (*forecast, foretaste*). 2. front (*forehead*). 3. preceding (*forefather*). 4. superior (*foreman*).

graph- to write (*graphite, graphic*).

hemi- half (*hemisphere*).

hemo- blood (*hemoglobin*).

hyper- excessive (*hypercritical*); overly (*hypertension*).

hypo- under (*hypodermic*); below (*hypothermia*).

il-[1] (another form of **in-**[1]) in, into (*illuminate*).

il-[2] (another form of **in-**[2]) not (*illegible*).

im-[1] (another form of **in-**[1]) in, into (*immigrate*).

im-[2] (another form of **in-**[2]) not (*impossible*).

in-[1] in, into; on (*income*).

in-[2] not (*inaccurate*).

inter- between or among (*intercity, intercollegiate*).

intra- within (*intraspecies*).

intro- inside (*introduce*).

ir-[1] (another form of **in-**[1]) in, into (*irradiate*).

ir-[2] (another form of **in-**[2]) not (*irreducible*).

kilo- thousand (*kilometer*).

mal- bad (*malfunction*).

mega- 1. huge (*megalith*). 2. one million (*megahertz*).

meta- after, along with, beyond, among, behind (*metabolism, metamorphosis, metaphor, metaphysics*)

micro- 1. small (*microorganism*). 2. restricted in scope (*microhabitat*). 3. one millionth (*microgram*).

milli- 1. one thousand (*millipede*). 2. one thousandth (*millimeter*).

mis- 1. wrong (*misprint*). 2. the opposite of (*mistrust*).

mono- one, single (*monarch, monochrome, monocle, monotonous*).

multi- many, much (*multicolored, multivitamin*).

neo- new (*neonatal*).

neuro- nerve (*neurosurgeon*).

non- not (*nonviolent, nonpayment*).

octa- eight (*octagon*).

omni- all (*omniscient*).

ortho- straight, correct (*orthodontics*).

pan- all (*panorama, pantheism*).

para- 1. beside (*paragraph, parabola*). 2. beyond (*paradox*). 3. abnormal (*paranoia*). 4. assisting (*paralegal*).

penta- five (*pentagon*).

per- through, completely (*perfect, pervade*).

peri- 1. around (*perimeter, periscope*). 2. surrounding (*pericardium*). 3. near (*perihelion*).

petro- rock (*petrology*).

photo- light (*photosynthesis*).

poly- many (*polyphony*).

port- to carry (*portable, porter*).

post-   after, behind (*postwar, postscript*).

pre-   before (*predict*), in front of (*preface*), surpassing (*preeminent*).

pro-[1]   **1.** forward (*proceed, promote*). **2.** bringing into existence (*procreate*). **3.** in place of (*pronoun*). **4.** favoring (*pro-choice*).

pro-[2]   **1.** before (*prognosis*), in front of (*proboscis*). **2.** early form (*prosimian*).

proto-   earliest form of (*protoplasm*).

pseudo-   **1.** false (*pseudonym*). **2.** closely resembling (*pseudopod*).

psycho-   soul, mind (*psychedelic, psychiatry, psychology*).

pyro-   fire (*pyrotechnics*).

quasi-   resembling (*quasi-scientific, quasiparticle*).

re-   **1.** action in a backward direction (*recede*). **2.** action in answer to or reversing a situation (*respond, restore*). **3.** action that is done over (*recapture*).

retro-   back, backward (*retrogress*).

semi-   **1.** half (*semicircle*). **2.** partially (*semiformal*).

sex-   six (*sexpartite*).

sub-   **1.** under (*subway*). **2.** just outside of (*subtropical*). **3.** less than (*subhuman*). **4.** secondary (*subplot*).

super-   **1.** above (*superstructure, superficial*). **2.** exceeding customary levels (*superman*).

sur-   over, in addition (*surcharge*).

syn- (or **sym-**)   with, together (*synchronize, symphony*).

tele-   far (*telegraph, television*).

theo-   god (*theology, theist*).

trans-   across, through (*transfer, transform, trans-Siberian*).

tri-   three (*trilateral*).

ultra- beyond (*ultraviolet*); extremely (*ultramodern*).

un-[1] not (*unemployment, unfair, unformed*).

un-[2] **1.** reversal of an action (*unfasten*). **2.** intensifying the meaning of a verb (*unloose*).

under- **1.** a place beneath (*underbrush*). **2.** lower in rank (*understudy*). **3.** of lesser degree (*undersized*). **4.** too little (*underfed*).

vice- in place of; deputy (*vice president*).

vita- life (*vital, vitality*).

COMMON SUFFIXES
and
THEIR MEANINGS

-able, added to verbs to form adjectives meaning "capable of, fit for, tending to" (*teachable*).

-aceous, made of (*herbaceous*).

-acious, tending to (*loquacious*).

-acity, used after roots to form nouns meaning "tendency toward" (*tenacity*).

-ade, result of an action (*blockade*).

-age, used to form noncount mass or abstract nouns **1.** from other nouns with meanings such as "collection" (*coinage*) and "quantity or measure" (*footage*). **2.** from verbs, with meanings such as "process" (*coverage*), "the outcome of or the remains of" (*spoilage; wreckage*), and "amount charged" (*towage, postage*).

-al¹, added to nouns to form adjectives meaning "relating to, having the form of" (*autumnal, natural*).

-al², added to verbs to form nouns meaning "the act of" (*denial*).

-an, 1. added to names or places or people to form adjectives and nouns meaning **a.** "being connected with a place" (*Chicagoan*); **b.** "having membership in a group of" (*Episcopalian*). **2.** used to form adjectives meaning "of or like (someone); "supporter of or believer in" (*Christian, Freudian*). **3.** used to form nouns from words ending in *-ic* or *-y* meaning "one who works with" (*electrician, comedian*).

-ance, quality or state of (*brillance*).

-ant, 1. used after some verbs to form adjectives meaning "doing or performing (the action of the verb)" (*pleasant*). **2.** used after some verbs to form nouns meaning "one who does or performs (the action of the verb)" (*applicant, servant*). **3.** used after verbs to form nouns meaning "substance that does or performs (the action of the verb)" (*coolant*).

-ard, used after verbs and adjectives to form nouns that refer to persons who regularly do an activity or who are characterized in a certain way (*dullard, drunkard*).

-arian, 1. used after nouns and adjectives to form personal nouns (*librarian, seminarian, veterinarian*). **2.** used after roots to form nouns meaning "a person who supports or practices the principles of" (*authoritarian, totalitarian*).

-ary, 1. used after nouns to form adjectives meaning "relating to" (*honorary*). **2.** used to form personal nouns or nouns referring to objects that contain things (*library*). **3.** used after nouns to form adjectives meaning "contributing to or for the purpose of" (*inflationary, complimentary*).

-ate, 1. full of (*passionate*). **2.** cause to become (*activate*). **3. a.** group of people (*electorate*). **b.** area ruled by (*protectorate*). **c.** office of (*consulate*).

-ation, state or process of (*starvation*).

-ator, person or thing that does the action indicated by the verb (*agitator*).

-cian, having a specific skill (*magician, optician*).

-cracy, used after roots to form nouns meaning "rule, government" (*democracy*).

-crat, used after roots to form nouns meaning "ruler, member of a ruling body" (*autocrat*).

-cule, very small (*minuscule, molecule*).

-cy, 1. used to form abstract nouns (*accuracy*) or action nouns (*vacancy*). **2.** used to form nouns meaning "office of" (*captaincy*).

-dom, 1. area ruled (*kingdom*). **2.** collection of persons (*officialdom*). **3.** rank (*earldom*). **4.** general condition (*freedom*).

-ee, 1. used to form nouns indicating the person who is the object of the action of the verb (*addressee*). **2.** used to form nouns indicating the one doing the act of the verb (*escapee*). **3.** used to form nouns indicating the one who is or does (*absentee*).

-en, 1. a. be or make (*harden*). **b.** cause to be or have (*lengthen*). **2.** used to form adjectives that describe material (*golden*).

-ence, quality or state of (*abstinence*).

-ent, 1. doing or performing (*different*). **2.** one who does something (*student*).

-ery (or **-ry**), used to form nouns referring to things or people as a group (*greenery, peasantry*) or to an occupation or condition (*dentistry, rivalry*) or to a place where an activity takes place (*bakery*).

-escent, in the process of (*adolescent, convalescent*).

-ese, 1. used after nouns that refer to place names: **a.** to form adjectives to describe things made in or relating to the place (*Japanese, Viennese*). **b.** to form nouns that describe in an insulting or humorous way the language characteristic of the base word (*Brooklynese, journalese*).

-ess, female (*poetess*).

-esque, in the style or manner of (*Kafkaesque, Lincolnesque*).

-fest, an assembly of people engaged in a common activity (*songfest*).

-fold, having the number of kinds or parts or multiplied the number of times (*fourfold, manyfold*).

-ful, 1. used after nouns to form adjectives meaning "full of or characterized by" (*beautiful, careful*). **2.** used after verbs to form adjectives meaning "tending to" (*harmful, wakeful*). **3.** used after nouns to form nouns meaning "as much as will fill" (*cupful, spoonful*).

-fy, 1. used to form verbs meaning "to make" (*purify, simplify*). **2.** used to form verbs meaning "to cause to conform to" (*citify*).

-gon, side, angle (*polygon*).

-gram, something written or drawn (*epigram, diagram*).

-graph, written down or drawn (*homograph, photograph*).

-hearted, used after adjectives to form adjectives meaning "having the character or personality of" (*coldhearted, lighthearted*)

-hood, 1. the state or condition of (*likelihood, childhood*). **2.** a group of persons of a particular class (*priesthood*).

-iatrics (or **-iatry**), the medical practice of (*geriatrics, pediatrics, podiatry, psychiatry*).

-ible, capable of, tending to (*credible, reducible*).

-ic, used after nouns to form adjectives meaning "of or relating to or having the characteristics of" (*metallic, Byronic*).

-ics, used after roots to form nouns meaning "body of knowledge or principles" (*ethics, physics*).

-ier, used after nouns or roots to form nouns meaning "person or thing that does something" (*financier*) or "person that is in charge of something" (*hotelier*).

-ine, used after roots or nouns to form adjectives meaning "of, relating to, or characteristic of" (*equine*) or "made of" (*crystalline*).

-ion, used to form nouns that refer to action or condition (*union*).

-ish, 1. used to form adjectives meaning **a.** "relating to; in the same manner of; having the characteristics of" (*brutish*). **b.** "of or relating to the people or language of" (*British, Swedish*). **c.** "like, similar to" (*babyish, girlish*). **d.** "addicted to; inclined to" (*bookish*). **e.** "near or about" (*fiftyish*). **2.** used after adjectives to form adjectives meaning "somewhat, rather" (*oldish, reddish*).

-ism, 1. used after verb roots to form nouns (*baptism*). **2.** used to form nouns showing action or practice (*adventurism*). **3.** used to form nouns showing state or condition (*alcoholism*). **4.** used after roots to form nouns showing the names of principles or doctrines (*Darwinism, despotism*). **5.** used to form nouns showing an example of a use (*witticism, Americanism*).

-ist, used to form nouns referring to a person who practices or is concerned with something (*novelist, terrorist*).

-ite, 1. used to form nouns meaning a person associated with a place or a set of beliefs (*Manhattanite, Laborite*). **2.** used to form nouns meaning mineral or fossil; explosive; chemical compound or drug product (*anthracite, dynamite, sulfite*).

-itis, used after roots that refer to an inflammation or disease affecting a certain part of the body (*appendicitis, bronchitis*).

-ive, used to form adjectives meaning "having a tendency or connection with" (*active, sportive*).

-ize, 1. used to form verbs meaning "to cause to become" (*sterilize*). **2.** used to form verbs meaning "to change to a state of" (*dramatize*). **3.** used to form verbs meaning "to subject to" (*hospitalize*).

-less, 1. without (*careless, shameless*). **2.** that cannot be (*countless*).

-let, 1. used after a noun to form a noun that is a smaller version of the original (*booklet*). **2.** used after a noun to form a noun that is a band or ornament worn on the part of the body mentioned (*anklet*).

-ling, 1. used to form a noun that indicates a feeling of distaste for the person or thing named (*hireling*). **2.** used to form a noun that is a smaller version of the base word (*duckling*).

-logy, used after roots to form nouns meaning "field of study or discipline" (*anthropology, biology*).

-ly, 1. used after adjectives to form adverbs (*gladly, gradually*). **2.** used after nouns that refer to units or time, to form adjectives and adverbs meaning "at or for every (such unit of time)" (*daily, hourly*). **3.** used after nouns to form adjectives meaning "like (the noun mentioned)" (*saintly, cowardly*).

-mania, used after roots to form nouns meaning "enthusiasm, often extreme" (*bibliomania*).

-ment, 1. used after verbs to form nouns that refer to the action of the verb (*government*). **2.** used after verbs to form nouns that refer to a state or condition resulting from the action of a verb (*refreshment*). **3.** used after verbs to form nouns that refer to a product resulting from the action of a verb (*fragment*).

-ness, used after adjectives and verbs to form nouns that refer to the quality or state of the adjective or verb (*darkness, prepared-ness*).

-off, used to form nouns that name or refer to a competition or contest (*cookoff, runoff*).

-oid, used to form adjectives and nouns meaning "resembling or like," with the suggestion of an imperfect similarity to the root element (*factoid, humanoid*).

-onym, word, name (*homonym, pseudonym*).

-or, used to form nouns that do or perform a function (*debtor, projector, sensor, traitor*).

-ory[1], **1.** of or relating to (*sensory*). **2.** providing (*satisfactory*).

-ory[2], used to form nouns referring to places or things that are used for something (*crematory, observatory*).

-ose, used to form adjectives meaning "full of" (*verbose*) or "tending to" (*bellicose*).

-ous, used to form adjectives meaning "possessing or full of" (*glorious, wondrous*).

-phile, used to form nouns meaning "lover of, enthusiast for" (*Francophile, bibliophile*).

-phobe, used to from nouns that refer to persons who have a fear of something named by the root or preceding word (*Anglophobe*).

-phobia, used to form nouns meaning "dread or fear of" (*agoraphobia, xenophobia*).

-phobic, used to form adjectives or nouns meaning "(a person) having a continuous, irrational fear or hatred toward" the object named (*xenophobic*).

-ship, 1. state or quality (*friendship*). **2.** position or rank (*lordship*). **3.** skill or art (*horsemanship*).

-some[1], like (*burdensome*) or tending to (*quarrelsome*).

-some[2], collection of objects (*threesome*).

-ster, used to form nouns, often implying a bad or negative sense, and referring esp. to one's occupation, habit, or association (*gamester, trickster*).

-tion, used to form nouns that refer to actions or states (*relation, abbreviation*).

-tious, used after roots to form adjectives (*fictitious, ambitious, cautious*).

-tude, used to form nouns that refer to abstract ideas (*exactitude*).

-ty, used to form nouns that refer to state or condition (*ability*).

-ure, used to form abstract nouns that refer to action, result, instrument, or use (*legislature, fracture*).

-ville, 1. city or town (*Charlottesville*). **2.** used after roots or words to form informal words that characterize a condition, place, person, group, or situation (*dullsville, gloomsville*).

-ward, used to form adjectives or adverbs meaning "toward a certain direction in space or time" (*backward*).

-ways, used to form adjectives or adverbs meaning "in a certain direction, manner, or position" (*sideways*).

-wide, 1. used to form adjectives and adverbs meaning "extending through a certain space" (*worldwide*).

-wise, 1. used to form adjectives and adverbs meaning "in a particular manner or direction" (*clockwise*). **2.** used to form adverbs meaning "with reference to" (*timewise*).

-worthy, 1. used to form adjectives meaning "deserving of" (*newsworthy*). **2.** used to form adjectives meaning "capable of travel in or on" (*seaworthy*).

COMMON ROOTS
and
THEIR MEANINGS

-acr-   sharp (*acerbic, acrid*).

-acro-   high (*acrobat, acrophobia*).

-act-   do, move (*action, transact*).

-ag-   move (*agitate*); do (*agent*).

-agon-   struggle (*agony, antagonist*).

-agr-   farming, field (*agriculture, agronomy*).

-alg-   pain (*analgesic, neuralgia*).

-ali-   other, different (*alias, alien*).

-alte-   other, different (*alternate, alternative*).

-alti-   high, height (*altitude, exalt*).

-am-   like, love (*amiable, paramour*).

-ambl-   walk (*amble, ambulatory*).

-ampl-   enough (*ample*), enlarge, (*amplify*).

-andro-   male, man (*androgynous, android*).

-anima-   spirit, soul (*animate, equanimity*).

-ann-   year (*annual, anniversary*).

-anthro-   human (*anthropocentric, anthropology*).

-apt-   fit, proper (*adapt, aptitude*).

-arch- **1.** leader, ruler (*archbishop, matriarch, anarchy, monarchy*). **2.** first, original (*archaeology, archaic, archetype*). **3.** used to form nouns that refer to persons who are the most notable or most extreme examples of the following noun (*archconservative, archenemy*).

-arm- weapon (*armada, armament*).

-astro- (or **-aster-**) star (*asterisk, astronomy*).

-athl- contest (*athletic, pentathlon*).

-aud- hear (*audible, auditorium*).

-bat- beat, fight (*battle, combat*).

-bell- war (*antebellum, belligerent*).

-bene- well (*benediction, benefit*).

-biblio- book (*bibliography, bible*).

-bio- life (*biography, biology*).

-brev- short (*abbreviate, brief*).

-cap- take, hold (*capture, caption*).

-carn- meat (*carnivorous*).

-caut- care, careful (*caution, cautious*).

-cede- (or **-ceed-** or **-cess-**) go, yield (*accede, proceed, succession*).

-ceive- get (*conceive, receive*).

-celer- quick (*accelerate, celerity*).

-cent- one hundred (*century, centigrade*).

-cep- get, receive, take (*accept, perception*).

-cert- sure, true (*certain, certificate*).

-chor- sing (*choir, choral, chord*); dance (*choreograph*).

-chrom- color (*chromatic, monochrome*).

-chron- time (*chronic, chronology*).

-cide-[1] kill (*genocide, homicide*).

-cide-[2] fall, happen (*accident, incident*).

-cise- cut (*incision, scissors*).

-claim- call out (*exclaim, clamor*).

-clos- close (*cloister, closet*).

-clud- (or **-clus-**) close, shut (*include, seclusion*).

-cord- heart (*concord, cordial*).

-corp- body (*corporal, corpse*).

-cosmo- universe (*cosmic*), world (*cosmopolitan*).

-crac-, -crat- ruler (*democracy, autocrat*).

-cred- believe (*credential, creed, incredible*).

-cres- grow (*crescendo, decrease*).

-crypt- hidden (*cryptogram, cryptic*).

-culp- blame (*culpable, culprit*).

-cur- (or **-cour-**) run (*current, courier, curriculum, occur*).

-cura- care (*accurate, curator*).

-cycle- circle (*bicycle, cyclotron*).

-dei- god (*deity, deify*).

-demo- people (*democracy, demography*).

-dent- tooth (*dentist, denture*).

-derm- skin (*dermatology, hypodermic*).

-dict- say, speak (*benediction, contradict, dictionary, dictator, predict*).

-doc- teach (*doctor, doctrine, document*).

-dox- belief (*doxology, orthodox*).

-du- two (*duel, duplex, duplicity*).

-duc- lead (*abduct, induce, introduce, produce, reduce, seduce*).

-dur- hard (*durable, endure*).

-dyn- power (*dynamic, dynamite, dynasty*).

-ego- self (*egotist, egomania*).

-equa- (or **-equi-**) equal; the same (*equilibrium, equivocal, inequity*).

-fac- (or **-fic-** or **-fec-**) do, make (*facsimile, manufacture, fiction, prolific, affect, infect*).

-face- face (*deface, facade*).

-fed- group, league (*confederate, federal*).

-fend- strike (*defend, offend*).

-fer- carry (*differ, transfer*).

-fess- declare; acknowledge (*confess, profession*).

-fid- faith, trust (*confidence, fidelity*).

-fil- thread (*filament*).

-fin- end or limit (*confine, final*).

-fix- fastened (*fixation, prefix*).

-flat- blow; wind (*deflate, flatulence*).

-flect- (or **-flex-**) bend (*deflect, genuflect, flexible*).

-flor- flower (*floral, flourish*).

-flu- flow (*affluence, fluctuate*).

-foli- leaf (*defoliate, folio*).

-form- form, shape (*conform, uniform*).

-fort- strong, strength (*comfort, fortify*).

-frac- break (*fraction, fracture*).

-frat- brother (*fraternity, fratricide*).

-fug- run or flee (*fugue, refuge*).

-fus- pour, cast (*fuse, diffuse*); mix or blend (*confuse, transfusion*).

-gam- marriage (*bigamy, gamete*).

-gen- birth, born, produced (*congenital, gender, gene*).

-geo- earth, ground (*geography, geology*).

-gest- carry, bear (*gesture, suggest*).

-glot- tongue (*epiglottis, glossary*).

-gnos- knowledge (*agnostic, recognize*).

-grad- degree (*centigrade, undergraduate*).

-graph- written down, printed, drawn (*biography, graphic*).

-grat- pleasing, thankful (*congratulate, gratuity*).

-greg- group, flock (*congregate, gregarious*).

-gress- step, move (*congress, progress*).

-gyn- wife, woman (*gynecology, misogyny*).

-hab- live, reside (*habitat, inhabit*).

-habil- handy; able (*ability, rehabilitate*).

-hale- breathe (*exhale, halitosis*).

-hap- luck, chance (*haphazard, perhaps*).

-helio- sun (*aphelion, heliocentric*).

-here- (or **-hes-**) cling (*adhere, coherence, adhesive*).

-hetero- the other of two; different (*heterogeneous, heterosexual*).

-hexa- six (*hexagon, hexameter*).

-holo- entire (*holograph*).

-homo- same (*homogenize, homonym*).

-hum- ground (*exhume, humility*).

-hydr- water (*dehydration, hydrant*).

-jac- (or **-jec-**) throw or place (*adjacent, inject, project, trajectory*).

-jour- day (*journal, sojourn*).

-jud- judge (*adjudicate, prejudice*).

-junc- join, connect (*adjunct, injunction*).

-jur- swear (*abjure, jury*).

-jus- law or right (*justice, maladjusted*).

-lab- to work (*collaborate, labor*).

-lat-[1] carried (*correlate, relate*).

-lat-[2] line, side (*equilateral, latitude*).

-lax- loose, slack (*laxative, relax*).

-lec- gather, choose (*collect, elect*); read (*lectern, lecture*).

-leg- law (*legislate, paralegal, privilege*); read (*legend, legible*).

-lev- lift (*elevate*); be light (*levity*).

-liber- free (*liberal, liberty*).

-libr- book (*library, libretto*).

-libra- balance; weigh (*deliberate, equilibrium*).

-lig- tie, bind (*ligature, obligate, religion*).

-lim- line, edge, threshold (*illimitable, sublime*).

-lin- string, line (*delineate, lineage, linen, lingerie, patrilineal*).

-ling- tongue (*bilingual, linguistic*).

-lit- letter; word (*alliteration, literary*).

-lith- stone (*megalith, paleolithic*).

-loc- place (*allocate, location*).

-log- speak; word (*eulogy, logo*).

-loq- (or **-loc-**) speak; say (*soliloquy, circumlocution*).

-lu- (or **-lav-**) wash (*dilute, lavatory*).

-luc- light (*elucidate, lucubrate*).

-lud- (or **-lus-**) play or playful (*allude, ludicrous, illusion*).

-lys- break down, loosen (*analysis, hydrolysis*).

-man-[1] hand (*manual, manuscript*).

-man-[2] stay (*permanent, remain*).

-mand- order (*command, demand*).

-mater- mother (*maternal, matriarch*).

-mech- machine, tool (*machination, mechanic*).

-medi- middle (*immediate, mediator*).

-mem- mind; memory (*commemorate, memorial*).

-men- mind (*mental, mention*).

-merc- trade (*commerce, mercenary*).

-merg- (or **-mers-**) plunge or dip (*submerge, immerse*).

-meter- measure (*barometer, metric*).

-migr- move to a new place (*immigrate, migrant*).

-min- least (*diminish, miniature*).

-mis- send (*dismiss, missile*).

-misc- mix (*miscellaneous, promiscuous*).

-miser- wretched (*commiserate, miserable*).

-mit- send (*commit, submit*).

-mne- mind, remembering (*amnesty, mnemonic*).

-mob- move (*automobile, mobilize*).

-mod- manner, kind (*immodest, model*).

-mon- warn (*admonish, monitor*).

-monstr- show (*demonstrate, monstrance*).

-mor- custom (*moral, morale*).

-morph- form; shape (*amorphous, metamorphosis*).

-mort- death (*immortal, mortgage*).

-mot- (or **-mov-**) move (*automotive, removal*).

-mut- change (*commute, mutation*).

-nat- (or **-nasc-**) born, birth (*innate, nativity*).

-naut- sailor, traveler (*astronaut, nautical*).

-nav- boat, ship (*navigate, navy*).

-nec- (or **-nex-**) tie, bind (*connect, nexus*).

-neg- deny, nothing (*negative, negligible*).

-noc- (or **-nox-**) harm, kill (*innocent, noxious*).

-noct- night (*nocturnal, nocturne*).

-nom-[1] custom, law (*astronomy, economy*).

-nom-[2] name (*denomination, misnomer*).

-norm- rule, pattern (*enormous, normal*).

-nov- new (*innovation, novel*).

-null- none (*annul, nullify*).

-num- number (*enumerate, supernumerary*).

-nunc- call, say (*annunciation, enunciate*).

-nym-, -onym- name (*synonym, acronym*).

-ocul- eye (*binocular, monocle*).

-odonto- tooth (*orthodondist*).

-oper- work (*cooperate, opera, operate*).

-opt- choose (*adopt, option*).

-opti- light; sight (*autopsy, myopic, optic, optometry*).

-ord- order, fit (*extraordinary, subordinate*).

-ori- rise, begin (*orient, origin*).

-pac- peace (*pacific, pacify*).

-pact- fasten (*compact, impact*).

-par- equal (*apart, compare*)

-pare-[1] prepare (*apparatus, preparation, separate*).

-pare-[2] bring forth (*parent, postpartum*).

-pass- step, pace (*compass, impasse, passport*).

-pat- (or **-pass-**) suffer (*compassion, patient*).

-path- suffering, disease (*pathology, psychopath*); feeling (*empathy, pathos, telepathy*).

-patr- father (*paternal, patriot*).

-ped-[1] foot (*centipede, pedestrian*).

-ped-[2] child (*pedagogue, pediatrics*).

-pel- drive, push (*expel, propeller*).

-pen- wrong (*penalize, repent*).

-pend- hang (*append, independent*).

-phil- love (*philharmonic, philosophy*).

-phon- sound (*cacaphony, microphone, phonics, phonograph*).

-phys- natural science (*physician, physics*).

-plac- please (*complacent, placid*).

-plan- flat (*plantation, plane*).

-plen- (or **-plet-**) full (*plenary, plenty, complete, replenish*).

-plex- fold (*complex, duplex*).

-plic- fold, bend (*complicate, explicit*).

-pneum- lung (*pneumatic*).

-pod- foot (*podiatrist, tripod*).

-point- point, pierce (*appoint, midpoint*).

-poli- smooth (*polish, polite*).

-polis- city (*cosmopolitan, politics, police, policy*).

-pon- put, place (*component, postpone*).

-pop- people (*populace, popular*).

-port- carry, bring (*export, portable*).

-posit- put, place (*deposit, position*).

-pot- power (*impotent, potential*).

-preci- value (*appreciate, precious*).

-prehend- grasp (*apprehend, comprehend*).

-press- squeeze, press (*compress, depression, impressive*).

-prim- first (*primary, primate*).

-pris- grasp (*comprise, prison*).

-priv- separated (*deprive, private*).

-prob- prove (*improbable, probation*).

-propr- one's own (*appropriate, property*).

-prov- prove (*approve, disapprove*).

-prox- near (*approximate, proximity*).

-psych- soul, spirit, mind (*psychic, psychology*).

-pter- wing (*helicopter, pterodactyl*).

-pugn- fight (*impugn, pugnacious*).

-puls- push (*expulsion, impulse*).

-punct- point, pierce (*acupuncture, punctual*).

-pur- pure (*expurgate, purge*).

-quad- four (*quadrangle, quadruplet*).

-quer- (or **-ques-**) seek (*conquer, query, quest*).

-quie- quiet, still (*acquiese, quietude*).

-quir- (or **-quis-**) seek, look for (*acquire, inquiry, inquisitive*).

-quit- release (*acquit, requite*).

-quot- how many (*quota, quotient*).

-rape- carry off by force (*enrapture, rapid, rapine*).

-rase- scrape (*abrasion, raze*).

-ratio- reason, judgment (*ratify, rational*).

-real- in fact (*reality, surreal*).

-rect- right, straight (*direct, rectangle, rectify*).

-reg- rule (*regular, regimen*).

-rend- give (*render, surrender*).

-roga- ask, demand (*arrogant, prerogative*).

-rota- round (*rotary, rotunda*).

-rupt- break (*corrupt, rupture*).

-salv- save (*salvation, salvage*).

-san- health (*insane, sanitary*).

-sanct- holy (*sanctify, sanctuary*).

-sat- full, enough (*dissatisfy, saturate*).

-scend- climb (*ascend, condescend*).

-sci- know (*omniscient, science*).

-scope- see (*microscope, telescope*).

-scrib- write (*describe, scribble*).

-script- writing (*description, scripture*).

-sect- cut (*bisect, section*).

-semble- seem, appear (*dissemble, semblance*).

-sene- old (*senate, senile*).

-sens- (or **-sent-**)   sense, feel (*extrasensory, sensation, sentient*).

-seq-   follow (*consequence, sequential, obsequious, sequal*).

-serv-[1]   slave (*servant, servile, service*).

-serv-[2]   save (*conserve, observe, reservoir*).

-sid-   sit; stay (*preside, residual*).

-sign-   sign; have meaning (*assign, design, insignia, signal*).

-simil-   alike, similar (*assimilate, facsimile, simulate, simultaneous*).

-sist-   remain, stand (*inconsistent, subsist*).

-soc-   partner, comrade (*associate, society*).

-sole-   alone (*soliloquy, solitary*).

-solv-   loosen, release (*dissolve, resolve*).

-som-   body (*chromosome, psychosomatic*).

-son-   sound (*consonant, sonata*).

-soph-   wise (*philosophy, sophisticated*).

-spec-   look at (*inspect, perspective, spectacle, species, suspect*).

-spir-   breathe (*expire, spirit*).

-stab-   stand (*establish, stable*).

-stan-   stand, remain (*inconstant, distant, substantive, stanchion*).

-stat-   stand, remain (*interstate, photostat, static, statue*).

-strict-   draw tight (*constrict, stricture*).

-stroph-   turn, twist (*apostrophe, catastrophe*).

-sum-   take or pick up (*assume, presume*).

-tact- (or **-tang-**)   touch (*contact, tactile, tangible*).

-tail-   cut (*curtail, tailor*).

-tain-   hold (*attain, maintain*).

-tech-   skill (*polytechnic, technique*).

-temp- time (*contemporary, tempo*).

-ten- hold (*content, tenable*).

-tend- stretch (*tendon, extend*); proceed (*tendency*).

-term- end, limit (*determine, terminate*).

-terr- earth (*terrain, territory*).

-test- witness (*attest, testimony*).

-theo- god (*atheist, theology*).

-therm- heat (*hypothermia, thermometer*).

-tom- cut (*atom, vasectomy*).

-ton- sound (*atonal, undertone*).

-tort- twist (*distort, torture*).

-tox- poison (*intoxicated, toxic*).

-trac- pull (*attract, traction*).

-turb- stir up (*disturb, turbulent*).

-type- impression (*archetype, typical*).

-ult- beyond (*ulterior, ultimate*).

-uni- one (*reunion, unicorn, unit, unique*).

-urb- city (*suburb, urban*).

-vac- empty (*vacant, vacuum*).

-vade- go (*invade, pervade*).

-val- worth (*valor, value, validate*).

-var- change (*variable, variety*).

-ven- come (*advent, convent, covenant, event, souvenir, venture*).

-ver- true, truth (*veracity, verity*).

-verb- word (*proverb, verbose*).

-verg- turn, bend (*converge, diverge*).

-vert- (or **-vers-**) turn (*divert, adverse, vertebrate, incontrovertible, perversion*).

-via- way, route (*deviant, viaduct*).

-vict- (or **-vinc-**) conquer (*evict, victory, vincible*).

-vide- (or **-vis-**) see (*evident, video, visit, invisible, vision*).

-vit- live, alive (*revival, survivor*).

-voc- call (*evocative, revoke, vociferous*).

-vol- wish or want (*benevolent, voluntary*).

-volv- (or **-volut-**) turn, roll (*evolve, revolution*).

-vor- eat (*carnivore, devour*).

-vot- vow (*devout, vote*).

-voy- send (*envoy, voyage*).

GLOSSARY OF TERMS

Accent the relative emphasis that may be given to certain syllables in a word. The term is also used for similar patterns of phonetic prominence inside syllables and for symbols placed over vowels of certain foreign words.

Acronym an abbreviation, such as NATO, laser, or IBM, that is formed using the initial letters of words or word parts in a phrase or name.

Action verb a verb that describes mental actions as well as physical actions.

Active Voice the person or thing represented by the grammatical subject that performs the action represented by the verb.

Adjective a word that modifies a noun or a pronoun.

Adjective clause a subordinate clause that modifies a noun or pronoun.

Adjunct part of a sentence that modifies the verb to show time, manner, place, frequency, and degree.

Adverb a word that modifies a verb, an adjective, or another adverb.

Adverb clause a subordinate clause that modifies a verb, an adjective, or an adverb.

Adverbial conjunction an adverb that connects independendent clauses such as *moreover, nevertheless, then,* or *therefore.*

Animate noun a noun that refers to people, animals, and living beings.

Antecedent the noun, phrase, clause, or sentence to which a pronoun refers.

Apodosis a term for the main clause in a conditional sentence.

Appositive a word or a phrase appearing next to a noun or pronoun that explains or identifies it.

Article a word that combines with a noun to indicate the type of reference being made by the noun. The three main articles in the English language are *the, an,* and *a.*

Auxiliary a verb that functions to give further information about the main verb that follows it. *Have, do,* and *be* are the three main auxiliaries.

Case the form of a noun or pronoun that shows how it is used and how it relates to other words in a sentence.

Clause a part of a sentence that contains a subject and a verb. It is connected to the other part of the sentence by a conjunction.

Collective noun a noun that names groups of people or things (e.g., *flock).*

Common noun a noun that names a class of people, places, or things (e.g., *city).*

Comparative the form of an adjective or adverb used to compare two things.

Complement the part of a sentence following the verb that is needed to make the sentence complete.

Compound adjective an adjective that is made up of two or more words.

Compound noun a noun that is made up of two or more words.

Compound sentence two or more independent clauses joined together.

Compound-complex sentence a sentence that has at least two independent clauses and at least one dependent clause.

Complex sentence a sentence that contains one independent clause and one or more subordinate clauses.

Conjunction a word used to connect words, phrases, or clauses.

Conjunctive adverb an adverb that connects two clauses or sentences by describing their realtionship to each other, such as *also, anyway, next,* or *thus.*

Copula or **linking verb** a verb that describes an occurrence or a state of being by connecting parts of a sentence.

Dangling modifiers words, phrases or clauses where it is unclear which element of the sentence they are modifying, because they could either be modifying the subject or object.

Declarative mood the normal form of a verb, in contrast with the imperative and the subjunctive.

Definite article A word used to restrict the meaning of a noun. "The" is the definite article in English.

Demonstrative words that indicate which entities a speaker refers to, and distinguishes those entities from others, such as *this, that, these,* and *those.*

Demonstrative pronoun a pronoun that is used to point out nouns, phrases, or clauses.

Dependent (subordinate) clause a clause that functions as a part of speech that relates to an element in the main clause.

Determiner sometimes called a *noun marker*, a word that determines the use of a noun without actually modifying it. Determiners are placed before nouns or noun phrases.

Diacritic a mark added to a letter to change the pronunciation; it can appear above or below the letter.

Direct object the noun, pronoun, or word acting as a noun that completes the meaning of a transitive verb by receiving the action.

Elliptical clause a subordinate clause that is grammatically incomplete but nonetheless clear because the missing element can be understood from the rest of the sentence.

Ergative verb a verb that allows the subject of the intransitive form to be the object of the transitive form.

Euphemism the substitution of vague language for language that is considered to be harsh, blunt, or offensive.

Future progressive a verb tense that is used to show continuing future action. It is formed with *will* plus *be* plus the present participle.

Gerund the -*ing* form of the verb (swimming, snoring) used as a noun.

Homophones Words that are spelled differently but sound the same.

Indefinite article an article such as "a" or "an" that is used before a singular noun. "A" is used before a consonant sound and "an" is used before a vowel sound.

Indefinite pronoun a pronoun that takes the place of a noun but does not have to have a specific antecedent.

Independent (main) clause a clause that can stand alone as a complete sentence.

Indirect object a noun or pronoun that names the person or thing that something is done to or given to.

Infinitive the infinitive of a verb is its basic form with or without the particle "to."

Intensive pronoun a pronoun that ends in *-self* or *-selves* and adds emphasis to a noun or pronoun.

Interjection a word used to express strong emotion.

Interrogative pronoun a pronoun used to ask questions, such as *which* and *what*.

Intransitive verb a verb that does not need a direct object to complete its meaning.

Modal verb a verb that expresses ability, possibility, obligation, permission, intention, and probability, such as *might* and *would*.

Mass noun a noun that names qualities or things that cannot be counted and do not have plural forms.

Nominative case the form of a pronoun that functions as the subject of a sentence.

Noun a word used to name a person, place, thing, idea, state, or quality.

Noun clause a subordinate clause that acts as a noun.

Noun phrase a phrase that contains a noun and one or more modifiers.

Object complement a noun or adjective immediately following a direct object.

Objective case the form of a personal pronoun that acts as a direct object, indirect object, or object of a preposition.

Participle a verbal form used as an adjective.

Past perfect progressive a tense used to show that a continuing past action has been interrupted by another. It is formed with *had* plus *been* plus the present participle.

Past progressive a tense used to show an action or condition continuing in the past. It is formed with the past form of the verb *to be* plus the present participle.

Person Pronouns used as the subject of a verb. English uses the first person (I, we); second person (you); and third person (he, she, it, they).

Personal pronoun A pronoun such as *I, me, my,* and *mine* that refers to the one speaking, the one spoken to, or the one spoken about.

Phonetics the study of the sounds of the spoken language.

Phrasal verb a combination of a verb and one or more adverbs or prepositions.

Predicate nominative the noun or pronoun following a linking verb that renames the subject.

Preposition a word used to connect and relate a noun or pronoun to some other word in the sentence.

Present Perfect Progressive a tense used to show that an action or condition is continuing from the past into the present and/or the future. It is formed with the present form of the verb *to have* plus *been* plus the present participle.

Present progressive a tense used to show continuing action or condition. It is formed with the present form of the verb *to be* plus the present participle.

Progressive forms verb phrases that show continuing action.

Pronoun a word that takes the place of a noun.

Proper adjective an adjective derived from a proper noun.

Proper noun a noun that names specific people, places, and things.

Reflexive pronoun a pronoun that ends in *-self* or *-selves* and shows that the subject of the sentence also receives the action of the verb.

Relative pronoun a pronoun used to tie together or relate groups of words.

Run-on sentence a sentence including two complete thoughts that are incorrectly joined.

Sentence adverb an adverb that modifies or comments on the sentence as a whole.

Subject complement a noun, pronoun, or adjective that follows a linking verb and gives further information about the subject of a sentence.

Subjunctive case the form of a pronoun that is used to state wishes or desires, requirements, suggestions, or conditions that are contrary to fact.

Subordinating conjunction a word that connects two thoughts by making one subordinate to, or dependent on, the other.

Superlative degree an adjective or adverb that indicates the greatest degree of difference or similarity by comparing three or more different things.

Tense something used to show the relationship between the action described by the verb and the time, which is reflected in the form of the verb.

Transitional phrases expressions that are used to link complete ideas.

Transitive verb a verb that requires a direct object to complete its meaning.

Verb a word that expresses an action, an occurrence, or a state of being.

Verbal a verb form—a participle, a gerund, or an infinitive—used as another part of speech. Verbals can function as nouns, adjectives, or adverbs.

Verb phrase a phrase that contains a main verb and an auxiliary verb.

INDEX

Abbreviations, 268, 287–291, 313–314
Acronyms, 253, 290
Action verbs, 21–22, 25
Active voice, 64–65
Adjective clauses, 97
Adjectives, 67–69
  after direct objects, 72–73
  after linking verbs, 71–72
  for comparisons, 73–75
  compound, 68–69
  distinguished from adverbs, 70–71
  irregular, 75–76
  nouns and pronouns as, 67–68
  placement of, 71–72
  prepositional phrases as, 80
  proper, 68
  in series, 259
  special, 68–69
  use of, 67
Adverb clauses, 97–98
Adverbs, 69–70
  after direct objects, 72–73
  for comparisons, 73–75
  conjunctive, 85–86
  distinguished from adjectives, 70–71
  irregular, 75–76
  placement of, 71–72
  prepositional phrases as, 80–81
  sentence, 70
Age, and terms for older individuals, 220

Agreement
  of nouns and pronouns, 20
  of pronoun and antecedent, 123–125
  of sentence parts, 117–125
  of subject and verb, 117–121
Antecedents, 6, 9, 123–125
Apostrophe, 277–279
Appositives, 10, 258, 265
Auxiliary verbs, 26

Bibliographies, 318–320
Brackets, 268–270

Capitalization, 282–284
Case, 9–10
  nominative, 10–11
  objective, 11–12, 18–19, 20
  possessive, 14–16
  subjective, 10
Clauses, 96–99
  adjective, 97
  adverb, 97–98
  conditional, 61–62
  dependent, 96–97
  elliptical, 98–99
  independent or main, 96, 255, 261, 262
  nonrestrictive, 257–258
  noun, 98
  restrictive, 257
  subordinate (dependent), 13, 96–97

Collective nouns, 5, 122–123, 133–134
Colon, 262–264
Comma, 255–260
Common
  commonly confused words, 186–214
  errors, 153–185
  nouns, 4
  prepositions, 78
  pronoun mistakes, 17–21
Comparative degree, 74
Comparisons, 19, 73–74
  completing, 76–78
  double, 76
  superlative, 76
Complements
  object, 103
  sentence, 102–104
  subject, 25, 71, 103–104
Complex sentences, 105–106
Compound
  adjectives, 68–69
  nouns, 5
  sentences, 105
  words, 280
Compound-complex sentences, 106
Conditional, 60–61
Confused, words often, 186–214
Conjugations, verb, 37–53
Conjunctions, 81–87
  coordinating, 81–82, 87
  correlative, 82–83
  subordinating, 84–85
Conjunctive adverbs, 85–86, 256–258
Coordinating conjunctions, 81–82, 87
Copula, 23–25
Correlative conjunctions, 82–83

Dangling modifiers, 114–115
Dash, 264–266
Declarative sentences, 107–108
Degree
  of adjectives and adverbs, 73–74
  comparative degree, 74
  positive, 73
  superlative, 74
Demeaning expressions, avoiding, 222
Demonstrative pronouns, 8, 68
Dependent clauses, 96–97
Depersonalization of persons with disabilities or illnesses, avoiding, 221–222
Determiners, 66
Direct objects, 11–12, 72–73, 102–103
Direct quotations, 135–136
Disabilities or illnesses, preferred terms for persons with, 221–222
Double
  comparisons, 76
  superlatives, 76

Ellipsis, 99, 266–267
Elliptical clauses, 98–99
Ergatives, 22–23
Errors
  common, 153–185
  sentence, 109–116
Ethnic terms, 219–220
Exclamation point, 255
Exclamatory sentences, 108–109

First-person pronouns, 6–7
Footnotes, 308–309
  articles in periodicals, 311–312

books, 309–311
common abbreviations in, 313–314
sample, 314–317
subsequent footnote references, 312–313, 317
Forward slash, 276
Fragments, 109–111
Fused sentence, 111–112

Gender-neutral language, 217–218
Gerunds, 15, 19
gerund phrases, 94–95
as verbals, 66, 94
Glossary, 351–358
Grammar, 1–150

Helping verbs, 26
Hyphen, 279–282

Illnesses, preferred terms for persons with, 221–222
Imperative
mood, 62
sentences, 108
Indefinite pronouns, 8–9
Independent clauses, 96, 255, 261–262
Indicative mood, 62
Indirect objects, 12, 103
Indirect quotations, 135–136
Infinitives, 27–28
infinitive phrases, 94–95
as verbals, 66
Insensitive language, avoiding, 215–223
Intensive pronouns, 7
Interjections, 87–89

Internet
citing Internet sources, 319–320
research for term papers, 305–306
Interrogative
pronouns, 7
sentences, 108
Intransitive verbs, 22
Inverted sentences, 102
Irregular verbs, 30–37
Italics, 274–276

Language that excludes or emphasizes differences, avoiding, 223
Library research, for term papers, 304–305
Linking verbs, 11, 18, 23–25, 71–72
Lists, parallel, 140

Mass nouns, 5
Misplaced modifiers, 113–114
Modal auxiliaries/ verbs, 26
Modifiers
dangling, 114–115
misplaced, 113–114
squinting, 116
Mood
imperative, 62
indicative, 62
shifts in, 128–129
subjunctive mood, 62–63
of verbs, 62–63

National origin, terms for, 219–220
Nominative case, 10–11

Nonrestrictive phrases and clauses, punctuation with, 257–258
Noun clauses, 98
Noun marker, 66
Noun phrases, 93
Nouns, 3, 4–5
  as adjectives, 67–68
  case, 9
  collective, 5, 122–123, 133–134
  common, 4
  compound, 5
  mass, 5
  pluralization of, 89–90
  predicate nominative, 11
  proper, 5
Number, shifts in, 132–134
Numbers, rules for using, 291–293

Object complements, 103
Objective case, 11–12, 18–20
Objects
  direct, 11
  indirect, 12
  of preposition, 12
Offensive language
  avoiding, 215–223
  dash as replacement for, 266
Older individuals, terms for, 220
Omissions. See Ellipsis
Outlines, parallel, 140

Parallelism
  parallel items in series, 139
  parallel outlines and lists, 140
  parallel structure, 137–139
Parentheses, 267–268

Participles
  past, 29
  present, 26–27
  verbals as, 66, 94
Parts of speech, 3–92. See also specific parts of speech, e.g., Nouns
Passive voice, 64–65
Past form, of regular verbs, 28–29
Patronizing or demeaning expressions, avoiding, 222
Perfect infinitives, 28
Perfect tenses, 56–58
Period, 253–254
Person
  of pronouns, 6–7
  shifts in, 129–131, 133
Personal pronouns, 6–7
Perspective, shifts in, 131–132
Phrasal
  prepositions, 79
  verbs, 26–27
Phrases, 93–95
  noun, 93
  prepositional, 94
  verb, 93
  verbal, 94–95
Pluralization, 89–92
Positive degree, 73
Possessive case, 14–16
Predicate nominative, 11
Predicates, subjects and, 100
Prefixes, 323–328
Prepositional phrases, 79, 94
Prepositions, 78–81
  and adverbs, 80–81
  common, 78
  phrasal, 79
  placement of, 80
  pronouns and, 18
  subordinating conjunctions vs., 85

Progressive, 58–59
Pronoun-antecedent agreement, 123–125
Pronouns, 6–21
  as adjectives, 67–68
  agreement of sentence parts, 117
  ambiguous references, 16–17
  case, 9–16
  common mistakes, 17–21
  demonstrative, 8, 68
  indefinite, 8–9
  intensive, 7
  interrogative, 7
  nominative case, 10–11
  personal, 6–7, 218
  predicate nominative, 11
  reflexive, 7
  relative, 8
Pronunciation, 284–286
Proper
  adjectives, 68
  nouns, 5
Punctuation, 251–293. *See also* specific types, e.g., Comma

Question mark, 254
Quotation marks, 270–274
Quotations
  ellipsis in, 266–267
  shifts in, 135–136

Race, ethnicity, and national origin, preferred terms for, 219–220
Reflexive pronouns, 7
Regular verbs, 30
Relative pronouns, 8
Restrictive phrases and clauses, punctuation with, 257

Roots, 337–350
Run-ons, 111–113

Second-person pronouns, 6–7
Semicolon, 260–262
Sentence adverbs, 70
Sentences, 100–125
  agreement of parts, 117–125
  complements, 102–104
  complex, 105–106
  compound, 105
  compound-complex, 106
  conditional, 60–61
  declarative, 107–108
  errors, 109–116
  exclamatory, 108–109
  formation of, 104–107
  fragments, 109–111
  function, 107–109
  fused, 111–112
  imperative, 108
  interrogative, 108
  inverted, 102
  modifiers, 113–116
  objects, 102–103
  parts of, 100–102
  punctuation, 255–293
  run-on, 111–113
  simple, 104–105
Series
  colon in, 263
  comma in, 258–259
  parallel items in, 139
  parallel structure in, 139
Sexist language, avoiding, 216–219
Sexual orientation, terms for, 221
Shifts, 126–136
  in mood, 128–129
  in number, 132–134
  in person, 129–131

Shifts *(continued)*
  in perspective, 131–132
  in quotations, 135–136
  in tense, 126–127
  in tone and style, 134–135
  in voice, 127–128
Slash, 276
Solidus, 276
Speech, parts of, 3–92. *See also*
  specific parts of speech, e.g.,
  Nouns
Spell-checker, 243
Spelling
  rules of, 233–235
  words often misspelled,
  235–243
Squinting modifiers, 116
Style, shifts in, 134–135
Subject complements, 25, 71,
  103–104
Subject-verb agreement, 117–121
Subjective case, 10
Subjects
  agreement of sentence parts,
  117–121
  complement, 25, 71, 103–104
  hard-to-locate, 101–102
  and predicates, 100
Subjunctive mood, 62–63
Subordinate clauses, 13, 96–97
Subordinating conjunctions,
  84–85
Suffixes, 329–336
Superlative comparisons, 76
Superlative degree, 74

Tense
  future, 56
  future perfect, 57–58
  past, 55
  past perfect, 57

  perfect, 56–58
  present, 54–55
  present perfect, 56–57
  sequence of tenses, 59–62
  shifts in, 126–127
  simple, 53–56
Term paper, writing a, 303
  bibliographies, 318–320
  footnotes, 308–317
  Internet research, 305–306
  library research, 304–305
  outline, 306
  subject, 303–304
  writing, 306–308
Third-person pronouns, 6–7
Tone, shifts in, 134–135
Transitional phrases, 86–87,
  256–257
Transitive verbs, 22

Underlining, 274–276
Usage, 151–250

Verb phrases, 93
Verbal phrases, 94–95
Verbals, 66, 94
Verbs, 3, 21–66
  auxiliary, 26
  conjugations, 37–53
  copula, 23–25
  ergative, 22–23
  forms, 27–30, 66
  infinitives, 27–28
  intransitive, 22
  irregular, 30–37
  linking, 11, 18, 23–25,
  71–72
  modal, 26
  mood, 62–63
  participles, 29–30

past form, 28–29
perfect infinitives, 28
phrasal, 26–27
progressive forms, 58–59
regular, 30
tense of, 53–63
transitive, 22
voice, 64–65
Virgule, 276

Voice
shifts in, 127–128
of verbs, 64–65

Who and whom, uses of, 12–14, 19
Word division, rules of, 243–245
Words often confused, 186–214
Writing, 299–320